BALM IN GILEAD

BALM IN GILEAD

The Story of Hadassah

by MARLIN LEVIN

Foreword by GOLDA MEIR

SCHOCKEN BOOKS · NEW YORK

Photo credits: The pictures are from the Hadassah Archives;
many were taken over the years by Hazel Greenwald
Berkowitz, whose work documents more than any other
person the life and times of Hadassah.

To
Betty
Sara
Oren
Don

Contents

CONTENTS

*Sections of photographs appear on pages 47–50,
136–140, and 240–244.*

Foreword
by Golda Meir

LOOKING back at the changes in American Jewish life which I myself witnessed, I would put the growth and influence of Hadassah high on the list. Out of a little volunteer group of Zionist women organized some sixty years ago has come a force of great dimensions, a force for health, education and the salvation of human beings. Hadassah has been making a contribution of basic importance to the development of the State of Israel and—clearly because of this—to the survival and enhancement of the Jewish community in the United States. Notably it has at the same time developed in thousands of women skills and talents unknown even to themselves.

All this emerges in rich detail from the pages of *Balm in Gilead*. Interweaving the story of Hadassah with the unbelievable, often tragic, political struggle of Jews in Palestine, the book shows Hadassah's efforts in true perspective, not as philanthropy but as nation-building in the face of great odds. Beginning at the turn of this century, Mr. Levin makes us see and feel the filth, poverty and disease of Turkish-ruled Jerusalem. This was the distress that inspired Henrietta Szold to make of American Jewish women "the healing of the daughter of my people."

Those American women were to bring the neglected land modern medicine at its most advanced—hospitals, the training of doctors and nurses, university medical research. It is a great and daring story, from 1913 when the first two nurses came, to 1918 when the Medical Unit arrived in the war-stricken, starving country, to vital aid in successive outbreaks of anti-Jewish rioting. Medicine was supplemented by vocational education and the magnificent Youth Aliyah program that saved thousands of Jewish children from the extermination camps which snuffed out the lives of a million of their young brothers and sisters in Europe.

I cannot forget the meeting I participated in during the siege of Jerusalem in 1948, when Hadassah's representatives decided to hold on to their hospital on Mount Scopus as long as possible and so helped to divert the brunt of Arab attack from the Jewish Quarter of Jerusalem. Till the liberation of Jerusalem in 1967 we were cut off from Mount Scopus where so many Arabs had been healed by Hadassah. Having lost Scopus, Hadassah energetically planned and built its hospital complex in Ein Karem. Later, many of its medical staff were lent to Asian and African developing countries, as I know very well from my days as Israel's foreign minister. And sadly, though gloriously, the Hadassah Hospital at Ein Karem is known to so many of us in Israel as the place that cared for hundreds upon hundreds of wounded soldiers during the Six-Day War and thereafter.

This is the record of an extraordinary alliance between Jewish women in the United States and their people come to life again in the Land of Israel—one of the great chapters in the integral relationship between the State of Israel and Jews throughout the world.

A Story Behind the Story

SHE is one of America's most successful women. With a single directive she can call into action 325,000 loyal members in every state. She can be found conferring in the halls of the United Nations, the State Department, and Congress. And on occasion she is at the White House.

She is one of America's busiest women. She thinks nothing of calling an 8 o'clock breakfast meeting or of phoning a colleague after midnight to discuss an idea. Normally, her day begins at 9 A.M. in a five-story, blue-white office building off Manhattan's chic Madison Avenue. There, she is enveloped in planning, organization, and negotiation until she rushes home for dinner. After dinner, her family is not surprised to see her run off to address a rally, attend a conference, or appear on a radio interview program.

She is a member of the National Board because she is forceful, quick-witted, dedicated, articulate, single-minded, pragmatic, personable, and tough.

Her rewards are intangible. She receives no pay because, above all else, she is a volunteer. One of the ground rules of the organization is that all the credit accruing from her labors goes to the benefit of one name—Hadassah.

The rank-and-file—all 325,000 of them—are likewise volunteers. To those even in the remote towns in states like Idaho and New Mexico, Hadassah is a way of life. Under Hadassah's banner they study their Jewish heritage of ethical and moral values and their American heritage of struggle for freedom and equality; at the same time, they mobilize money for a great medical center halfway around the world in Zion. In the cities Hadassah is all that and one thing more: an impressive example of the constructive power of women.

Among Hadassah members one finds movie stars and astrophysicists, diplomats, optometrists and cardiologists, but the backbone is fashioned of many, many housewives.

Early in this century the Hadassah woman rejected the male monopoly of public life, and while Betty Friedan and Gloria Steinem were still at their mothers' breasts, she had already made an impact in the man's world. True, the trousered class was at first contemptuous, but after suffering thereby, men began asking her to join their councils and committees. Because of her success in the organization she has been sought out in America to help run campaigns for various causes and serve on committees for everything from symphony orchestras to museums.

But that is by no means the whole picture of a Hadassah personality, as I was to learn one hot evening in June, 1958, in Jerusalem. On a feature assignment for *The Jerusalem Post*, I had gone to the home of Madeline and Sam Lewin-Epstein. Madeline, a nurse, and Sam, a dentist, had been members of the Hadassah-organized American Zionist Medical Unit that ventured into submarine-infested waters during World War I on a relief assignment to Palestine. Madeline, a matriarchal type, kept me alternately spellbound and amused with her tales of derring-do at the war front: her adventures in cholera-stricken Tiberias and her unfortunate confrontation with a British officer who tongue-lashed her because she had dropped a pair of panties in the gasoline tank of one of his military vehicles. Sam told me how he had carried gold to the starving Palestine Jewish community during the war.

This was a different Hadassah from the one I was familiar with. In 1960, an opportunity to resume the research came when *Time* scheduled an article on the Ein Karem medical center. Nuggets of stories similar to those I had heard from the Lewin-Epsteins fell into my notebooks: real-life tales of Hadassah men and women fighting for life in the midst of riot, plague, and starvation, building hospitals on war fronts, engaged in political combat, clutching children from concentration camps, dying horribly in ambush, airlifting supplies into a battle zone, creating art history, pathfinding new ways in education and science. I mused to an old and dear friend, former Hadassah President Rebecca Shulman, that someone ought to be commissioned to do a book. This volume, in short, is the result of that comment.

Few authors will admit that their book was easy to do. This one, I submit, was harder than most, simply because of the times in which it had to be written. The years from 1960 to 1973 were a period of high tension in the Middle East and my work as Jerusalem correspondent for *Time* necessarily had priority. The research and the writing were interrupted for significant periods by cascading news stories far more times than I care to remember. On one occasion I gave up altogether. But at that point another old Hadassah friend, the gracious Esther Gottesman, gently but persistently made demands on my conscience that I could not resist, and so I went back to work.

Space does not permit me to name here the nearly two hundred persons who kindly granted me interviews. Many are mentioned in the narrative. Nor is it possible for me to list all my sources. I must ask the reader for his trust while giving assurance that all the material herein has been checked and cross-checked. Inevitably errors must creep in, and for those I apologize in advance. I must, however, acknowledge the invaluable guidance and assistance from the following: the incomparable Judith Epstein, who took the book down the editorial home-stretch with me at a pace I found difficult to match; Shulamith Schwartz-Nardi, an accomplished writer and adviser to the president of Israel, who contributed both to the book's genesis and to its completion; friends of my youth, Marian Kay Lewin-Epstein, for transcribing the taped interviews; and Shirley Raskin Abelson, who appeared in Jerusalem from her home in Minneapolis just in time to give the manuscript a careful and critical reading; Hadassah stalwarts Annabelle Yuval, Esther Passman Epstein, Lillian Gold-Shpiro, Jeanette Leibel Lourie, and Hannah L. Goldberg, for guidance and logistical support; Emma Ehrlich, personal secretary to Henrietta Szold, for sifting through letters and papers; Elaine Farbenbloom, who besides her regular duties at the *Time* office found time to organize material and type the many versions of the manuscript. Of course, I also wish to acknowledge the daughters, mothers, and grandmothers who, without ever being mentioned, implement the plans and the projects and but for whom there would never have been a Hadassah or a book.

Apart from the standard reference books, I found of great value the following: Chaim Weizmann's autobiography *Trial and Error* (New York: Schocken paperback, 1966); Christopher Sykes' fascinating and well-balanced history *Cross Roads to Israel* (New York: World Publishing Co., 1965); *Women of Valor* by Irving Fineman, (New York: Simon and Schuster, 1961); *Henrietta Szold: Life and Letters*, by Marvin Lowenthal (New York: Viking Press, 1942); *Henrietta Szold, Record of a Life*, by Rose Zeitlin, (New York: Dial Press). Others that were helpful for background and checking were Walter Laqueur's handy *The Israel-Arab Reader* (New York: Bantam Books); Dov Joseph's *The Faithful City* (Tel Aviv: Schocken); *The Arab Awakening*, by George Antonius (New York: Capricorn Books, 1965).

Particular thanks are due to the editors of *The Jerusalem Post* and to the staff of the Zionist Archives, Jerusalem, for use of their files, and to the New York and Jerusalem staffs of Hadassah for aid in digging out old documents, records and published articles. A very special word of gratitude is also due to my superiors at *Time* for their encouragement.

I save the dearest for last. My personal Hadassah family played a key role in this book's creation. To Rose Levin Green, a woman of keen intuition and extraordinary courage, who wisely insisted that I remain in Jerusalem during the war of 1948 when other American mothers were demanding of their sons to return home, a son's lasting love and respect. To Zelda Levin Elinoff, my deep gratitude for work done that shall remain a confidence between brother and sister.

And to Betty, who over the years suffered quietly while this book was being gestated, who eased crises with loving assurances, and who sat patiently by my side through long lonely nights as I worked, I am eternally indebted, as I am to our children, Sara, Oren, and Don, for having paid for this book in many hours of missed companionship with their father.

M. L.

Jerusalem, July, 1973

I BELIEVE THAT WHEN THE HISTORY OF ZIONIST
RESETTLEMENT OF THE LAND COMES TO BE
WRITTEN, THE CHRONICLER WILL HAVE TO SAY
OF THE HADASSAH UNDERTAKING: IT BEGAN AS
A MERE WAR RELIEF MEASURE, IT ENTERED INTO
THE FABRIC OF PALESTINIAN LIFE, INTO ITS WEB
AND WOOF, AS A PART OF THE RENEWAL AND
REHABILITATION ZIONISM STANDS FOR. FROM
FIRST TO LAST, IT REMAINED TRUE TO ITS
MOTTO, "THE HEALING OF THE DAUGHTER OF
MY PEOPLE."

—HENRIETTA SZOLD, APRIL, 1929

1.

Mission: 32° Latitude, 35° Longitude

JERUSALEM emerged from the nineteenth century with the eyes of the Western world focused upon it. In 1799, Napoleon Bonaparte stormed the gates of Acre and Jaffa, pushed inland and reached Nazareth where he spent a night in prayer. But his conquest was short-lived. The Ottomans on land and the British at sea defeated his overextended troops and prevented his triumphal entry into the Holy City. Bonaparte's presence in the Holy Land nevertheless electrified Europe, and by the first half of the nineteenth century, pilgrims were on a new crusade.

Jerusalem has, over the centuries, been called by a hundred names: City of Heaven, City of Peace, Navel of the World. To Europeans it was more than a city of flesh and blood; it was not really of this earth, but a gleaming golden, fantasy city of sun-burnished castles guarded by hovering angels. The first pilgrims who followed Bonaparte indeed found Jerusalem sublime in its natural beauty, but hardly the glittering capital of some celestial realm. To their dismay they found that the God who reigned over its indolent residents from beneath a golden dome on the Temple Mount was Allah. Except for some shrines, Jerusalem was in fact a neglected city—its venerated streets defiled by stinking heaps of sewage and bowel, and built upon layers of refuse that had accumulated to a height of over fifty feet since

the days of the Second Temple. The sanitary condition of the
City of God was such that anyone who sought to spend his last
days on earth there could look forward to fulfilling that ideal with
dispatch.

The word of Jerusalem's degradation soon spread to the religious councils of Europe. Missionaries and emissaries rushed to
the scene from Russia and Britain, Prussia and France. These self-
sacrificing souls, unaccustomed to either the ways or the filth
of the Middle East, nonetheless attacked disease and ignorance
with fervor. But their primary aim was spiritual salvation. By
1840 the local population of 7,000 Jews and 5,000 Moslems looked
upon the rapidly increasing number of Christians in Jerusalem
(3,000 in 1840) as the beginning of the insidious crusade. To the
Orthodox Jew and Moslem the threat of conversion was much
more real than the danger from flies, mosquitoes, or microbes. Just
as disturbed by the missionary menace were the medicine men
who balmed the sick and dying with amulets and talismans. As
missionary schools, hospices, and clinics began to appear in the
walled city, bitter murmurings spread through the market places
and the houses of worship.

"Ha! Christians, you say? Nonsense. Not with names like
Gershtman and Bergheim. Converts! May their names be erased!"

"At the English Mission a Jew will step inside with a fever
and come out cured of both his fever and his Judaism."

The physician Gershtman and the pharmacist Bergheim arrived in 1838. By the early 1840's the sick and the lame—Jew and
Moslem alike—were trooping regularly to mission clinics and
getting quicker cures than they could ever expect from the quacks.
As conversions multiplied, the rabbis sent frantic messages to
Jewish notables in Europe. One of the first to reply was the
Italian-born British philanthropist Sir Moses Montefiore, who had
been to Jerusalem in 1827 and 1830. Sir Moses sent a Chelsea
physician, Shimon Frankel, with medical supplies, but Frankel did
not stay. The missionaries did, and the Jews of Jerusalem wrote
more urgent warnings to their brethren on the continent. What
was in reality the forerunner of a European invasion of the Holy
Land was to them a Christian conquest of the Holy City. The
crisis for the Jews reached its peak by 1853 when the Crimean
War between Russia and Turkey erupted. As a result, *halukah*
(charity) from Russia, on which half the city's Jewish population

depended, came to a halt, and their alternative to starvation was to take the free food, medicine, and clothing dispensed by the missionaries. The situation was similar in Tiberias, Safad, and Hebron. As the seers of Palestine saw matters, it was now only a question of time and pills before Jewry in Eretz Israel would silently disappear.

In that year of 1853 there appeared at the gates of Jerusalem a distinguished, bearded French-speaking gentleman who introduced himself as Baron Gustav de Rothschild. To the spiritual leaders of the community he was one of the city's hovering angels in disguise. The baron was appalled by conditions in which the Jews lived. He recognized the threat from the missions and sent his father in Paris an urgent message which said in essence: "All that our brethren in Jerusalem say is true. Their needs call for the most urgent action." In the French capital, his father, Baron James, summoned to his drawing room one of his most trusted friends, Albert Cohn, a scholar and a devoted Jew who directed the educational work of the Rothschild family. The baron gave Dr. Cohn a simple mandate: Save the Jewish community of Jerusalem.

In June, 1854, Albert Cohn left Paris for Vienna en route to Jerusalem. In the Austrian capital he called on Emperor Franz Josef I, who five years earlier had granted his Jewish subjects full civil rights. Dr. Cohn faced the emperor with this proposal: If Franz Joseph agreed to be the patron, a hospital would be built in Jerusalem with Rothschild funds that would serve all, regardless of race or creed, in the spirit of the empire's liberal new constitution. The Catholic Franz Josef readily assented, and with an empire firmly behind him, Dr. Cohn set sail for the Holy Land with a traveling companion, Michael Ehrlanger. They landed at Jaffa on July 7, and two days later they stood at Jerusalem's Jaffa Gate. There the entire Jewish community awaited them. Dr. Cohn wept both out of joy and grief, and paraphrasing the words of the prophet, he asked, "Is this the city that is more beautiful than the whole land and now is sighing?" Refusing to rest, he requested to be taken directly to the Western Wall where he wished to pray for the success of his venture. Every Jew in the city, Ashkenazi and Sephardi, infant and aged, man and woman, followed reverently in his footsteps.

Negotiations for the purchase of a hospital building began

immediately. The most suitable structure in the Jewish Quarter was a religious school belonging to the Sephardi community. It was located on the slope facing the Wall and the Al Aqsa Mosque. With £1,000 in gold available the negotiations were not unnecessarily protracted, but there was a fly in the ointment. Under Ottoman Law a European was not permitted to own property in Palestine. Dr. Cohn suggested that he take a lease on the building on condition that when the Rothschild Hospital moved to other quarters the premises would be returned to the Sephardi community. Thirty-five years later, in 1888, that is actually what happened. The Rothschild Hospital moved outside the walled city and the Sephardi community replaced it with its own Misgav Ladach Hospital.

Only seventeen days after Albert Cohn arrived, the conversion of the Sephardi yeshiva into a hospital of eighteen beds (nine for men, nine for women) was completed. It was Rosh Hodesh Menahem Av, July 26. The dedication on that hot, dry summer day was done in the typical Rothschild manner. Turkish and Arab dignitaries of the city attended. So did the consuls of Austria, England, France, and Prussia. So did the tailors and the rabbis, the beggars and the carpenters, the scribes and the yeshiva boys. Dr. Cohn spoke in faultless Hebrew, Arabic, French, and German. He gave notice that the hospital was under the protection of Franz Josef's flag and that it would be open to the sick of all faiths. The Talmud Torah children, proud to appear before so distinguished an audience, lustily sang Psalm 119 (the longest in the Psalter) and the equally proud rabbis beseeched the Divine to pour His blessings on the sultan, the kings of Europe, and the Rothschild family. The hospital was a declaration of status, a symbol to the non-Jewish residents of the city of Jewish determination to survive. Just as important, it was an assurance to the Jews that they had not been forgotten by their fellow Jews in the Diaspora. In turn there was little doubt that they would ever forget the Rothschilds. On the courtyard gate they put up a Hebrew sign transliterated in Latin characters which read: "For MAYER ROTHSCHILD FROM HIS SONS AMSCHEL, SOLOMON, NATHAN, KARL, JAMES BARRANE VON ROTHSCHILD." From each of the eighteen beds in the green-walled wards hung a plaque bearing the names of members of the family plus those of Sir

Moses Montefiore and Lady Judith, Albert Cohn and his wife, Mathilde.

Before leaving Jerusalem later that month, Dr. Cohn provided funds for the establishment of a boys' vocational school and a girls' school. The latter was named for Evelina de Rothschild and is still in existence in western Jerusalem. Prior to embarking from Jaffa, Dr. Cohn addressed a letter to the Jews of Jerusalem in which he pointedly summed up his month-long stay. He wrote, "Ashkenazim and Sephardim! No longer need you ask the missions for aid." On his way home he called on the Turkish minister for foreign affairs in Constantinople and received an unusual letter assuring the Rothschilds that all rights accorded to the Gentiles of Jerusalem would likewise be accorded to the Jews. He stopped in Vienna to report to Franz Josef and invited him to visit the hospital which, in fact, the emperor did sixteen years later. Back in Paris he arranged for a steady flow to the Rothschild Hospital of pharmaceuticals, surgical equipment, and a substantial supply of hernia belts. To the schools he shipped libraries in five languages.

The hospital itself was always crowded. Medical care was free. Anyone could visit the out-patient clinic three times a week and obtain all medicines without charge. The Rothschild Hospital doctor was permitted to take a fee only for house visits: two francs during the day and four francs at night. Administration of the hospital was turned over to a mixed Ashkenazi-Sephardi committee, but such were intercommunal squabbles that the committee was finally disbanded and the hospital was turned over to Dr. Bernard Neumann, who had been resident in Jerusalem for seven years. In Paris, Dr. Cohn received regular reports of the institution's progress. At the end of the first year he happily informed Baron James that of the 542 patients served by the hospital, 502 walked out cured. In that first year, men of many faiths and nations were served. The meticulously kept records include among the patients 33 Moldavians, 21 Italians, and 2 Americans. A glance at the occupations of some Jewish patients is revealing: 1 painter, 2 watchmakers, 5 bakers, 6 laundry women, and 83 scribes, among others. Expenses were listed down to the last sou: of the 14,510 francs expended the first year, 9,490 were spent on food and administration. Albert Cohn returned in 1856 and went away heartened. A year later Alphonse de Rothschild (brother of Gustav) paid a visit and took back to Paris a stirring report that both the death and conversion rates of Jews had fallen. Baron Alphonse set up a fund of 250,000 francs from which the annual interest of 14,000 francs would keep the hospital operating on a permanent basis. In gratitude the *yishuv* promised that the memorial prayer for the dead would be recited annually in the synagogue hospital for all Rothschilds.

The Rothschilds' word being as sound as their checks, the hospital never lacked means of support. Obligations were kept, sometimes in bizarre ways. During the Franco-Prussian War, for example, Paris was cut off by siege. In September, 1870, Dr. Cohn wrote the following letter to the hospital's administrator in Jerusalem:

> This letter will reach you by means of a balloon, if it reaches you at all. We are under siege this Sunday, September 18. Today is the 33rd day of the siege but we are well, thank God.
>
> My two sons are in the army. God has protected them until now. Just now I have written by balloon post to London and I have asked Mrs. Lionel de Rothschild to send by way of the London branch to Mr. Valero in Jerusalem 5,000 francs that we will repay, God willing, after the siege is lifted.

In the same year that the Rothschild Hospital was opened, a will was probated in New Orleans, Louisiana, that had a decisive effect on the fortunes of Jerusalem's Jewish community and their hospital. It was the will of the shipowner and philanthropist Judah Touro. He, too, had heard the agonizing cries that came from the Holy City and so provided $60,000 from his $1.5 million estate for settling the Jews outside the walls of Jerusalem so that they would be assured "the inestimable privilege of worshiping the Almighty according to our religion, without molestation." Except for monks who lived in seclusion in fortress monasteries, no one lived beyond the walls of Jerusalem nor dared to venture beyond them at night. Beasts and brigands, both real and imaginary, roamed the barren hills of Judea. But life within the walls had become so intolerable, a break finally had to be made. Touro's bequest was given to Sir Moses Montefiore who directed the construction of "almshouses" across the Valley of Hinnom, which in Biblical times was used by the Canaanites for human sacrifice. There, only a few hundred yards away, the walled city was close enough for comfort, yet sufficiently distant to escape the ministrations of missionaries and the fevers of plagues. A year after the Rothschild Hospital was in operation the almshouses were dedicated. They were beautiful homes for their times; so well built, in fact, that more than a century later they were still being used. Touro's money soon ran out but Sir Moses kept them going. The British philanthropist built a windmill on this site and his name, not Touro's, was later given to this key landmark in Jerusalem's modern history: *yemin Moshe* (right-hand of Moses).

In 1875, money for the almshouses was completely gone, and the poor moved back to the Old City. The wealthy Jews of Jerusalem rented their own homes within the walled city and moved into the almshouses, living in them rent-free and paying only for their upkeep. In that same year the new head of the hospital began to press the Rothschilds to move the institution outside the walls. Recurrent epidemics made administration difficult, and the more well-to-do Jews were leaving the Old City to build new homes beyond the ramparts. The hospital, the pioneer director reasoned, should be in the vanguard of Jewish settlement. The arguments made sense to Alphonse de Rothschild, who got the necessary firman from Sultan Abdul Hamid II, and work soon began on a one-and-one-half acre plot not far from the Russian Orthodox Church compound. One week before Rosh Hashanah, in 1888, the hospital—a dignified, three-story edifice costing 211,-000 francs and described by a diarist as "the nicest building in our city"—was ready. Originally, the hospital was fitted out with eighteen beds but was quickly enlarged to twenty-four. Later, a children's ward was opened which permitted mothers to live in with their infants. By the turn of the century the hospital could boast of the city's first maternity ward and its own ophthalmologist who was taken on to combat the rocketing incidence of trachoma. Baron Alphonse increased the capital fund for the hospital from 250,000 francs to a round 1 million and the income increased accordingly. In 1904, Alphonse began receiving reports of budget "irregularities"—money for the hospital was ending up in private pockets—and ordered the physician in charge to turn over the administration to a special committee "appointed from among the best Ashkenazim and Sephardim." He sent a physician from Paris to assume control of the medical organization, but such were the antagonisms between the communities that the committee could not function effectively. The baron, by now old and ill, threw up his hands and turned over the hospital administration to Kol Israel Haverim (known better now as the Alliance Israelite), the Jewish communal organization in Paris. Within a year the books were straightened out, and in 1905 the hospital boasted thirty-three beds, two physicians, and an administrator, as well as separate quarters for the three men and their families.

To most Diaspora Jews, as to the Gentiles, Jerusalem had become a mystical, dreamlike place. For the Jews the city's glories were in its history—in the chronicles of the kingdoms of David and Solomon, in the heroism of the Maccabees, in the magnificence of the Second Temple. *Yerushalayim* was a holy word to repeat in prayers; and its rebirth in this world would be a gift brought by the Messiah. Then in the mid-nineteenth century the crucial mission of a man named Cohn served to change Jewry's view of Jerusalem. He had come to save a remnant, and as a result the city again stirred for Jews everywhere. With the passage of time ordinary Jews began to acknowledge the fact that on top of the weather-beaten, treeless Judean hills, at the end of an aimless road located on this globe at 32° 45′ latitude, 35° 13′ longitude, Jerusalem breathed.

It would be ludicrous to imply that Jerusalem of the Jews was restored only because the Rothschild Hospital of eighteen beds was established. There is little question, however, that it was a significant beginning. Later on, other hospitals were established, but in the first fifty years none of them managed to prevent epidemics or even undertook large-scale public health campaigns. Jerusalem still suffered from malaria, trachoma, cholera, typhus, typhoid, ringworm, malnutrition, and pox. But at least the city's Jewish population could have good care without paying for it either with money or with their consciences. There was another important development, too. Mothers began going to hospital to have their babies, and infant mortality dropped.

The Rothschild Hospital helped lift Jerusalem out of the Middle Ages, brought it into contact with the medical sciences of the Western world, and, perhaps as important as anything else, provided the focus from which Jerusalem would be catapulted into the best that medicine of the twentieth century could offer. But that would not take place until after World War I and until after a few brave pioneers in skirts came to Jerusalem and looked into the sad, sick eyes of its children.

2.

Flies in November

November, 1909.

On the uneven stone pavement outside the Old City wall, on Jaffa Road, three women stood for a moment chatting in a foreign tongue. From where the barefooted beggar woman sat, up against the wall of the apothecary, she could see that the eldest of the three had tears in her eyes. These were definitely Ashkenazim from a foreign land, judging by their clothes. The beggar woman adjusted the scrawny dozing infant in the crook of her arm, extended her hand a bit farther and pleaded, "Matliq, matliq."

The old Ashkenazi matron sent one of the younger women over with a coin. The beggar looked up into a face that was grim, into eyes that were as sharp as the bite of mosquitoes. The mouth of this Ashkenazi lady was saying something in a strange Hebrew: "Why don't you brush the flies from the child's eyes?" As the lady deposited the coin she swooshed her hand past the baby's fly-infested eyes. The baby jerked its head as though something familiar were being snatched from it. The beggar woman's own watery, squinting eyes lost some of their vapidity for a moment as she began to explain, "They will only come back." They were part of her abysmal life, like begging and like her chronically ill husband who had to stop work in the carpentry shop because of his consumption. What did these strangers want, that a poor mendicant should do the sultan's work for him and rid Jerusalem of its flies! "May God bless you and keep you well and give you a safe return home." The matron called out, "Come on, now, we have only a few hours to the Sabbath, Henrietta, and we want to make it to the Wailing Wall." Henrietta Szold, then only a month from her forty-ninth birthday, turned and lost in thought, walked off mechanically to join her mother and friend. Soon they were lost in the crowds of the market place.

Not far from the beggar woman a haughty, elderly doctor was receiving patients from the back of his ragged brown mule. "What is *your* complaint?" he asked with a touch of annoyance in his voice.

"Doctor, doctor," half-cried the young man holding his hand to his brow, "My brains feel like they are boiling."

The doctor bent low to probe for the patient's spleen and muttered the diagnosis, "Ague," in the tone of a magistrate fining a hungry thief for stealing bread. He scribbled a prescription on a piece of note-pad paper, took the *grush* that was extended to him, and looking at his watch, shouted, "Next!" An elderly man complained of loose bowels and terrible cramps. "Bismuth for you. Next! Hurry up! The Sabbath is approaching."

Prescriptions in hand, the sick turned and stepped past the beggar woman into the pharmacy. In the opening years of the twentieth century in Jerusalem, quinine and bismuth were the magic cure-alls. Physicians took up their stations outside pharmacies because it was both practical and profitable. Doctors and the druggists cooperated as partners-in-trade.

In the first years of the century not more than a dozen Jewish doctors with fairly good training practiced in Jerusalem. Because there was no medical association or effective health department to control standards, quackery and medicine existed side by side. Even physicians who had genuine diplomas scoffed at new methods of diagnosis and treatment. A thorough medical examination was unknown. When one young physician arrived with a lab microscope from Europe as late as 1914, the resident doctors laughed in ridicule. What kind of doctor has to examine blood specimens before he diagnoses malaria?

As for the pharmacists, not all, to put it mildly, had academic training. A large number learned the rudiments of the profession as apprentices. Turkish law did require a certificate showing professional competence before issuing a license to open a drugstore, but this regulation was easily circumvented. All one had to do was to pay a practicing pharmacist to open another shop in his own name. He would then permit his young apprentice to run the apothecary. Then the novice would offer the premises to a physician or, failing that, to a quack. Working together they could make a good living.

One of the most popular pharmacies of the day in Jerusalem was that of the Greek Kaitonopoulos, well-located just off Jaffa Road. There the medicine men would gather. The well-to-do would work from the backs of mules. The younger men would sit on stools, smoking waterpipes, near the beggars and while waiting for patients exchange the latest in the world of witch-doctory. Understandably, some patients had more faith in pharmacists than in doctors. The druggists had the advantage of being less expensive; going straight to the pharmacist was like bypassing the middleman. When there were no physicians near, pharmacists would encourage direct contact. "Why ask the doctors?" a druggist would confide to a patient, "I can do as well." Medical problems were simply solved. Complaints were put into a few general categories. Every pharmacist knew that a few drops of silver nitrate would cure trachoma, and if the eye disease was already in a chronic stage, then a touch of the copper stock, serving as a cauterizing agent on the conjuctiva, would give relief. It was as simple as that.

Jerusalem had four Jewish hospitals. But Jewish mothers placed their faith primarily in traditional preventive measures and remedies. In late summer, for example, the children should be very careful of ripe melons. Melon juice must not be rubbed into the eye. If the juice gets into the eye, it will become sticky with the sickness. And if the children did contract trachoma, the best relief was egg yolks and mustard plasters over the temples. If the baby's sleep is disturbed at night because of stomach pains, burn white herbs of the field under the cradle. The fragrance, seductive as a lullaby, will caress the child back to sleep. If the pains continue, then drive them away with a burning stick applied to the chest or the stomach.

Basically, all ills had their roots in the evil eye and there was no safer, better guardian than a well-prepared amulet. Going into hospitals was so risky! Is it not a fact that many who go in never come out alive? If you are going to die, then what better place than in your own bed, among your own sympathetic family. It is better to die peacefully than to take your chances in the French,

German, Greek, Russian, or British mission hospitals. They may
serve kosher food, but they are the devil's delicatessens! The
government hospital? Who would ever think of putting his life
into the hands of the Turks. Jewish hospitals? They were probably the safest of the lot but better wear the cameo and stay well.

There was another segment of the population—less primitive,
more courageous and willing to take a chance—that would call a
physician or a quack to the home; whether the former or latter,
depended on the family's financial position. If the doctor's advice
did not immediately cure the patient, then another doctor was
called the following day. After a number of physicians were con-
sulted, then all the prescriptions were taken to the pharmacy and
the pharmacist was asked which he thought was the most effective.

A relatively small community of enlightened souls took advantage of the few reasonably good doctors and hospitals in Jerusalem. They went to the excellent eye hospital established by the
Order of St. John of Malta. They entered the Jewish institutions,
which for all their administrative problems gave exceptional medical care. But the best of medicine in Jerusalem was only palliative
in the face of enormous problems. When Henrietta Szold and her
seventy-seven-year-old mother stared at the flies in children's eyes
in Tiberias, Jaffa, and Jerusalem—a scene that invariably brought
tears to the eyes of Mrs. Szold—they were looking at a problem
whose dimensions were social and educational as much as medical.
The need for a vast public health program screamed out. Mamma
Szold and Henrietta heard the cry. Throughout their month-long
trip to the Holy Land in November, 1909, as they visited schools
and religious sites and saw beggars in squalid streets, it was tearful
Mamma who prodded Henrietta, "Here is work for you. This is
what your group ought to be doing."

Henrietta's group was a study circle that was formed as the
Daughters of Zion by Emma Gottheil in 1898. Emma had accompanied her husband, Semitics Professor Richard Gottheil, to Basel
where he was a delegate to the Second Zionist Congress. While
there, Emma met Theodor Herzl, who encouraged her to organize
American women in the cause of Zionism. On her return home
she invited young women from New York's East Side to study
Zionist and Jewish subjects at her elegant Fifth Avenue home. A
few years later, at the suggestion of some of the participants in
the group, the name was changed from Daughters of Zion to

Hadassah in memory of Hadassah Gottheil, Emma's mother. Similar study groups sprang up in Harlem, then a center of Jewish life in New York City. Most of them were called Daughters of Zion, and a few, Hadassah. They were small and met sporadically. The girls, who were in their late teens or early twenties and had some Hebrew education, were concerned about their identity as Jews. In their discussions they eagerly sought Judaism's answers to such problems as social inequality and militarism.

One of the better known group leaders was the brilliant but complex Jessie Sampter, a pacifist and intellectual, who traveled to Zionism and back to Judaism by a devious route, through the Ethical Culture movement, Unitarianism, and socialism. She influenced a number of young women who later were to become leaders on the American Zionist scene. One of the more successful study circles called Hadassah was formed by Lotta Levensohn at the encouragement of Rabbi Judah Leib Magnes, of Temple Emanu-El, for whom she worked in his capacity as honorary secretary of the Federation of American Zionists (later to become the Zionist Organization of America). In discussing prospective members for the group, whose purpose was primarily to acquaint Jewish women with Zionism and Palestine, Rabbi Magnes suggested to Lotta that his prestigious pacifist friend Henrietta Szold be asked to join—in an honorary capacity, of course. Little Lotta was frightened stiff at the idea of approaching so eminent a scholar and editor as Henrietta Szold and pleaded with Rabbi Magnes to make the approach. He did and Henrietta replied that she would be happy to join but as an active participant not as an honorary do-nothing member. That assured the success of this particular study group which held its meetings from their inception, in the autumn of 1907, in the YMHA on Lexington Avenue in New York City.

Henrietta was twice the age of most of the girls, and it was natural that she should be their leader. Later, she brought in a few older women ("They will keep me company," she told a friend), among them Emma Gottheil and Mathilde Schechter, wife of the president of the Jewish Theological Seminary. Henrietta set the tone of these meetings. "Wherever she sat," Lotta Levensohn recalled years later, "Henrietta Szold became the head of the table."

On returning from the Palestine adventure in January, 1910,

Henrietta lost herself more and more in Zionist work. She served as honorary secretary of the predominantly male Federation of American Zionists. But after eight months of trying to straighten out the organization's hopelessly desperate financial affairs, she gave up. That experience coupled with her mother's urging to "do something" and her own poignant recollections of life in Palestine quickened within her the idea that a national women's Zionist organization must be formed to carry out practical projects. She arrived upon the scene at the right moment.

Women from the former study groups of Harlem created the nucleus. There was Emma Gottheil, the third woman of the triumvirate that toured Jerusalem. There was Gertrude Goldsmith, with whom Henrietta worked closely on the early plans of a national organization. And there were Mathilde Schechter, Lotta Levensohn, Sophia Berger, and Rosalie Phillips. "I would be ashamed to attend another Zionist Congress," Emma would say, "and report that we did nothing but talk." That was the sentiment of the hour and it was embodied by these seven Zionist women in the brief invitations sent out to prospective members in the second week of February, 1912. "The time is ripe for a large organization of women Zionists," their invitation read. Their purpose? "The promotion of Jewish institutions and enterprises in Palestine and the fostering of Jewish ideals."

Sometime after 8:00 P.M. on February 24, 1912, in the vestry room of Rabbi Magnes' Temple Emanu-El there gathered a group of women (the precise number is not known, but there were probably less than twenty). Henrietta Szold spoke of her trip to Palestine and of the need for a "definite project." Eva Leon, who had been to Palestine more recently and was Emma Gottheil's sister, brought home the need for wider maternity service in the Holy Land. One such service, she reported, was run by the Christian missionary London Jews' Society whose price of admission to the hospital was the agreement of mothers to baptize their babies on departure.

A constitution was drawn up. Article I gave the old familiar name Daughters of Zion to the projected national organization, but Henrietta held that the organization could not really be considered national in scope until more chapters were established. This constitution, then, was really the by-laws of a New York chapter which would be called Hadassah (Hebrew for "Myrtle"). The name was a natural if only because the founding meeting was held on the Feast of Purim, and Hadassah was also the Hebrew name of the Biblical heroine Queen Esther. In the spirit of the holiday the opening session decided that all future chapters of Hadassah would likewise take on the names of Jewish heroines. (It was historic justice that in later years the Jewish heroine Henrietta Szold would be among the most popular of all Hadassah chapter names.) Other articles in the constitution spelled out the purpose of the organization and provided for associate membership to women who did not consider themselves Zionists. Later, associate membership was dropped when the constitution was amended to foster Zionist ideals in America.

At that first meeting there was a discussion on numerous projects that the Daughters of Zion might initiate: a day nursery, a girls' workshop to make lace, a maternity hospital, a school to train midwives, a district nursing scheme, sending nurses to Palestine. Finally, Henrietta Szold was elected president and nineteen members were made either officers or members of the board. Altogether thirty-eight women were listed as founding members. At the first board meeting, held at the home of Mathilde Schechter on April 4 and chaired by Henrietta, the ten members present agreed that if practical projects were not to be mere flights of fancy, the organization would need a membership of three hundred. By the end of the first year, that goal had not been reached: there were 157 regulars and 37 associates, and the cash box had $542.00 from dues. But the organization did have a motto taken from Jeremiah 8:22 (*Arukhat Bat Ammi*—"Healing of the Daughter of My People" *), which was suggested by the Jewish Theological Seminary's Professor, Israel Friedlander. And it had an emblem—a Star of David—on which the motto and Hadassah in Hebrew were superimposed. This was the work of Victor Brenner who gave the United States the design for the Lincoln penny. In February, 1913, Hadassah Chapter finally had sufficient money— "tribute" as Henrietta Szold described it sarcastically—to affiliate with the Federation of American Zionists. In June of 1914 the first and last Daughters of Zion national convention was held in Rochester, New York, where seven of the eight chapters were

---

* Although this has been a standard translation and was especially appropriate for Hadassah, the phrase is probably more accurately rendered without "the Daughter."

represented (Boston's Deborah was missing). At that convention
Rabbi Magnes took an active part. His lasting contribution was to
urge the delegates to adopt the more concise Hadassah as the name
of the national organization. It was done and Daughters of Zion
became a footnote in Zionist history.

Apart from its founding day, there is no date in Hadassah's first
years that was so significant and hopeful for the organization as
January 1, 1913. On that day an extraordinary meeting of the
board was called at the home of Emma Gottheil. There, Henrietta
Szold brought the exciting news that the department-store magnate
and philanthropist, Nathan Straus, had agreed to help finance both
traveling expenses and four months' salary for a trained nurse, to
be chosen by Hadassah, to open a health station in Palestine. But
he set two conditions: one, after the first four months Hadassah
would have to pay the nurse's salary—that would mean $2,500 for
two years—and, two, that she would have to be ready to leave for
Palestine with him and Mrs. Straus by January 18.

Hadassah was facing its first crisis. "When I heard the proposal, I was terrified," board member Alice Seligsberg wrote many
years later. With only a few hundred dollars in the till these
women were about to undertake a major responsibility that could
through failure make them the laughing stock of the Jewish community. Already, male Zionist leaders were grousing that the
women were dividing the movement. An undercurrent of feeling
grew at first among board members that it was too big a bite to
chew for so young an organization. But Henrietta and Emma were
insistent. They swung the other members with their self-confidence
and when a vote to underwrite the mission was taken, all ten hands
went up in favor. Everyone was aware that should they fail, the
organization would be badly crippled. But should they make a
success of it, chances were good of winning over large numbers of
American Jewish women.

Henrietta Szold was sold on the idea of establishing in Jerusalem, for a start, a district home-nursing system. She wanted to
model it after Lillian Wald's Settlement House and District Visiting Nurses, then being tried with success in New York City.
Nathan Straus, too, was aware of the need. He visited Jerusalem
in 1912, and on the spot set up a soup kitchen and a health bureau.
The latter was run by a German-Jewish doctor, Wilhelm Bruenn

who, on his own, had been fighting malaria, trachoma, and black water fever.

There was also a political side to the quick opening of the health bureau. When Straus appeared in Palestine, the German government, foreseeing a war in Europe, was sending doctors and sanitary engineers to Jerusalem. The kaiser considered Palestine strategic because it protected the flank of the Berlin–Constantinople–Baghdad railroad line. It was therefore necessary to clean up the area for the German soldiers who might have to be stationed there. The kaiser ordered the Hamburg Tropical Institute to send doctors and sanitary engineers, one of whom was known to the Jews of Jerusalem as a dangerous and rabid anti-Semite, to close cisterns and give quinine prophylaxis. It was this added factor—to provide a counterweight to the German activity —that convinced Straus to answer the urgent call of Dr. Bruenn and the Jewish community.

When Nathan Straus returned from Jerusalem, he told Henrietta Szold in explanation of opening a soup kitchen, "Once long ago, I suffered the pangs of hunger. I was starving; I had no money for even a single meal. I have never forgotten the sensation. In so far as lies within my power, no man that crosses my path shall go hungry." He then told Henrietta that he had heard about her desire to initiate a nursing project in Jerusalem. "Why don't you do it?" the philanthropist asked Henrietta.

"But we have only $283 in our treasury," she replied.

"That doesn't matter," both Strauses said in unison. "Start!" Nathan Straus commanded.

Henrietta insisted there was no money, and Nathan Straus repeated, "That has nothing to do with it!" Henrietta was befuddled for a moment. Then her eye caught Lina Straus standing behind her husband's chair nodding frantically as if to say, Henrietta later recalled, "The Lord will provide." Henrietta thought she got the message and was encouraged. But doubt still lingered.

The day after that confrontation took place, the Strauses called at Henrietta's apartment. They went through the same "start work —no money" routine until Nathan Straus finally broke it off with the offer that Henrietta somewhat breathlessly reported to her board on January 1. The Lord had, indeed, provided.

In the following weeks, hectic interviewing took place. Henrietta talked to twenty-one applicants. In the midst of the search for a suitable nurse came a bombshell message from Eva Leon. Non-Zionist friends in Chicago, she reported, offered to grant $2,000 a year for five years to send a nurse to Palestine, and they insisted that Hadassah choose and supervise the nurse. The crisis was over. It was now possible to send two nurses with the Strauses and possibly a third and fourth later on.

On January 18, as planned, the Strauses sailed again for Palestine taking with them Eva Leon and two trail-blazing Hadassah nurses—Rose Kaplan and Rachel Landy. Little more than two months later, on March 23, 1913, Hadassah for the first time brought healing to Jerusalem.

3.

War, Disease, Starvation, Death

THE four horsemen of the Apocalypse had already begun their long, wild ride in the Balkans when the two nurses set sail for Palestine in the bitter cold winter of January, 1913. Highly skilled as the nurses were, they were not prepared for the hardships ahead.

Short and stocky, Russian-born Rose Kaplan was the older of the two and had a long distinguished career in nursing at Mt. Sinai Hospital in New York. Tall and blonde, Cleveland-born Rachel Landy, was a light-hearted, fun-loving woman who had supervised nurses at Harlem Hospital Dispensary in New York. Rose signed up for two years, Ray for two-and-a-half. The assumption was that they would introduce a district nursing system under the guidance of Dr. Bruenn, head of the Straus Health Bureau. Things turned out differently.

When the nurses, together with the Strauses and Eva Leon, arrived in Jerusalem, public health work was being done by a number of independent organizations. Dr. Bruenn had gone to Tiberias to fight a cholera epidemic, then left for Germany. An eye clinic, Lema'an Zion, was functioning under a popular young German-Jewish physician, Albert Ticho. Antitrachoma clinics were operating under the Austrian-Jewish doctor Arieh Feigenbaum. Rose and Ray hardly knew where or with whom to begin. With financial aid from the Strauses they furnished a stone house located in the ghettolike, ultra-orthodox quarter of Mea Shearim, opposite the Hungarian Houses, and distinguished by a fragrant lemon tree in its quaint courtyard. They put a Hebrew-English sign on the iron gate: "American Daughters of Zion Nurses Settlement HADASSAH," and—as fate would decree—at Purim time, on March 23, 1913, accepted their first patients. In the beginning they took maternity cases, but trachoma was so rampant that under the guidance of their neighbor, Dr. Ticho, they began to care for the sick eyes of Jerusalem. One year later, they reported back to Hadassah that they had treated five thousand children for eye diseases, 20 per cent of them trachoma.

The Strauses and Eva Leon, who was asked by Henrietta Szold to represent Hadassah in Jerusalem, soon left. Hard work and loneliness took a double toll of the nurses' spirits. They had hoped they would be accepted with open arms by the community. In fact, they were greeted with suspicion and skepticism by both residents and professionals, because in those days nurses who went to Jerusalem were nuns. Rumors were spread that Rose and Ray were spies who had come to infiltrate the Jewish community. They plugged away nevertheless against Jerusalem's spiritual and bodily malignancies. Their monthly reports contained an encyclopedia of illnesses: enteritis, dysentery, typhoid, paratyphoid, trachoma and, as they wrote in one, "starvation." What disturbed them most was the high maternal mortality rate. It seemed that at least every other mother died while giving birth. They found one source of the problem in the untrained women who were acting as midwives. Ray and Rose were horrified to discover that these "midwives" would supervise births without even washing their hands. To ease difficult labor the ignorant attendants would pour impure oil into the womb and unintentionally induce septicemia, which was usually fatal.

The nurses immediately scoured Jerusalem for Jewish women who had received some training abroad in obstetrics. They discovered four, all graduates of Viennese and Constantinople schools, and employed them to pay regular visits to pregnant Jewish women in the city. Rose and Ray also formed a class for "big sisters" to whom they taught personal hygiene and child care.

When they were not in the settlement house tending to patients, the two nurses helped destitute families with a little money or food, sometimes giving them linen or a layette, and generally building confidence and faith in genuine medical practices. Where

they could not help with medicines or money, they would ease
social problems with sympathy and understanding. Gradually a
feeling of kinship grew between the nurses and the Jewish community, and soon they were among the most loved visitors in
Jerusalem. Their warm, gentle manner, their easy Yiddish talk had
won out. Where once they were called spies, they were now
called angels. In schools, where teachers had refused to permit the
nurses to examine the children's eyes, they now eagerly greeted
them. With the pupils Rose was gravely persistent; Ray was
smilingly insistent. The nurses' personalities were complementary
and they got along well. (Ray always had an added inducement
in her pockets when the going got rough with the children: hard
candies.)

When they diagnosed serious eye trouble, their most difficult
task was to convince the patients, or the parents in the case of
children, to enter Dr. Ticho's eye clinic for treatment. Once the
patients did risk it, they found the cure well worth the treatment.
As a result fear and prejudice gradually declined, and the queues
outside the settlement house grew longer from week to week. One
of Ray's favorite stories to her stubborn patients was about a
Bedouin who brought his young wife to Dr. Ticho's clinic. The
Arab asked the doctor whether he could restore the sight of his
bride's one bad eye. Ticho found that her sight had been impaired
by tissue that had grown over an old inflammation, and he operated. A short time later the woman could see well again. Her
proud husband, profuse in his gratitude, said to Dr. Ticho, "I took
a chance and I won, thanks to you. I bought this woman cheaply
because she had one bad eye. Now she is worth twice as much."

Jerusalem had a deep effect on the nurses. Rose was no Zionist
when she left for Palestine, and she never seemed to have considered the possibility of settling in the Holy Land. But in her
letters home she wrote of the joy she felt when she visited schools,
particularly the secular Gymnasium, where she saw hundreds of
bright and alert children, who had emigrated with their parents
from Eastern Europe. She also wrote despairingly of the poor
children she treated in Jerusalem's Tin Quarter, so-named because
the hovels in which they lived were made from discarded Standard
Oil Company tin cans. So bad were conditions of other Jewish
families living in cramped, underground cavelike rooms, she said,
that even a little bit of sunlight would have made an immense

difference in preventing and curing illnesses. She reported back to
Hadassah the general feeling of the small professional community
that social conditions of hygiene were the prime factors influencing
the health of the Jewish community, but the problems were so
enormous that a large-scale public health effort would be needed
to change the picture.

A few months before World War I erupted, the noted Baltimore eye physician, Harry Friedenwald, spent two months' volunteer service in Jerusalem. He saw that the nurses were doing fine
work, but there was no over-all coordination, and health institutions were duplicating each other. Besides four Jewish hospitals
there were the Straus Health Bureau and the Pasteur Institute and
Dr. Ticho's Lema'an Zion and Dr. Feigenbaum's clinics and Hadassah. Competition among them caused personal animosity and friction. For their part, the nurses worked around the clock. In the
schools, at the settlement house, in Dr. Ticho's clinic, with pregnant women, teaching midwives. In the United States it was impossible for Hadassah leaders to get a clear picture of what was taking
place. Frantic correspondence went back and forth over the 6,000
miles between New York and Jerusalem. Hadassah was troubled
that the nurses were fighting trachoma in schools when they should
have been setting up a district nursing system, and besides why
wasn't the Straus Health Bureau doing the antitrachoma work?
The fact was that so much had to be done by so few competent
people that everything was being done on an emergency basis. It
was clear even before Dr. Friedenwald arrived in Jerusalem that
two more nurses were urgently required. Eva Leon reported to
Hadassah early in 1914 that the nurses needed help to get their
district visiting system underway. She said she planned to return
to help them. After hearing Eva's report in January, 1914, Hadassah's central committee in New York adopted two principles
that fixed the guideposts for its future work in Palestine. In agree-
ing to Eva's return, it requested her to send frequent reports and
to consult on essential matters first with the home office, "even at
the risk of delay." The reason for the latter principle was simply
that even as early as January, 1914, Hadassah was thinking in terms
of a permanent presence in Palestine and that final responsibility
for all the work overseas had to reside with the home organization.
Hadassah was to be no mere fund raiser but a dynamic American-
based Zionist movement.

The war exploded in August, 1914. Communications with Palestine were broken. Eva Leon did not return as planned. The additional nurses could not sail. Dr. Friedenwald reported his experiences to Henrietta Szold and suggested that Hadassah establish a lying-in hospital in Jerusalem. His was the first serious suggestion that Hadassah build a hospital. Henrietta reported this to the central committee in October. By then the war was two months old. The committee decided to ask Rose Kaplan to consider remaining at her post until a replacement could be sent. Ray Landy's contract was to expire in July, 1915, and by then, it was felt, the war would be over. The request never reached Rose, and her letters pleading for instructions never arrived in New York.

Living and work conditions in Jerusalem were fast deteriorating. The war added another misery to the lives of the city's Jews. They were panic-stricken at the thought of being trapped on a potential battlefield, but even more so that sons and fathers would be drafted into the sultan's army. Hundreds of families packed their bags and prepared to flee to Egypt. The Turks expelled all non-Turkish citizens. The French physician heading the Rothschild Hospital, Jacob Segal, returned to Paris and joined the army. Dr. Bruenn, of the Straus Health Bureau, sailed for Germany to enlist. Bruenn's successor, Abraham Goldberg, was inducted into the Turkish forces. Later on, Ticho and Feigenbaum would have to leave the city on perilous adventures. The prospects were not bright for the American nurses. The Jewish agronomist, Aaron Aaronsohn, world-famed for discovering the original species of wheat in eastern Galilee, and a British spy, warned the nurses to return home. Rose was in a dilemma. The last ship was about to sail from Haifa. She was not aware that Hadassah urgently wanted her to remain. Her contract was expiring. Refugees were pouring out of Jerusalem. She had little money left and no prospects for getting more. Aaronsohn, who was aware of the international political situation, pleaded with her to go. Rose bent to the pressures, but with a purpose in hand. She sailed with the Jewish refugees, meaning to care for them in three camps set up in Alexandria. Hadassah was completely in the dark about Rose. Then, while the central committee was meeting in New York on February 15, Rose walked in. The committee members were startled. What they soon learned was that Rose could not stay on in Egypt because she needed urgent medical care. After an operation, she insisted on returning to the refugee camps in Alexandria. She set sail in November, 1915, but the Greek steamer she had taken sank in the Atlantic as a result of a fire in the engine room. She was rescued and finally got to Egypt early in 1916. There, she served in the camps until, on August 3, 1919, she died of cancer.

Ray kept on with the maternity and antitrachoma work in Jerusalem after Rose's departure. "Although it is not very pleasant living here alone, especially just now," she wrote to Alice Seligsberg in January, 1915, "I am perfectly willing and satisfied to keep up the Hadassah work, as long as I have funds."

Bravely and lonely, in a tense, unpredictable situation where the Turks were becoming daily more anti-American, Ray tried to maintain a normal regimen of work. Every Thursday morning she continued to give classes in what she called her "School of Home Nursing."

> I find these classes very interesting. We have taken bed-making with and without a patient in bed—lifting helpless patients. I gave one of the children a bed-sponge bath. We have made linseed poultices, mustard pastes and foot baths. The girls are very clever, and enjoy the classes very much. The last few weeks I have been teaching bandaging, so as to be up-to-date. We all find it very fascinating. I just give practical work and then give them notes. The girls are from 15 to 17 years of age—only seven of them—but small classes are always better . . .

Around Ray's island of normalcy, the whirlwind of terror grew daily. Jews in Jerusalem were a suspected alien element. They were liable to sudden arrest, banishment, torture. They were at the will and whim of Jamal Pasha, a tyrant who was answerable exclusively to the sultan and, on occasion, only to Allah. Little wonder that anyone who could get out of the city did so. So many left that midway during the war only three Jewish physicians remained. And hard as they worked they were helpless in the face of chain-reaction epidemics. Malnutrition set in on a large scale soon after the hostilities began. Day in, day out, families lived on *tzibile mit shires* (onions dipped in sesame seed oil), a few spoiled vegetables that were brought to market by Bedouin, a bit of bread, and a little goat's milk. Children suffered from a lack of vitamins, and as the war continued, their stomachs bloated. They were a pathetic picture as they walked the streets of Jerusalem searching garbage cans for scraps of food. Ray never forgot the scene:

> Never in my life will I forget these last few weeks. You should see the people in the streets. They are perfect studies of pain, misery and starvation. I never saw such faces. You can imagine how it feels to meet people who you can see are hungry, yet you don't like to approach them and they are ashamed to approach you. The Straus soup kitchen is open. What a blessing it is! I passed it one morning, and I never witnessed a more pitiful sight. You can imagine the number of applicants—such screaming and pushing—women fainting . . . I was watching some children of the Sepharad Talmud Torah eat their mid-day meal yesterday. Some had a piece of bread and the green leaves and stalks which come off a head of cauliflower. I have often wondered how these children can be happy—for they really seem to be. They are very amusing—perfect little devils. I have a right jolly time with them once in a while . . .

Two weeks later: "It is all I can do to treat the Sepharad Talmud Torah. The children seem to be getting smaller and thinner every day. They are developing idiotic expressions on their faces, and are such pitiful sights."

Then the locusts came. Voraciously, as though they too were victims of the growing famine, they ate fabrics, curtains, rugs. Infants had to be protected with heavy clothing. They fastened on to the garments—even the underwear—of adults.

Debilitating diseases became widespread—diarrhea and intestinal ailments were common, spread by unattended cesspits that poured rivers of sewage into the streets. Few residents boiled their water. Paratyphoid, typhoid, typhus swept across the city in waves. In summer, water in the cisterns sank low. Arabs would fill the cisterns by bringing supplies in *tennikes* (oblong oil tins), strapped to the backs of donkeys. A whole day's work would fill a cistern, but the wells were left uncovered and the anopheles thrived in the water. The Old City of Jerusalem swarmed with mosquitoes, and few escaped malaria. Trachoma cases multiplied and Jerusalem became known, along with its seventy traditional names, as the City of the Blind. Spotted fever made an appearance, then cholera. On and on rolled the list of diseases and the registers of the dead.

Jerusalem was a dying city. In mid-morning, Jaffa Road was deserted except for the movement of military traffic. A few old people, who were immune to death, showed up regularly to sweep the streets. Men of military age dared not go out lest they be pulled into the sultan's forces by Jamal Pasha's police, which was worse than a thousand plagues.

The situation might have been somewhat relieved if sources of money had not dried up. But Jerusalem was as poor as it was sick. Soon after the war began, families sold furniture, pillows, bed sheets, and rugs to buy food. They would barter it to the Bedouin who came in out of the desert with vegetables. As the war went on, families were left living in bare houses, sleeping on stone and tile floors with nothing but the clothes they wore.

At this time, Ray wrote in one of her letters, "There is a lady physician here, an obstetrician, and I have asked her to help us in our maternity work."

Helena Kagan was her name. Spurned and scorned by professional colleagues when she first arrived in Jerusalem from Switzerland in 1914, she was later to carry on the nurses' work when they left and to treat Jerusalem single-handedly when the last two Jewish male physicians were forced out of the city. She was to become a legend in her own time.

In those days Helena Kagan kept a cow in her backyard for no other purpose than to provide milk for the children who visited her clinic. But it was only a drop in an ocean of need. To save the Jews of Jerusalem transfusions of money and supplies were needed on a grand scale. They arrived in a most dramatic way.

Young as it was, Hadassah was making urgent inquiries at top political levels in Washington to send relief to the Jews of Palestine. Acting on its behalf was Louis Levin, a noted social service worker and brother-in-law of Henrietta Szold. Levin knew that a Navy collier, the *Vulcan*, was about to sail for the Middle East. He asked the Navy Department whether Hadassah could send along a physician and supplies. Inexplicably, the *Vulcan* was not permitted to take a physician but space was made for 900 tons of food and medicines, sent by Mary Fels, a member of the famed soap manufacturing family. Levin and a young dentist, Samuel Lewin-Epstein, were authorized to ship along with the relief.

The *Vulcan* put into Jaffa port four days after Passover in 1915, too late for its supplies of *matzot* to grace holiday tables. Awaiting the *Vulcan* were the Turkish police with orders to arrest Levin and Lewin-Epstein the moment they set foot on shore. The charge was that they were agents of the Allies who had come to incite a revolt against the Turkish regime. But the Turks were stymied by the American consul in Jerusalem, Otto Glazebrook, an Episcopalian minister, who went aboard and announced that the two men had the diplomatic protection of the neutral U.S. government. The two men handed to Glazebrook $100,000 in gold which they had brought from American Zionist organizations for the Jews of Palestine. The consul returned immediately to Jerusalem with Lewin-Epstein who put in later at a Jerusalem hotel. Levin remained with the *Vulcan.* One day, Jamal Pasha called on Lewin-Epstein and in the presence of the consul, invited him to dinner. Suspecting that the Pasha intended a plot against the American, Ellis Gillette, the interpreter, stepped on the foot of the consul and said, "But Dr. Glazebrook, you already have asked our guest for dinner." With that Lewin-Epstein was rushed to the safety of the consulate. In a few days, the *Vulcan* was to sail for home. Lewin-Epstein had to make the ship, but the consul had been warned that Jamal Pasha was not going to let him leave the country alive. It was suggested that he leave in disguise, but the proud Glazebrook would have none of it. "He arrived here as an American. He will leave as an American." Telegraphic messages passed urgently between Jerusalem, American Ambassador Henry Morgenthau in Istanbul, and the State Department. Finally, Glazebrook was authorized to inform Jamal Pasha that if Lewin-Epstein was harmed before he reached the *Vulcan,* the U.S. cruiser *Tennessee,* steaming off the coast of Palestine, would fire its guns on the port of Jaffa. Jamal Pasha quickly indicated that the man need not worry about traveling to Jaffa. The ride to Jaffa port went off without incident.

Back in Jerusalem Jamal Pasha's agents began searching for the gold. Glazebrook had handed it over to David Yellin, then chairman of the Va'ad ha-Kehila (committee of the Jewish community), whose headquarters were located in the Street of the Prophets, not far from the Rothschild Hospital. One night, Yellin raced across the street to Helena Kagan, hauling the hot gold. He pleaded with her to hide it, arguing that the Turks would not lower themselves to searching the premises of a single, young woman. Years later, Dr. Kagan recalled, "I almost fainted when I saw all that gold, because I knew that if I were ever found with it, I would have been hanged." Working at night, she and Yellin dug a hole next to a palm in her back yard and buried the money there. From time to time, as they needed it, Dr. Kagan would dig it up and turn as much as was needed over to a special committee of the community. The treasure did not last too long. Nor did the relief supplies, half of which were confiscated by the Turks.

Through the summer of 1915, Ray Landy worked together with Helena Kagan. Her own money was down to practically nothing. Hadassah sent messages through Ambassador Morgenthau to Glazebrook to find out how she fared. Ray replied that even though her contract had run out, she was willing to stay on if everyone at home agreed. But Ray's parents in Cleveland were terrified by news reports from Palestine and implored Hadassah to recall their daughter. Finally, the central committee cabled: "Come Home." Ray could hardly believe that she was to seal the doors of the settlement house. She wrote to Hadassah, "I don't know whether I had malaria or whether my fever was due to your telegram, but my temperature went up to 39 degrees C. [101.6] and stayed there off and on until I sent you a reply."

Ray settled her affairs, distributed supplies that she had received from the *Vulcan*, and closed the settlement house. But she remained in Jerusalem until the very last moment. She disliked Jaffa so much that she asked Consul Glazebrook to telegraph her from the port precisely when the ship would leave. As she sat for several days waiting, she wrote, "I still wish I would be obliged to stay until you could send nurses. I don't know whether it is Jerusalem or these trying times, but I have become so attached to everything and everybody that it gives me a sinking feeling when I think of leaving it all at this stage, especially since I have been through the worst. It upsets me very much to break up the Settlement. I had looked forward to leaving it in a different fashion."

Her last words from Jerusalem in September were to ask Hadassah to raise the salaries of the two local "probationers." Wrote Ray, "No matter what or how much I asked them to do, they always did it cheerfully." And the midwives were underpaid, too, she wrote. She hung on, but finally the moment of her departure was at hand. At the specific request of Hadassah, Dr. Kagan and Dr. Ticho continued the medical work. Glazebrook took fond leave of Ray. He had written Hadassah, "Miss Landy is one of the most useful people in Jerusalem. She is a splendid woman and is accomplishing most excellent work. I congratulate your society on having such a representative."

In New York, Hadassah had no word after it sent the "Come Home" cable. What happened to Ray? It sent more cables to Glazebrook through Morgenthau. "Why does Landy not come home?" Finally, on October 8 a telegram arrived from Ray in Naples. Two words: "Sailing Cretic." The *Cretic* left two days later, and Ray was home two weeks later. The following day she reported to a meeting of the committee. It was a gathering full of emotion and pride, and of some disappointment too. Ray reported that Albert Ticho was continuing with the antitrachoma work. In one school she had visited, she said, trachoma had been eradicated, but it would return. Helena Kagan was caring for the maternity cases. Ray pulled a letter out of her purse written by Dr. Kagan in which she asked that a small polyclinic for female diseases be established. At a later meeting the committee accepted the suggestion on condition that the work be done in the name of Hadassah and in Dr. Kagan's office, and that she submit monthly reports.

But back in Palestine there was little hope of setting up such a clinic. Through 1916 and 1917 the community of Jerusalem dwindled. Corpses lying in the street were becoming a common sight. The new Jaffa suburb of Tel Aviv, begun with great hope and spirit in 1909 on the sands north of the port, was inhabited by ghosts. When the war broke out, Jamal Pasha ordered the evacuation of all Jews. Some ran back into Jaffa, others fled north, but most sought refuge in Alexandria. Tel Aviv, then consisting of nothing more than four main streets, was left without population. By the beginning of 1917 it looked like a deserted set of a Western film. Papers and packing materials were whisked up and down the sand-covered streets by the winds blowing in from the sea. Doors banged and echoed through the hollow town. Empty windows looked out on empty streets. Occasionally a guard from Jaffa shuffled through the quarter, coming and going like a mirage out of the dunes.

In November, 1917, the Balfour Declaration was issued, promising a Jewish National Home in Palestine. But the Jews of Palestine knew nothing of it, and even had they known, they would have despaired that the only Jews left by the time the British could arrive would be dead ones. The Turkish authorities were aware, of course, of the declaration. General Allenby was on his way from the south at the head of hard-fighting troops. It would be a month more till he entered Jerusalem commanding a victorious army. The Turks became increasingly suspicious of the Jews who remained in Jerusalem. Of a prewar population of over 50,000 fewer than 25,000 remained, most of them women and children, old men and some frightened young men, many of them in hiding. As Allenby's men took El Arish and were on their way to Beersheba, Jamal Pasha insisted that every Jewish male of Jerusalem be called into service. Turkish police rounded up any man who could walk. A few young Americans studying in yeshivot were told to report to the police station to register as aliens. When they found they had been tricked into the Turkish army, they protested and waved their American passports. That brought sneers of contempt. They were corralled with all the rest.

Rothschild Hospital was taken over by the Turks and was then closed altogether. Three other Jewish hospitals remained open but had no funds and no nurses and could do little for patients.

Shortly before the British entered Jerusalem, Jamal Pasha arrested the heads of the Jewish community. Consul Glazebrook used his influence to have them released on the pretext that they had to hand over the affairs of the Va'ad ha-Kehila to others. Once out of prison they ran into hiding. A favorite refuge, as we have already seen in the case of the gold, were the quarters of Helena Kagan.

A sharp rap on the door scared the wits out of Dr. Kagan, that cold, rainy night of December 7. At first she refused to reply, fearing that the Turkish army had decided to conscript women as well. The knock came harder and harder, again and again. The pounding became unbearable. Helena opened the door to prevent it from being broken. Meekly, she asked who stood out there in the dark. Through the crack she could make out two figures. One was Rachel Feigenbaum and her father, Yosef Baran Meyouhas, one of the leaders of the Jewish community.

Said Meyouhas, "Helena, I must hide here. They won't look for me in your house. I must stay the night."

Helena hesitated, then reluctantly agreed. She went to her kerosene stove to warm food for a drenched, shivering Meyouhas.

Then, a brisk knock came at the door. Meyouhas ran for cover inside the house.

Helena opened nervously. Another member of the Va'ad, Siegfried Hoofien, was looking for refuge.

"I'm coming from Glazebrook," whispered Hoofien. "He said he could not keep me another minute. Let me in. Quick."

"Where is Thon?" Helena asked. Ya'acov Thon was then head of the Palestine office of the World Zionist Organization.

"Over at Hadassah House."

Helena ordered Hoofien to take cover with Meyouhas. She then wrapped a shawl around her shoulders and ran over to Hadassah House (as it was then popularly known). On the way she slipped through lines of Turkish soldiers moving out of the city. She banged violently on the door, but the frightened Thon refused to open. She continued knocking and shouting until he finally relented.

"Meyouhas and Hoofien are at my place. Come with me. Quickly."

Thon followed her back through the storm. Once all were together she bedded one of the men in her clinic, another in an empty house next door, and a third in the flat of Dina Meyer. Helena asked Meyouhas for news of Arieh Feigenbaum, the eye specialist. Meyouhas said he heard Feigenbaum had been taken prisoner and was being held with hundreds of others in the Dominican monastery near Damascus Gate.

At dawn the next day, December 8, Helena Kagan headed for the monastery. Her plan was to bribe the guards to release the opthalmologist. But the place was empty when she arrived. She found a deaf mute and wrote out an instruction to take one hundred pieces of gold to Feigenbaum. She figured that since the messenger could not talk, he would not be questioned. The deal was that if he brought back a note from Feigenbaum saying that the doctor had received the money, he would receive a reward of ten gold sovereigns. It was taking a chance, of course, but two days later, the honest deaf mute was back at her home with the note from Feigenbaum whom he had met on the road to Jericho.

Dr. Feigenbaum had been arrested while making his rounds of the Old City. When asked why he was being taken to the *nookta* (police station), the policeman replied, "Doctor Feigenboom, you are a Zionist. The British have promised Palestine to the Jews. Therefore, you Jews are the enemy of the sultan." It was the first inkling that any Jew of Jerusalem had of the Balfour Declaration.

On the way to Jericho, the miserable group of men—Moslem Arabs, American Jews, Palestinian professionals and beggars—were strafed by British planes. They walked all the way to Jericho, a distance of twenty miles. En route one night they were held in an empty cistern. From Jericho they were taken across the Jordan River in German lorries to e-Salt. Then they marched to Dera'a and boarded a train to Damascus. In all, it was an eight-day trip. They found chaos in Damascus and many escaped, among them, Feigenbaum. He moved south, walking, hitching rides, and got as far as Kfar Saba where he waited for the British advance. But it was long in coming. He saw horrible scenes of men and women dying of starvation. The fleas were incredible. People dropped dead everywhere from typhus.

Dr. and Mrs. Ticho had, in the meantime, fled to Damascus on their own, and kept on going to Istanbul, returning to Jerusalem after the war on a refugee ship.

On December 9, 1917, Allenby took the surrender of Jerusalem in what is today the Romema Quarter of the city and signed the peace terms in Sha'are Tzedek Hospital. For the Jews of Jerusalem, the war was over, but it still raged farther north, and it would be yet another year until the Armistice stopped all fighting. An American Red Cross unit moved in with the British forces, but it was woefully inadequate to deal with the dreadful health problems of Jerusalem. What the *yishuv* needed was radical and complete medical rehabilitation, not just supplies and pills.

It would be another eight months, and a long hard winter, before that kind of aid would arrive. Unknown to the survivors, it was on the way.

4.

The Unit

BROADWAY was neither gay nor white that second week of June, 1918. Fourteen months previously, President Woodrow Wilson asked Congress for a declaration of war. Now, twenty-five American divisions were already in France, and fresh ones were leaving weekly. In Belleau Wood, the green American Marines were stopping the massive German thrust toward Paris. Mightier, bloodier battles were still ahead, but the stand of the Marines was welcome relief to the growing numbers of casualties that would total more than 100,000 American dead and twice that number wounded before armistice five months hence.

The group of Hadassah doctors and nurses who gathered on 42nd Street in the early evening of June 11 were making an effort to be happy and carefree their last day on home soil. At midnight they would report at the pier for duty overseas.

One of the keyed-up young nurses suggested, "Let's all go to see the 'Garden of Allah.'"

A young physician had a less romantic proposal. "You girls can watch a Broadway show if you like. We'll be in Allah's garden for a whole year. What I want to do is say goodbye to the biggest, juiciest steak I can find." And with that he, and two concurring colleagues, went off to a restaurant.

Two other nurses demurred as well. They wanted to go to

Coney Island to have their fortunes told, and off they flitted in a shower of gleeful titters.

Even at midnight the weather was hot and humid. Tense, heavy-eyed, the small band of doctors and nurses gathered at the wharf beneath the looming troopship. In peacetime she was the luxury liner S.S. *Megantic*. Now, great and grey, her only marking was a giant number "19" on her prow.

"How was the show?"

"How was your steak?"

"Could've been better, but there *is* a war on, you know?"

"What did the fortune teller have to tell you?"

"I'm going on a long trip and I will marry a dark, handsome man . . ."

"So what else is new?"

"And there will be a tragedy before it's over. And I will not come back."

Only a sharp call to get moving up the gangplank saved the nurse from being dumped into the river.

Three thousand American men and women moved into the ship. Most were soldiers in khaki. Others were Red Cross and social welfare personnel. Forty-four, most of them doctors and nurses, wore a badge that no one had ever seen before: a red star of David encircled by the words "American Zionist Medical Unit." At 4:00 A.M. on June 12, number 19 cast off from her moorings, joined eleven other ships in the predawn haze, and sailed in convoy into the U-boat–infested Atlantic.

AZMU—as the Unit was popularly known—was long overdue. It was born two years previously, in June, 1916, when the World Zionist Organization in Copenhagen cabled an urgent appeal to the Provisional Executive Committee for General Zionist Affairs, set up in New York City after the start of the European war, to send a medical force to Palestine. The committee passed the request on to the Federation of American Zionists, which in turn fielded the ball to Hadassah. That July, Hadassah was holding its third national convention in Philadelphia. The treasurer reported that the organization was in the black to the tune of $2,880.65, and membership was at a record high of 1,937. The goal of 2,000 members would certainly be reached before the end of the year. Henrietta Szold, who was also Hadassah's representative on the Provisional

Executive Committee of WZO, disclosed that money had been raised to send two more nurses to Palestine. And then in the name of Hadassah's central committee she announced that what was really needed from Hadassah was to organize and contribute to the dispatch of an entire medical unit. The Federation of American Zionists had set a budget of $265,000, of which Hadassah would be required to raise only $25,000. "Only!" whispered a horrified delegate from Boston. "Only eleven times more than we have in the bank!" Henrietta made it sound simple. If every member saved on carfares, each could certainly donate up to $15. And that would do it. Henrietta's leadership won the day. The world had gone mad, so why should Hadassah be an exception. The project was endorsed.

Across the nation as far as Kansas City, then Hadassah's westernmost chapter, and Galveston in the South, Hadassah women saved nickels and dimes for the project. Henrietta had once said to her New York chapter, "The emergency should be used as an opportunity." It was. AZMU became a cause to believe in and work for. Membership rose. And so did costs. By the end of 1917, Hadassah sent out word that its share in the project was now $30,000.

But money was only one of the problems in forming AZMU. Transport was another. Trans-Atlantic shipping was scarce for all but the military; AZMU was to aid Palestine—a low priority—when, for America, the war was in Europe. Visas were a problem because the Turks held Palestine. Then, when the British issued the Balfour Declaration in November, 1917, an entry permit from the Turks was unthinkable. In December, after Jerusalem was conquered by the British, the Unit's organizing committee began to negotiate with the British ambassador in Washington. By March, 1918, authorization for the Unit had been received from Washington and London through the personal intervention of Supreme Court Justice Louis Brandeis, a leading Zionist. At first, the plan was to send AZMU to Palestine via the Cape of Good Hope, but finally sanction was given to permit the medical team to sail directly to Europe, on an American troopship. Adolph Hubbard, who had been active in obtaining passports for the Unit, wrote later, "This passport matter was not altogether simple. It was wartime and everybody was subject to suspicion, so that in a number of instances it was necessary to cut corners." Most problematic was Alice Seligsberg, a pacifist, who was granted her passport only hours before sailing time.

Originally, the Unit was planned for two doctors, two nurses, and a half-ton of supplies. By the time it got underway, there were twenty nurses, a dermatologist, obstetricians and gynecologists, an orthopedist, pathologist, pediatricians, dentists, a pharmacist, eye-ear-nose-and-throat specialists, and a sanitary engineer. Five administrators were assigned to the Unit. The manager, white-goateed Eliahu Lewin-Epstein, who was secretary of the Provisional Executive, had sailed on ahead. Alice Seligsberg, a children's welfare leader in New York, represented Hadassah.

Henrietta Szold wanted to go but stayed behind to help raise funds. She chose Alice to replace her, a friend whom Henrietta described as "a rare human being, wise, devoted to duty to the point of self-effacement." However, Henrietta refused the pleas of another friend Jessie Sampter, to join the mission. To Jessie, a poet, she wrote, "What your pen could add would not, to my mind, be so valuable as to justify changing what I conceive the character of the Unit should be—a strictly professional undertaking."

The pharmacopoeia and supplies that were shipped separately included 2,000 cases of medicines, 2 ambulances, 8 vehicles, uncounted gallons of antilouse fluid, instruments, blankets, linen, and clothing—all told enough to open a 50-bed hospital. A great deal of thought went into the choice of summer and winter uniforms. The women had light cotton greys with panama hats and veils (to protect sensitive skins) for summer wear. Dark grey woolens and velour hats were the uniform for winter. According to prevailing fashion the hemline was maxi—just above the ankles. The men wore khaki cottons or woolens. For shipboard emergency, each member was given an outlandish life-saving unit that was as big as a tent when inflated. When the commanding officer of the troop-ship saw the lifesavers, he exploded. "Anyone who inflates one of those tents in an emergency will be shot on the spot." He had a point. The suits were so expansive that they would have blocked the ship's companionways.

For all Henrietta Szold's meticulous preparation, the Unit went off without a medical director. Dr. Isaac Max Rubinow, a medical statistician from Washington, who had accepted the post, suddenly backed out at the beginning of June at the insistence of his family. Szold appealed to Adolph Hubbard to go as an administrator in charge of equipment, personnel, and finances. He agreed.

Thirty thousand Americans sailed in convoy that day, but only AZMU and a group of American Judaeans (who volunteered to fight with the Jewish Legion in Palestine) would be required to navigate three submarine zones—the Atlantic, the English Channel, and the Mediterranean. The two-week crossing of the Atlantic was hard from the outset. Homesickness was aggravated by seasickness, which in turn was brought on by violent storms that lashed the ship for the first few days. Anxiety over submarines was so great that few of the members of the Unit undressed to sleep. Most climbed into their berths even with boots and overcoats on and kept lifebelts at arms' length. Lifeboat drills two and three times daily did nothing to reassure them.

At 4 o'clock one morning, close to Scotland's shore, sirens sounded the submarine alert. Members of the Unit hurried to their lifeboat stations.

> We waited in silence. It was dark except for a thin glow of light on the horizon to the east. The minutes passed by in agony. Three thousand men and women thinking of a single thought. Most of them were soldiers who had to be there. They had no alternative. But we were volunteers. We could have remained home. We nurses were all about 25 years old. Most of us never ventured beyond our home states. Some of us had gone for the adventure. When we finally faced it, we were scared. Some were here because they simply got bored at home doing not much of anything and this was one way of serving both our country and our fellow-Jews. The pay was certainly good. One hundred dollars a month and maintenance for nurses. For the doctors, two hundred and twenty-five dollars. But at four o'clock in the morning, standing on top of a hunted ship, the pay was not so good as it first seemed. . . . We heard muffled explosions off in the distance. Our escort cruiser, the *San Diego*, spotted the sub and sank it. The eternity was over. All-clear sounded. Later, when we learned that the *San Diego* went down in the Atlantic while returning home, we all cried a little.

That was how, many years later, one of the nurses recalled the terror of that night.

Blacked-out Liverpool was a blessed sight. It was the night of

June 24. The nurses marched down the gangplank waving tiny British and American flags. Two of the girls were taken to hospital on stretchers, one with pneumonia and one with Spanish flu.

In London, the Unit split up, some bedding down at the Regent Palace in Piccadilly, the others at the Strand. With Vera Weizmann, Chaim Weizmann's wife, and Rebecca Sieff as their hosts, the nurses quickly got their fill of sightseeing, theaters, parties, and teas. Wherever they went they were greeted as the AZMU's. One night at a vaudeville show the noted comedian George Robey greeted them from the stage to the applause of the crowd.

But the most remarkable welcome of all took place in the regal London Opera House on the afternoon of July 14. Posters all over London proclaimed: "A Public Meeting to Welcome the American Zionist Medical Unit on its Way to Palestine."

Zionists who packed the opera house were in high spirits. The previous November, the British government had sent Lord Rothschild a short note saying that it looked with favor on the establishment of a Jewish home in Palestine. As a follow-up Chaim Weizmann had gone off to Palestine in March as head of the British section of the Zionist Commission to survey conditions in preparation for implementation of the Balfour Declaration. In June, Weizmann had his first meeting with Emir Feisal, leader of the Arab world, with whom he was to come to an understanding on Arab acceptance of a Jewish state. In two weeks, the cornerstone of the Hebrew University would be laid on Mt. Scopus in Jerusalem. Thus, the Zionist program was rolling forward rapidly and AZMU's presence in London added vigor to the momentum.

Lord Rothschild, who chaired the meeting, was interrupted nine times by applause and cheers during a five-minute opening welcome address, "I consider the sending out of a fully-equipped Jewish Medical Unit as a very great tribute to the progressive means by which modern Zionists are seeking to solve the problems of the new Palestine."

The most rousing speech of the day, however, was made by a non-Jew, the Member of Parliament George Barnes who represented the war cabinet. In a long-forgotten, but nevertheless highly significant address, he said to mounting crescendos of hand clapping, "The British Government proclaimed its policy of Zionism, because it believed that Zionism was identified with the ideals for which good men and women are struggling everywhere. That policy is the policy of the Allies with us in this war. It is the policy to which we are pledged. It is the policy which we believe accords with the wishes of vast numbers of the Jewish people." Barnes glorified the Unit: "They are taking help and hope and succour to people long-oppressed and down-trodden. . . . They are taking to a liberated East the knowledge and science of the modern West."

Another cabinet member, Sir Alfred Mond (later to become Lord Melchett) followed: "What we have been promised, in a declaration of policy made on November 2nd by the British Government, and which has since been gladly endorsed by the Governments of our gallant allies, France and Italy, is the establishment in Palestine of a Jewish National centre, to which Jews from all over the world, who wish to unite in spreading the influence of Jewish thought, Jewish industry and Jewish energy throughout Palestine *and the adjacent countries,* can do so in complete harmony with the other people living in that territory." Then Nahum Sokolow, the great Hebrew writer, and early Zionist leader, referred to the Balfour Declaration as the "Magna Carta of the Jewish people" and declared that the AZMU was the "beginning of the result of that Declaration."

Among the greeters was a member of the Armenian National Delegation who hoped the Unit would maintain "the high and noble Samaritan traditions of the American people," the highly popular and good-humored Colonel Josiah Wedgwood ("You are going to lay a foundation stone that will convert a race into a nation"), and Lloyd George who later became prime minister and had just come back from Palestine ("I have been working alongside the Arab Army and I want to say there is plenty of room in that country for the Jewish people, for the Arab people and for all the peoples that are in it").

Alice Seligsberg and Lewin-Epstein replied on behalf of the Unit. And the last to speak was Sergeant Gershon Agronsky (Agron) on behalf of the American Judeans. In the forthright manner that was later to make Agron a popular Zionist speaker as well as a magnificent editor of the Jerusalem *Post,* which he founded, he told the audience, "Bid us, if you will, good-bye or farewell but for a very short time, because we shall see you all in Palestine. In these circumstances, you cannot speak to us of homecoming in the sense of returning or of seeing us on a return when we shall pass through England again, because it is not our intention to come back."

Originally scheduled to remain ten days, the Unit was now in England three weeks. The meeting in the opera house had been arranged partly to keep up morale. It would be another week still before they could continue. Adolph Hubbard and a few others spent the time digging out as much information as they could on conditions prevalent in Palestine. Having learned something of the terrifying situation awaiting them, they thanked heaven that they had the foresight to take along about a half-ton of medical supplies, since the four hundred tons being shipped separately would most certainly be delayed en route. Now they could begin work the minute they stepped off the ship.

Finally, on July 22 the Unit was on the train to Southampton, and from there it sailed for Havre in what Hubbard called "a dirty little tub." More delays awaited the group at Havre, then the seat of a rump Belgian government. Hubbard was given a list of names, including his own and Alice Seligsberg, who were to be questioned by American Army Intelligence about their pacifism. But Hubbard used a ruse—he never revealed what it was—to bypass the investigation.

The group arrived in Paris past midnight to find a dozen army-requisitioned taxicabs waiting to take them in a grand convoy to their hotel near the Place de l'Opera. Only next morning did Hubbard learn that AZMU had been given the status of official guests by the French government because Baron Edmond de Rothschild had assumed "sponsorship" of the group. The war-bankrupted government, eager to maintain good relations with the financier, had laid out the red carpet. Hubbard, Alice, and engineer Louis Cantor called on the baron who was so impressed by their mission that he agreed to their request to turn over the Rothschild Hospital in Jerusalem to the Unit and to help maintain it financially. The baron authorized James de Rothschild, then serving with the Zionist Commission in Palestine, to draw up a contract. Addressed to Eliahu Lewin-Epstein on October 17, 1918, the agreement provided that while the Unit would be responsible for managing the hospital, it would always carry the Rothschild name. The three-year contract likewise provided that the furnishings and equipment would be returned to the Rothschilds on its expiration. But that provision was never invoked. At the end of three years the accord was not renewed, but the hospital remained in Hadassah's hands and subventions from the House of Rothschild were continued until 1940—300,000 francs in the first three years and 2,000 Egyptian pounds yearly thereafter.

Paris was gay, even in wartime, and French food made up for the grey, hard weeks of scarcities in London. On July 26, the little taxi convoy took the much happier contingent to the railroad station. But on the train, they had no facilities for washing, dining, or sleeping. Some tried dozing on the floor. The nurses had thoughtfully brought along tins of sardines and French cheese which the doctors generously helped themselves to. "Those doctors wanted to be mothered. So we mothered them, but the result was that *we* went hungry," one nurse remembered many years later. In Rome, they toured the catacombs, Vatican City, and the big synagogue on the Tiber where psalms of joy were sung in their honor by an organ-accompanied choir. A troubled Hubbard had no time for touring. "Nothing went right," he recalled later. "Most of our two days in Rome I spent getting our papers in order. Were it not for the aid of the British naval attaché, we would have had even more delays. And to prove that nothing could go right, when it came to get the final papers a clerk told us that he had orders for us to remain in Rome until the camp at Taranto, our next stop, was prepared to take us."

Hubbard was fed up. When he figured that it would cost about $350 more daily to remain in Rome, he charged ahead to the camp at Taranto, despite the orders. "I decided to go on, trusting to be able to talk us out of trouble, if trouble came."

Taranto was located on the burning sands of a gulf on Italy's heel and was the principal reception center for Allied troops and supplies moving from Europe to the Middle and Far East. The heat hovered around 120 degrees at times, but nothing was so fierce as the British commanding officer's temper on hearing that Hubbard's contingent had arrived against orders. The Unit remained only because no transport was available to take them back. According to Hubbard's itinerary, the Unit was to ship out to Alexandria within forty-eight hours. But a submarine raid in the Mediterranean delayed them for ten days. One evening a group of Palestinian and British officers discovered the Americans and serenaded them with Hebrew songs. One of the Palestinians was botanist Aaron Aaronsohn, soon to die in a mysterious plane crash.

Another was Major Ormsby-Gore (later to be colonial secretary), who had been hunting for the Unit high and low in his capacity as British military liaison officer to the Zionist Commission then in Palestine. From Aaronsohn and Ormsby-Gore the Unit received a sobering picture of raped Palestine. The war was still in a critical stage; Jerusalem was in British hands but northern Palestine was not. The American Red Cross unit, headquartered in Jerusalem, was not equipped to cope with Palestine's basic medical and rehabilitation problems. In sum, the Unit was desperately needed.

On August 9, AZMU shipped out on an Indian transport convoyed by three Japanese destroyers and an Italian hydroplane. As the ship slipped out of Taranto, the nurses and doctors glumly stared at the hulks of sunken vessels. The *Kaiser I. Hind* sailed into Alexandria two days later, but not without a fright. Several hours before arrival all hands were told to put on life belts and stand by at lifeboat stations. Submarines were lurking about at the entrance to the harbor, but the danger passed without incident. On hand for their first welcome to the Middle East was Chaim Weizmann who regretted the delay in the Unit's arrival and said that departure for Palestine would be given top priority even though most transport was then being used by the military.

The doctors and nurses spent four days in Alexandria and two in Cairo. The Unit put up at Cairo's Shepeard's Hotel, and the wealthy Mosseri family who dominated the Jewish community was their host. They dutifully visited the sixty-bed Israelite Hospital where the director told them, "If it were not for the Jews of Palestine who came to Egypt during the war, we would not have had this hospital. It was they who infused us with a new spirit and it was with that spirit that we built this institution."

There was just time enough for the group to see something of Egypt before they took off. The impressions never left them. They were horrified by the mud villages along the Nile, the oxen yoked to the water wheel, the sickly peasants ploughing the earth with scraggy camels. In the city itself, they tasted and smelled misery wherever they went. Poverty, filth, rotting refuse in the streets, dirty naked children, blind beggars, and everywhere flies—billions of flies spreading an invisible germ canopy over the teeming, milling metropolis. What made the experience grotesque was that, amid the destitution, fabulous wealth and luxuriant living and high culture were enjoyed by a small ruling clique. This then was the gateway to the lurid, alluring Levant, a loud and sluggish region, illiterate, indigent, a diamond on a garbage heap, intoxicating in its tawdriness, frustratingly inconsistent, magnetically enigmatic, a mosaic of contradictions that no Westerner would ever begin to understand.

By Saturday evening, August 17, 1918, the British had cleared space on troop trains to send AZMU on the last leg of its voyage to Palestine. Leaving one nurse behind to take charge of the camp of Palestine Jewish refugees in Alexandria, the group boarded double-decker berthed trains and, according to one scholarly version, traveled the route into the Holy Land chosen by Moses to take the Israelites out of bondage. Across the horizon as they chugged along in the bright moonlight, they could discern long caravans of camels. By early morning they crossed the Suez Canal and were in Kantara. The northern coast of Sinai, along the Mediterranean, was anything but romantic. A sand storm swirled up out of the desert and all views were lost in the gritty winds.

Eighteen hours after they started out, the train finally arrived in Lydda, a sandy tent town that could offer not a single shade tree against the August heat. The railroad terminal was a rickety shed. Sitting on valises for two hours, waiting for someone to greet them, left the group depressed. Several nurses fainted from the oppressive heat and fatigue.

Their presence in Palestine was a source of contention between the Zionist Commission and the British authorities. The British had decided that AZMU would not be quartered in Jerusalem. But Chaim Weizmann put their case before General Allenby who, while not overly sympathetic toward Zionist aims, was fair. Allenby argued that since the American Red Cross had already pitched its tents in Jerusalem there was no need for a second mission there. In the end, Weizmann's charm and persuasive arguments won out. As a compromise the two agreed that the Unit would split up with AZMU establishing its base in Tel Aviv and a detachment working in Jerusalem. But both certainly knew what would happen in the end. There was an air of permanence about AZMU, and only Jerusalem could then be headquarters for any Zionist organization.

Despite the agreement the largest number of AZMU members entrained for Jerusalem. The others—Executive Headquarters—set out by vehicles over the limestone road through the citrus groves for Tel Aviv. In Tel Aviv, the Unit occupied the only three houses located on what is now Allenby Street. These houses marked the limit of the town. Beyond, all was sand dunes. With emergency supplies that were brought along squads began work immediately. In Jaffa, a sanitary unit sprang into action to supervise garbage collection, food inspection, cattle examination at slaughter houses, malaria control. In a short time an emergency hospital of ten beds was operating.

Not long after the Unit was functioning, Tel Aviv stirred with military activity. Moving at night in long shadowy columns, British troops tramped through toward Petah Tikva. On the evening of September 18, two members of the Unit were returning from Lydda when they reported an extraordinary sight—an unending line of camels loping northward, each animal carrying two tanks of water. There were 25,000 camels. On a nearby road going in the same direction moved trucks and ambulances. The next day muffled booming of heavy artillery could be heard in the streets of Tel Aviv. Allenby's offensive to capture northern Palestine had begun. Later on, trains and ambulances brought in the wounded. Several of AZMU's physicians were put into service at the casualty clearing station set up in the Gymnasium on Herzl Street.

Soon the Turks were routed and the north of the country was open. The Unit now stood before a momentous challenge. All of Palestine waited to be cared for, and only the American doctors and nurses were prepared to cope with the long, bitter task.

1913. First American nurses sent by Hadassah to Jerusalem. Rose Kaplan, left, and Rachel Landy, right, with a visitor outside original Hadassah welfare station which provided maternity care and treatment of trachoma. Palestine, under Turkish rule, was so backward that Hadassah's Drop of Milk was delivered to mothers via donkey express.

1918. *Above:* First American Zionist Medical Unit on eve of departure. In the front row are members of the Central Committee of Hadassah, from right to left: Henrietta Szold, Alice L. Seligsberg, Dora Lefkowitz (Dorothy Leffert), Ruth Fromenson, Emma Gottheil, Bertha Weinheim, Ida Danziger, Libby Oppenheimer. Top two rows are the nurses. *Below:* Doctors, sanitarians, and other medical personnel. During World War I, Palestine and Egypt were under the British Middle East Command.

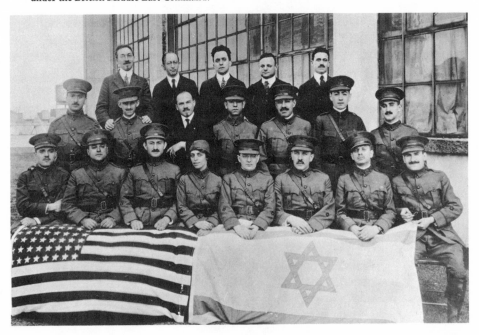

Above: November 3, 1918. British Army hands over keys of the Rothschild Hospital in Jerusalem to the AZMU, whose 44 members became the "founding fathers and mothers" of the Hadassah Medical Organization. Standing, center, James de Rothschild. The Rothschild-Hadassah Hospital moved to Mount Scopus in 1939, and this building eventually housed the first Alice L. Seligsberg Trade School for Girls, and is still part of Hadassah's educational complex. *Below:* 1927. Nathan Straus lays the cornerstone for the Nathan and Lina Straus Health Center in Jerusalem. Community health and education services radiated from here. Today building houses Infant and Child Care for High Risk Children, Hadassah Vocational Guidance Institute, and Hadassah Council in Israel.

Hadassah's school-hygiene program was another part of its systematic, coordinated program to wipe out trachoma and other endemic diseases. The school lunch program taught hygiene and good nutrition to thousands of children, who helped to change the eating habits of the home. The sanitarians created a safe environment. Before dredging, this is how the Huleh swamps were cleared of mosquitoes.

5.

Panties in the Gas Tank

JAMAL PASHA, the Turkish tyrant, could not have cared less about the miseries of Jerusalem when he retreated from the British in December, 1917. He told an aide, "There is enough bichloride of mercury [Mercurochrome] in the drug shops for all of them." Nine months later, the Holy City was a terminal patient suffering its last agonies. Rarely had microbes grown in such favorable conditions. Apart from the usual endemic ailments, cases of typhoid and meningitis were common. The men and women who could still walk were shells. Well did the Wailing Wall live up to its name. There, mothers lay on the stone pavement weeping, praying, beseeching the Lord to save their children.

The Unit sought out the sick. As they visited Jewish homes, one picture emerged. In unlighted hovels humans writhed on rag-covered floors. Their furniture was gone, sold to Bedouin for vegetables. Sunken-eyed, bearded men shook violently from chills. Disheveled women held scrawny infants at dried-out breasts. Even the houseflies were skinny. The stench was overpowering. One nurse commented at the time that living quarters were so bad it would have been necessary to fumigate to turn them into dog kennels.

The moral climate of the city was in raucous tune with the general war atmosphere. The army was an intoxicated troop. Off duty, the men's cry was, "Here today, gone tomorrow—so let's have a time, lads." Girls kept alive by turning to prostitution.

Jerusalem's most pitiful sight was its little army of orphans and abandoned children. Their mothers were either dead or too feeble to care for them, and their fathers were behind Turkish lines. The lot of one such typical tot has been recorded. His name was Yitzhak and his father was impressed into the Turkish army. No one knew who or where his mother was. A Hadassah doctor found him roaming the streets, emaciated and blind, begging for bread. When the air turned cool, Yitzhak knew it was evening, so he fell where he stood and went to sleep, to be awakened by the sun the following morning. He managed to stay alive because he was a familiar figure on the streets of Jerusalem and people saved crusts for him. Even when he had his fill of bread, he would still go on begging for more. It was his way of asking for love and care. The doctor picked up Yitzhak and took him into Roth-schild Hospital. He was cleaned, fed, and pampered, and a couple of days later his appetite was satiated. One afternoon the doctor asked him whether he wanted more bread.

"Neyn, neyn," he replied in Yiddish.

"Cake, perhaps?"

"Neyn, neyn."

"Well, then, what can we give you?"

Yitzhak raised his head and whimpered, "Ich vil meyn ey-gelach."

Yitzhak could not have his eyes, but his body was rehabilitated and he was eventually reunited with his family.

An estimated four thousand waifs roamed the streets of Palestine, most of them in Jerusalem. Alice Seligsberg, who had dedicated her adult life to solving the problems of neglected children in the United States, went about the country establishing orphanages and foster homes, and searching for parents.

From August until November, 1918, AZMU handled Palestine's unfortunates on a basis of emergency care. Before it could do more basic work, the Unit had to settle in and acclimatize. On their arrival in Jerusalem, the physicians were housed in the Hotel de France and the nurses in a small house on the Street of the Prophets. Their first few days were hectic. On the first morning after their arrival, the nurses awoke to find their faces dotted with red spots. Most thought they had caught a dread tropical infection. Others diagnosed it as measles. A doctor hurried over and after a quick examination announced his diagnosis to the women: "Sand flies! And don't be too hard on them because they haven't had the pleasure of such well-fed animals in years." Three days later a more serious affliction gripped the Unit: enteritis, or as most referred to it then, "Gyppie tummy." What made the affliction unpleasant was the lack of a modern plumbing system in Jerusalem. Water was carried by Bedouin to the nurses' quarters in goatskins. More fortunate householders had cisterns. Cooking was done on smelly kerosene stoves. Kerosene was likewise the source of lighting. Daily the Unit had to take quinine against malaria.

Language was a problem. Few AZMU members spoke Hebrew or Yiddish sufficiently well to make themselves understood. There was friction between the Unit's doctors and the few Jerusalem doctors who survived the war, the latter believing that the newcomers had no experience to handle the medical problems peculiar to the Middle East. At night there was no entertainment except for one cinema which played the same film for a solid year. In winter the unpaved streets turned into quagmires. In summer the air was polluted by clouds of gagging dust.

By September, 1918, the Turks were on the run. Nablus, Nazareth, and Haifa were all yielding. Refugees streamed southward into Jerusalem as they did to Jaffa and Tel Aviv. Then, Tiberias fell to the Allies and the flow of refugees to Jerusalem was even greater.

Friday, September 27, 1918, was a memorable day in Jerusalem. It brought the season's first rain. Those who escaped the Turks up north and had recently returned were in a better physical condition than the people who remained in the city. Elated, they walked through the muddy streets of the city observing the festival of Sukkot. They were a mixed crowd of Yemenites and Bokharans, Hasidim wearing their holiday *shtreymlach*, North African Jews in fezes—all singing and dancing lustily. The Sephardim carried their white-bearded *hakham* on their shoulders; Jewish soldiers of the British army whipped through the streets on horseback. It was bitter-sweet merrymaking because Jerusalem was nearly a ghost city, and the holiday jollity resembled a wake. In between the Sukkot processions bands of ragged Turkish prisoners, starved and gaunt, interspersed with the better fed, straight-backed Germans, ambled along to POW camps under the wary eyes of victorious Australian soldiers and bearded Sikhs in white turbans.

The more areas that were liberated from the Turks, the more the Unit was called upon to do. Its members traveled south to Hebron, the most orthodox Moslem town in all Palestine. One AZMU doctor recalled:

> I and my assistant and a nurse would leave at dawn in our Ford tin-lizzie. The car was crammed with medical and surgical supplies and basic food items. It was only 25 miles but it took us two hours in those days. On the way to the dilapidated, tumbling town of stone houses and narrow crooked streets we would pass a wayside tavern called the "Oak of Abraham." It was presided over by a bearded, one-eyed ogre, indescribably and wretchedly filthy. We had been told that to pass the ogre without partaking of his sickly sweet, syrupy coffee, would set off a signal to his henchmen who lay in ambush farther down the road. We always stopped. In Hebron, the Jewish hospital had been stripped of every movable item by the retreating Turks. We treated more Arabs than Jews. Their most common ailments were malaria and trachoma.

In the Jewish schools of Hebron about 40 per cent of the two hundred pupils were suffering terribly from malaria. "As night came on, we always had the choice of spending it in the vermin-ridden 'Oak of Abraham' tavern or returning to Jerusalem. We preferred returning despite the narrow, hilly roads, the sharp curves, the fog and our Ford's weak lights."

In that same month of September, the Sea of Galilee area was liberated. One day, the Unit's manager, Eliahu Lewin-Epstein, got an urgent call from Allenby's headquarters in Tiberias. He was told that a cholera epidemic had broken out in the wake of the Turkish retreat. Lewin-Epstein hired a droshka, fitted it with supplies and sent two doctors, a sanitary engineer, and three nurses. Along the way the evidence of the war was everywhere. The rotting bodies of Germans and Turks were a common roadside sight. On the desolate road the team was stopped by a British officer and an escort with rifles at the ready. "And where are you going at this time of night?" the officer asked with his pistol drawn.

He suspected that the doctors and nurses were disguised German spies returning from a behind-the-lines foray. The forgetful doctors had left their passports behind, but fortunately one of the nurses had hers. After sharing coffee from a Thermos with the reassured Tommies, they got a good send-off on the last lap of the trip. As it turned out, the route they were traveling was taking them straight into the German-Turkish lines. The British officer set them straight.

It was dawn when they arrived on top of the hills overlooking Tiberias and the Sea of Galilee. The trip had taken them forty-eight hours. The sun was just rising over the Golan Heights and the vast panorama below made them gasp. Never had they seen a picture so sublime, so full of nature's wonders. But even more surprising was the welcome they received. There before them on the road were scores of Jews. All night long they had waited in expectation of the "Amerikanim." Some were crying, some were laughing. All chanted in unison a single prayer: *sheheyanu, ve'kiyi-manu, ve'higiyanu lazman hazeh.*

The Unit was overcome both by the welcome and by the conditions in which the Jews lived. Dr. Joseph Krimsky wrote in his diary:

> In the main bathhouse, the water was changed only once in three days. Hundreds of people, many of them suffering from skin diseases immersed themselves in this water. It was an abomination. In the poorhouse, men, women and children reclined, haggard, sunken-eyed, hollow-cheeked with skin the color of yellow parchment, their eyes with lustrous feverish unnatural brilliance, lips graying blue, emaciated limbs. They could not sleep at night because of the vermin. They were fed only once a day. Even then they could not eat.

The team was horror stricken when they saw that before burial, corpses were being washed in the Sea of Galilee at the same spot where women were filling water jugs. Most of Tiberias' Jews were so weak that they could not dig graves deeply enough to bury the dead properly. Dogs and jackals scratched open the shallow graves and pulled out the corpses.

The Unit found that 75 per cent of the town had cholera, a disease transmitted by bad water and usually fatal if not checked within a few days. Hadassah's doctors immediately ordered the populace to stop using Sea of Galilee water, and the British army fenced off the most frequented sites. The entire town was placed under quarantine. Truckloads of food and medical supplies were sent by Hadassah from Jerusalem. Inoculations were given to hundreds. Most cholera patients were treated at home, but the Unit opened an emergency ward in a private house for forty of the most seriously ill. Ray Malin-Cutler, then one of the nurses, later recalled:

> I was the sole nurse in the house, but I had help from hired people who agreed to work only for very high pay. Taking care of the cholera patients was nothing more than hard, physical labor. No medications. Just drinks, drinks, drinks, and hot water bottles and massage, all day and all night long.

Wells were chlorinated. Overchlorinated to be exact. So much chlorine was dropped into the water that the distressed nurses found their hair standing stiff as chicken wire after they washed it. One of the doctors helpfully suggested they add lemon juice to the rinse. The Unit had more serious problems, however. A nurse fell ill with malaria and at one point was close to death. Working conditions were bad. Lice was the staff's nemesis. On one occasion it led to tragic-comic consequences. "We wore long flowing caps, like those of the British nurses," Nurse Madeline Epstein * recalled many years later. "Not only did the lice camp on our heads, but they traveled. The clothes we wore were conservative; you just couldn't scratch yourself wherever you wanted to. Nor was it easy to give a hypodermic with one hand and relieve an itch with the other. The steel corsets we wore were partly to blame for our discomfort."

One day as Madeline stood on the balcony of the Tiberias Hotel where the team was housed she noticed a long line of army trucks and cars parked outside. It dawned on her that they held the solution to the lice problem. Asking no one's permission she picked up a stick, hammered a nail into it, furtively headed for the trucks, opened the cap of a gas tank and then proceeded to dunk her underclothes in the gasoline. The solution was effective although somewhat irritating to the skin, but it was better

* Madeline was the young nurse to whom the Coney Island fortune teller had foretold she would not return and she would suffer a tragedy. She did not in fact return because she married Dentist Samuel Lewin-Epstein, son of the Unit manager, and lived the rest of her years in Jerusalem. Tragedy struck in the death of her father and, during World War II, in the death of one of her two sons. Her surviving son, Jacob, is at this writing Dean of the Hebrew University-Hadassah School of Dentistry in Jerusalem.

than the vagrant vermin. The daily rinsing of clothes in military gas tanks went along smoothly until one day Madeline carelessly let a pair of pink panties slip off the nail.

Early next morning, Nurse Epstein stopped short on her way to the dunking ritual. She saw a British officer severely reprimanding one of the army drivers. The soldier was pleading that he knew nothing "about it." Later that day, Madeline was ordered to report to the headquarters of the commanding officer. As she entered the staff room, she faced the granite faces of the C/O, his aide-de-camp, and officers in charge of military transport. The C/O was direct.

"Sister, do *these* belong to you?"

He held high a pair of pink panties, now bleached white.

"I suppose so," mumbled Madeline, pink-faced.

"Sister, can you explain this act of sabotage?"

The C/O listened patiently, drumming his fingers on the desk. When she concluded, he remonstrated in cold heat. "Do you realize that you put four Staff HQ vehicles out of commission. *Four!*" Only later that day did Madeline understand that the lice that she had killed in the gas tanks had clogged the feed lines of the vehicles. Next morning, a tin of petrol was placed at the door of her room marked "For Personal Use ONLY!"

Tiberias' off-limits status posed a problem as the British military machine pushed on toward Damascus and Constantinople. As it went, the conquering army freed more Palestinian Jewish refugees, and the road home for the war victims led through Tiberias. One morning a group of five hundred riding on hay wagons suddenly appeared at the city's gates. In the city, the health risk was great. The weather had turned stormy and the frail refugees could not continue to Jaffa and Jerusalem in their wagons. At the intercession of Nurse Epstein, the British agreed to send them to their homes in a military convoy. After being fed and housed by the Unit, the refugees trudged up Tiberias' hills to the takeoff point, which they reached by midnight. At 2:00 A.M. a message was received by the Unit at the Tiberias Hotel that the convoy was nowhere to be seen. Enraged, Nurse Epstein dressed, jumped on an unsaddled horse, and dashed after the truant convoy. She found the British officer-in-charge several miles beyond the appointed place, calmly shaving. He explained airily that he did not intend to take the civilians because they were not the responsibility of the British

army. A fierce argument ensued, with Nurse Epstein doing most
of the arguing and gesticulating. When she threatened to report
him to Army HQ in Jerusalem, he finally gave in, turned the convoy around, and picked up the refugees. It occurred to Nurse
Epstein only after she returned to the hotel at dawn that she
had rarely ridden a horse and never bareback. Frightened, she
pulled the covers over her head and went to sleep.

As Hadassah made it a rule never to distinguish between Arab
and Jew, so its doctors did not distinguish between British and
German or Turk in Tiberias. The British kept a large number of
ill POW's in an administration building behind the Scottish Mission Hospital, which had been turned into a general hospital.
Hadassah treated the prisoners—as they would a half century
later the wounded Arab terrorists brought to Jerusalem's Medical
Center—with high professional skill.

Members of the Unit soon moved north from Tiberias into the
Hills of Canaan where lay the mystic town of Safad, venerated
home of sages and kabbalists. No more charming site existed in
all the Middle East. But the war had left its scars. When a Hadassah doctor arrived in the winter of 1918–19, he headed straight
for a Jewish elementary boys' school. After the physician finished
examining the pupils, none more than ten years old, the teacher
addressed them softly: "Children, it's now time for *minha* [the
afternoon prayers]. Those of you who must go to synagogue
to recite *kaddish* [prayer for the dead] may now leave. Now run
along quickly."

The doctor looked up from putting his stethoscope in his
bag. He was shocked to see that half the class were leaving to
say *kaddish*. That night in his room in Safad he took out his
diary and wrote:

> Safad. 8,000 Jews before the war, only 3,000 left. 3,000 died
> of hunger and pestilence. The rest fled. Town is full of little
> orphans, many homeless, and destitute. Pitiful to see these thin,
> wizened children with their solemn appealing faces framed in
> straggling unkempt hair and long curly earlocks. Safad's Jews
> live off of *halukah*, sent from abroad. When war cut off the
> charity, they sold homes and belongings to Arabs. Problem of
> Safad is the problem of the entire Jewish population of Palestine.
> Healthful, liveable conditions and remunerative labor are the solu-

tion. Water must be provided. Marshes must be drained. On the way up to Safad we passed enough swamps and morass to poison an empire.

A typhoid epidemic had hit Safad early in 1919. AZMU provided the town with 3 physicians, 5 trained nurses, and 12 student nurses, who took over a 50-bed hospital that had been erected by the Rothschild family. The American Red Cross unit that was then disbanding sold AZMU their equipment, and by June, 1919, a 5-ward hospital was formally opened. It provided free out-patient service to all of Galilee, and did all the surgical work for the entire north of Palestine. Because of Safad's long dry season it was a favorite site for tubercular patients and by June, 1926, Hadassah Hospital had opened a ward for 28 consumptives.

At the western gateway to Galilee, in the little port town of Haifa, AZMU opened a clinic and introduced a school hygiene service soon after the war. But immigration so heavily taxed the city's resources that by 1922, Hadassah opened a small hospital which it continued to subsidize until the late 1930's. Between Safad and Haifa, the Jewish settlers of north Palestine were fairly well cared for. Tiberias was not to have a hospital until May, 1930, although money for the construction of an institution had been contributed by Mr. and Mrs. Peter Schweitzer as early as 1921. Maintenance funds were not available for nine years when finally Hadassah assumed responsibility.

Down in Jaffa in 1919, an epidemic of relapsing fever and bubonic plague suddenly broke out. AZMU opened an emergency ten-bed hospital in Mordecai Ben-Hillel Hacohen's two-story house. In the summer of 1920 an out-patient clinic and forty-five beds were added. Eight years later the Tel Aviv area would have its first modern, fully-equipped hospital. In the late 1930's Hadassah turned it over to the Tel Aviv municipality, but for more than fifty years the name Hadassah Hospital would linger on.

Jerusalem was still Hadassah's capital, however, and the immediate need in Jerusalem was to open the Rothschild Hospital, which had been entrusted to AZMU. "I shall never forget the first day we saw the hospital," said one nurse. "We walked right in and we walked right out." Jewish community leaders, expecting the Unit, had done their best to clean up the worst of the mess left

behind by the Turkish Army. Charwomen were not available, so
the nurses assaulted the building. The cleaning took nearly a
week and having been done, hundreds of cases of medicines,
instruments, and food were unpacked. Hadassah had forgotten
nothing, but the only item that was in oversupply was toilet
paper; it was several years before the original inventory was
depleted.

The official opening of the Rothschild Hospital took place
eight days before the end of the war—on November 3, 1918—
as part of the celebrations marking the first anniversary of the
Balfour Declaration. In retrospect, the presentation of the hospital to AZMU was a milestone in Palestine's medical history. Present at the ceremonies, held on the steps to the building, were the
Grand Mufti of Jerusalem, who blessed the project in Arabic;
the highest ranking British officers in Jerusalem at the time, headed
by General Arthur Money, and diplomatic and ecclesiastical representatives of France, Italy, Spain, Greece, and Armenia. The
United States was represented by the Spanish consul. For the
occasion Jerusalem's Bezalel Art School fashioned a silver key
which the goateed Eliahu Lewin-Epstein, looking all the while
like King George, accepted from the monocled Major James de
Rothschild.

By the end of 1918 the hospital had accepted 255 patients, but
conditions were far from ideal. In the first few months the atmosphere was more of a field hospital. In the operating theater,
kerosene lamps provided light. During an operation the task of
an unfortunate nurse was to hold the lamp high over the anes-
thetized patient.

At the official opening in November, 1918, the Rothschild
Hospital was an institution of 90 beds, 6 departments with out-
patient clinics and 3 laboratories. The two largest departments of
24 beds were set aside for internal medicine and pediatric patients.
The others were obstetrics, ophthalmology, dermatology and general surgery. An isolation hut, morgue, machine shop, garage, and
laundry were soon constructed, and bacteriological and patho-
logical labs were installed. The demand for beds was so great that
within a short time 22 were added. AZMU's most valuable innovation was the introduction of an X-ray institute. At first it was
poorly equipped and could provide only emergency services, but
by 1921 the institute had a specialist and new equipment provided

by the American Jewish Physicians Committee. It helped make Rothschild the most important medical institution in the country. In the four months of operation from September, 1918, to the end of the year, Hadassah treated 15,000 persons who had made 59,000 visits. (Within two decades the number would jump to 1,733,773 who would make 10,000,000 visits.) Another vital statistic: In the first full year of AZMU's work in Jerusalem, 15 out of every 100 patients were Moslems, 5 out of every 100 were Christian.

What emerges from this picture of AZMU's work is that the foundations for basic medical work had now been established. Hospitals had been activated up and down the country—probably a unique undertaking in medical history for a foreign, private volunteer women's organization. Twenty years later when Palestine's first medical center was opened on Mt. Scopus in Jerusalem by Hadassah, over 200,000 patients were being treated in Hadassah's institutions annually. That amounted to nearly 60 per cent of all Jewish patients treated in Palestine hospitals.

As early as January, 1919, AZMU had made a great impression in the United States. We may today read with wonder that Henrietta Szold in New York should write to Alice Seligsberg in Jerusalem:

> Are you noticing in Palestine the change that is taking place in the name of the Unit? Here Hadassah is fading out of sight and mind. The Unit is known only as the American Zionist Medical Unit. The *Palestine News*, I see, still refers to it as the Hadassah expedition. I should like to make a suggestion. Eventually the name Hadassah will have to disappear, but would it not be well and fitting if we could at least secure its attachment to the little hospital that Dr. Kagan established before the Unit came out? . . . If you think well of this suggestion and if the little hospital still exists, will you propose its keeping the name Hadassah Hospital as a memorial to our pioneer medical undertakings in Palestine? Would it not be lovely if Hadassah were to be memorialized through a children's hospital?

Alice must have reacted with astonishment to those words, for Hadassah was rooting itself deeply into the life of the country. As she read the letter, a sanitary commission made up of Hadassah doctors was on a six-week tour of the settlements to determine the health situation of the "colonies." Hospitals were fine institutions to build, but what was needed just as much by the *yishuv* was a network of preventive and educational services which only AZMU was in a position to create. This, the commission was to recommend and it was to lead to the beginning of nurses' training and school hygiene and mother and child care. Odd indeed were Henrietta's words. Perhaps they would have been different had she been with the commission when it stopped at seven-year-old Degania, mother of kibbutzim, and heard one of the settlers speak to it:

> The heat is unbearable, for as you well know this spot is located over 200 meters [600 feet] below sea level. To work in such heat requires superhuman effort. To sleep is well nigh impossible. We are constantly drenched with perspiration and we drink gallons of water. This pouring water into our systems while we are overheated as well as the poor quality of the food and the irregular hours of work and sleep have made everyone here a confirmed dyspeptic. . . . We are now confronted with this question: shall we continue or are we fighting a losing battle? We believe that we cannot carry on here much longer unless conditions are made more endurable.
>
> It is for you, gentlemen, to see that it is done. We colonists form the vanguard of our nation in Palestine. We are trying to hold a front which is unsanitary, unhealthful, unliveable. You must remedy these evils for us.

The commission found that blackwater fever, a pernicious type of malaria, had already claimed a number of. Degania pioneers. All the settlers had malaria, including the infants, and most suffered from anaemia. One of the commission members observed, "The colonists are all intelligent looking but have a yellowish pallor. They are our most promising forces. We must establish a system of public health and hygiene, and harness the Jordan River to drive every labor-saving motor in every farm and homestead in Palestine."

The commission continued its investigation, and Hadassah Dr. Joseph Shapiro noted in his diary:

> At Rosh Pina, 40 settlers, 100 hired labors. Sephardim, Persian, Ashkenazi Jews dressed in rags. Homes are one and two rooms in which five to 10 humans huddle. Diet: durrha bread, tea, green vegetables. No medical help except local druggist who dispenses quinine and eye applications.

Mishmar Hayarden: An old greybeard tells this heart-breaking story. . . . "Turks, Arabs, Germans, Arabs, British, Arabs followed one after the other and each contributed something to our destruction. Horses, cattle, food. All are gone. We are sick. We have no medicines."

Metulla: With adequate sanitation and mosquito control, this could be the health resort of Palestine.

Yesod Hama'ala: Pop. 200. Wide muddy streets with two rows of one-storey stone houses. We sink into the mud to our knees. All plans for sanitary improvement must take into consideration the Arabs in the villages around. Bad as is Jews' sanitation, the Arabs is one thousand times worse.

Poriya: A few Americans here among 60 settlers. Cisterns impure.

Sejera: Arab village of 300. Kurdi Jews among them. Misery, Misery.

Merhavia: 25 men and women. At least one member of every family down with fever. Despite fever, they work.

Zichron Ya'acov: Pop. 1,000 of whom are 100 Yemenites. Hospital built by Baron de Rothschild is neglected. They're waiting for him to come up with money to repair it. . . . Colonists are apathetic, indifferent, nursed on charity.

Shfeya, Karkur, Bat Shlomo, etc.: Malaria, trachoma, all the usual things.

Hadera: Turks destroyed 1,000 eucalyptus trees. Seven years ago, 300 enthusiastic Yemenites arrived. 200 died, some returned home, 70 left. Filth, poverty, overcrowding, low wages, malaria, trachoma, TB.

The six-week tour of the colony mapped the needs of the *yishuv*. The commission's findings showed that if the land was ever to be turned into a Jewish home as the Balfour Declaration had promised, more than curative and preventive medicine were required. Solutions and remedies had to be found for neglected children, ignorance and indolence, communal and intercommunal strife. As the war ended there was nobody on the scene capable of coming to grips with these problems except the American Zionist Medical Unit which was fast becoming known to everyone in Palestine as, simply, Hadassah. The Unit itself was beset by enormous internal administrative, personnel, and financial problems at the time. Financially, the Joint Distribution Committee played a life-saving role in keeping the venture going. Between 1919 and 1923, it provided over $800,000—first to AZMU and then to Hadassah when the name of the Unit was changed to Hadassah Medical Organization, a change authorized by the Twelfth World Zionist Congress at Carlsbad in 1921. But, more than anything else, Hadassah was kept alive by the *yishuv*'s need to survive. And Henrietta Szold would admit in 1929 that she had been wrong about Hadassah's name disappearing. Said she: "The Hadassah Medical Organization came into the country as a war relief organization and remained in the land as a peace organization."

6.

"Jew! Speak Hebrew!"

At nineteen, beautiful Shulamit Yedid-Halevy could be excused for having more nerve than sense. But her father, well-known and well-to-do in the Jewish community of Beirut, Lebanon, was at the point of exasperation. Girls of traditional families simply did not go in for nursing careers. That was a job for nuns, not for good Jewish daughters. But Shulamit inherited a healthy portion of her father's willpower, and she threatened that if he did not let her become a nurse, she would run away to some foreign school to study. So, as most loving fathers do, he compromised. She would remain at home in Beirut and study nursing at the American University Hospital.

The same determination that overcame her father's objections also helped Shulamit through a strange, even hostile, new environment in training. She was pained to be obliged to attend Christian prayer services in university chapel on Sunday mornings. The curriculum was based on church mission ideology, because nurses were expected to heal bodies and souls alike. In this foreign world she dreamt of going to Palestine where one day she would help organize a Jewish nursing school. As she studied late into the night her thoughts would meander, and she pondered that Jerusalem was so close—only 150 miles to the south—and yet so far.

In September, 1918, word had reached Beirut that the Hadassah Unit had reached Palestine. By then, Shulamit was a registered nurse. She satisfied her longings for Jerusalem by joining the Maccabee Zionist Organization. One day in December, the coastal vessel *Geula* (*Redemption*) called at Beirut. On board were war refugees returning to Palestine from Constantinople. Only males were permitted on board. The exception was the wife of a prominent eye specialist. Shulamit's cousin was emigrating to Palestine and Shulamit pleaded with him to take her along as a stowaway. In a moment of weakness he agreed and hid her on deck behind a stack of camp beds. Shulamit's cousin warned her to remain there for the overnight voyage to Jaffa. But when the returning Palestinians gathered on deck to sing and to dance, the temptation was too much for her. Shulamit came out of hiding to join the joyous males. Almost at once the captain roared, "Who's this young woman?" Discovering that she was taking a free trip, he ordered the helmsman to return to Beirut.

Shulamit ran to the doctor whom she found to be a Jewish physician returning to Jerusalem. He was Albert Ticho.

"Dr. Ticho," she pleaded. "I am a registered nurse. I know that the Zionists have come to Palestine from America to help, and I want to join them. Please influence the captain to let me go on."

The famed physician was at first dubious. How, he asked, could he know that she was telling the truth.

"My cousin is on board. You can ask him."

"He is your cousin, is he?" Dr. Ticho was skeptical.

Members of the Maccabee organization came to Shulamit's aid. They pleaded with Mrs. Ticho, who convinced her husband to vouch for the girl and her fare. The captain grudgingly ordered another turnabout.

On landing in Jaffa her joy was unbounded. She noticed signs everywhere addressed to immigrants, "Jew! Speak Hebrew!" Thanks to her father she had been given a good Hebrew education and could read easily. But Shulamit's joy was quickly eclipsed. When she applied to join AZMU, the doctor told her abruptly, "We don't need nurses." Shulamit could not know then how wrong he was. She had the choice of returning to Beirut or of taking a post as an operating nurse in the Catholic St. Louis Hospital and once again working under the sign of the Cross. She chose the latter. Then, about six weeks later, she noticed a doctor wearing a Star of David on his military uniform. He had come to St. Louis Hospital to observe operations and to seek out a Jewish nurse who he had heard was working there. He was pathologist Benjamin Roman, acting medical director of AZMU.

"We are in a predicament in Jerusalem, Shulamit. We have taken in forty students who want to be taught nursing—but only in Hebrew. The girls are refusing to attend classes if they are taught in any other language. Do you by any chance know Hebrew?"

Her heart pounding hard, Shulamit barely managed to say, "I do."

In February, 1919, Shulamit reported to Dr. Roman at the Hotel de France, Hadassah's headquarters in Jerusalem. She moved into the Hughes Hotel across the street where the nurses now lived. The following day she began teaching.

Shulamit's Hebrew was classic rather than colloquial, and she read better than she spoke. At first, she would write out lectures in English, then with the help of two Palestinian-born members of the staff, she would translate them, always keeping two lessons ahead of the class. Shulamit, who was soon to marry the Unit's sanitation engineer, Louis Cantor, would even write down replies to a long list of questions she was sure the students would ask her. They rarely did ask the ones she prepared.

As halting as her spoken Hebrew was, it was much better than that of the other nurses. Even the students themselves were not too good at the language, most of them being Russian and Polish immigrants. The Hebrew was fractured, but thanks to their tenacity, the Hadassah school became the first anywhere to instruct nurses in the language of the Book. It did present difficulties. No texts were available in Hebrew nor were there Hebrew typewriters to prepare them. So a scribe was engaged to transcribe the lectures and these were given to the students. Most members of the Unit not only had no knowledge of Hebrew, they had no readily available translations of scientific words. On occasion the father of modern Hebrew, Eliezer Ben-Yehuda, would sit up long nights with members of the staff creating Hebrew medical terms. Some words, such as "vitamin," defied translation and remained unchanged.

Professional standards were high, and the curriculum was wholly American. In charge at the beginning was Russian-born, American-educated Rose Klombers. Shulamit took charge for a

short time, and she was relieved by Anna Kaplan. Anna, a nurse
with long experience in New York hospitals, started out with the
Unit but remained behind in a London hospital, gravely ill with
flu. During her tenure as head of the Nursing School she broadened the curriculum, introduced textbooks, and established a
permanent staff of instructors. But not without periodic crises.

To begin with, the Americans on the staff and the others, like
Shulamit, were worlds apart in outlook. The Americans were
high and mighty about their superior training, and this often expressed itself in a supercilious attitude toward non-Americans.
Many picayune, personal battles were fought with non-American
staff members. Objection was raised, for example, to Shulamit's
wearing the same uniform and pin as the Unit's nurses, or even
eating together at the same table. Acting Director Roman did
much to calm tempers, but new irritations constantly appeared.

The European physicians at Rothschild had their own idio-
syncrasies. They objected strongly to a three-year period of
training for nurses, which they thought was overlong. They considered theoretical classroom work a waste of time. On the Continent, nurses learned all they knew in the wards, and were never
required to utter more than an obedient "Yes, sir" or "No, sir."
And here was Hadassah teaching them to give intramuscular in-
jections, to take blood pressure, to do all sorts of preventive work
that was the private preserve of the physician. The German-born
Jewish doctors, who had always worked with nuns, thought that
regular hours for nurses was madness. They could not quite ac-
custom themselves to the fact that nurses were human. The
Russian-born doctors objected particularly to nurses who had
something to say about the condition of the patient. On one occasion when a nurse reported a change in a patient's symptoms, a
European-trained doctor cried out in exasperation, "Nurses should
have feet, hands, and eyes! They are not supposed to think! They
should *do, see,* and *rush,* and *that's all!*"

Working and teaching conditions of nurses always leave something to be desired. But in Jerusalem in the early years after the
war they were downright primitive. Anna Kaplan recalled:

> We had no classrooms. We taught wherever we could find
> an empty room, even in the laundry. The Nurses' Home was some
> distance from the hospital. We had no transport, and the students
> had no suitable wearing apparel. When I opened the Surgical

Department, the plumbing was not yet completed. Equipment came from America but not furniture. We saved the shipping cases from the Palestine Supply Department and from these made bedside tables, chairs, and cabinets. Electricity was only a dream in those days. Ice was unheard of.

After the first year at the Hughes Hotel, we moved to more spacious quarters in the Musrara Quarter of the city, but even then there was considerable crowding with as many as five girls sharing a single room. A terrible snowstorm, unprecedented in Palestine, visited us—the roof caved in, two nurses were injured and the house was no longer fit for use. The snowstorm lasted twenty-four hours but it caused us trouble for weeks. During the storm the doctors and the nurses had to sweep the snow off the roof of the hospital for fear that it too would cave in.

The first class of student nurses was assembled on November 3, 1918, the same occasion on which the Rothschild Hospital was formally opened. What a group they were! Most came from rural areas. Some had been employed in menial jobs at the hospital. Few of them had as many as eight years of formal schooling. A number of the girls had sneaked through Turkish lines in northern Palestine after they heard a nursing school was being organized. They were a ragged, sickly group of refugees. But what they lacked in physical appearance they made up in high spirits. Matured by war and hardship, they were highly independent. On one occasion one of the girls took off without permission for an overnight trip to Tel Aviv together with a doctor of the Unit. She was temporarily suspended on her return. Her enraged fellow students, claiming that the Don Juan physician was at fault, went on strike. They won. Strikes were frequent among the nurses, but they did not always succeed. Their most successful protests opposed the use of Yiddish, English, and all languages other than Hebrew.

With it all Hadassah upheld its high, if martinet, standards: "You are expected to give respectful attention to your superiors," read the rules, "to obey orders promptly and unquestioningly, to refrain from carrying on conversations while on duty, to speak in a low voice, to move about gently, not to indulge in familiarities with patients or discuss their illness with them."

The school soon developed a strong feeling of responsibility among the students. Once the question arose before the five-member governing committee of the school whether a nurse should be punished for giving a patient the wrong medicine.

"Definitely not!" replied Anna Kaplan, to the shock of the committee members. "Nurses must not be afraid to report such errors. On the other hand, failure to report should be severely punished."

As the first year passed, the school insisted on more stringent screening of students. After Henrietta Szold arrived in 1920 to head Hadassah's work in Palestine, she personally scoured the country for candidates.

"Do you owe any debts to your parents or to anyone else, and how much do they amount to? Do you suffer from rheumatism, headaches, emotional upsets?"

These and twenty other questions were routinely asked. If the students' debts were too large they were disqualified, because they would then have to take on outside work to repay the loans. They had to be twenty years' old (today's requirement: seventeen), had to know Hebrew, the Latin alphabet, and remain on probation for six months. They were not permitted to treat sick relatives at home or in the hospital, except in the line of duty. They received a small allowance for the first six months. The working day was twelve hours with three hours off for homework and recreation. The students got one afternoon off a week and had a two-week vacation yearly. Lights-out was 10:00 P.M. (11:00 P.M. today) with late leave until 11:30 P.M. once a week. On graduation nurses were assured of work and a starting salary of the equivalent of $50 a month. And yet they did have a measure of self-rule. The girls had their own committee which dealt with complaints against both students and nurses, and could mete out light punishment for disciplinary infractions. The committee later grew into a national nurses student organization.

Only twenty-two nurses of the original forty made it through the first three years. But those who did graduate did well. Six became principals of schools or supervisors in hospitals. Several made excellent reputations in public-health nursing. Later on, Shulamit Yedid-Halevy Cantor, the stowaway from Beirut, would succeed Anna Kaplan and serve a long and distinguished career as Hadassah's supervisor of nurses and director of the school.

Graduation exercises are nothing to write home about, except for the students. But the rites of the first class were an exception. Since the school was dedicated on Balfour Day, 1918, it was decided to schedule the ceremonies for Balfour Day, 1921. In the last week of October, the Hebrew-English invitations were about to be dispatched by two Yemenite runners (they were more reliable than the local mail service) when a representative of the Zionist Executive asked Henrietta Szold to postpone the festivities. Rumors were wild that the Arabs would observe the anniversary as they did in 1920 and again at Passover in 1921 by shooting and stabbing Jews.

The rumors turned out to be true and fortunately Henrietta took the advice to delay the ceremonies for one week. On Balfour Day, November 2, bloodthirsty Arab mobs ran screaming out of the Old City of Jerusalem. They burned and pillaged. Before the day was out, five Jews were dead and twenty wounded. British Governor Ronald Storrs' police neglected to intervene energetically, though Storrs himself, whom Henrietta described as "an evil genius," had taken refuge in Hadassah Hospital during the Passover riots under the pretense of "protecting" the Jewish community. Zionist officials demanded his removal. But Storrs remained and riots continued periodically through the 1920's and 1930's. On November 4, 1921, a massive funeral procession left the Rothschild Hospital compound. More than one thousand persons marched in silence behind the stretchers on which the tallit-draped bodies were borne. When a month of mourning was declared, the graduation exercises were postponed again to December 7. But the graduation certificates still bore the date November 2. Henrietta insisted the date be left unchanged as a sign "of our unquenchable hope for the future of the Jewish people."

Dressed in crisp white uniforms and caps on which were emblazoned a blue Star of David, the graduating class of 1921 was led into the hall of Bet Aminoff, on Jaffa Road, the new nurses' home, by Anna Kaplan. Henrietta Szold presided and Lady Samuel, wife of the first British high commissioner, handed out the diplomas. Szold commented in her address:

> For this day you have waited three years, and across the ocean [in the United States] there are thousands of women who have waited for it nearly ten years. When they sent two pioneer nurses over here to inaugurate District Visiting Nursing, they

thought of this evening. When the summons came to enlarge the number of nurses from two to twenty, they rejoiced for the sake of this evening.

Now, as if in payment for the loan of the twenty-two nurses that America had sent before and after the war, the *yishuv* was contributing twenty-two of its own. And none too soon. Only two of the original AZMU nurses were still on duty at Rothschild Hospital by the time graduation had rolled around.

Immediately after the exercises were over, six-month courses were begun in midwifery, operating-theater nursing, and public health. Later, these would be integrated into the undergraduate studies.

By the end of the first decade, 135 registered nurses were graduated by the school, and the standards of the profession were fixed. In its eleventh year, the Hadassah School of Nursing was adjudged by the International Association of Graduate Nurses to be the finest in the Middle East.

Still, the demand for graduates was insatiable. Hadassah started courses for male orderlies partly to make up for the lack and partly to care for those Arab and Jewish Orthodox patients who refused to be tended by women.

Hadassah was the main source of highly qualified registered nurses until 1935 when Kupat Holim, the sick fund of the Jewish Federation of Labor (Histadrut), opened a school. A municipal school was opened in 1940 in Tel Aviv, and both these institutions drew heavily on Hadassah's experience and personnel.

But Hadassah was not always so readily accepted. There were times when the Americans were told they were simply wasting their time.

7.

"You're Wasting Our Time, Doctor!"

A YEAR after World War I ended the third great wave of Jewish immigration began to hit the shores of Palestine. It had also brought a small number of immigrants from the United States, among them Henrietta Szold and Golda Meir. Nearly 10,000 Jews from Central and Eastern Europe arrived in a single year. They left their homelands for many reasons, but essentially they had taken the Balfour Declaration literally, and they wanted to be in Eretz Israel for the founding of a Jewish state. The immigrants were rugged idealists. They trooped off to the marshes of northern Palestine, joined the colonists in building roads and draining swamps. By the end of 1920, more than sixty labor camps were organized throughout Galilee. Living conditions for the pioneers were primitive. The region was a morass that spawned malaria, typhus, and typhoid. Roving doctors and nurses from Hadassah provided the only medical aid. Public health teams from Jerusalem tried to teach elementary rules of hygiene, but the Hadassah workers soon found that if they wanted to subdue the louse, the fly, and the mosquito, they would first have to overcome the mulish, senseless opposition of the *halutzim*, the pioneers. As a matter of course, the laborers refused typhoid inoculations. Not even the offer of an American cigarette could entice them to submit to the needle. Some spurned an injection even when they were lying flat on their backs with roaring fevers.

The largest of the labor camps was located at Migdal, on the western shore of the Sea of Galilee.

"Your toilets are lousy," the enraged Hadassah public health doctor Joseph Shapiro spluttered in a mixture of weak Hebrew and Yiddish. "You've got to cover them. Besides that, you men have just got to stop taking your drinking water out of the Sea of Galilee because that is where your sewage is being dumped. You'll all soon be dead if you keep going on like this, and then what good will your Zionism be to anybody?"

The camp foreman gave a half smile. "Now look, Dr. Shapiro. We had worse conditions when we first came, and we've survived."

Of the five hundred men and women at Migdal, nearly every one of them had malaria. Yet the foreman insisted that they had come willing to struggle, and if need be, to die. Let the shop-keepers in Jerusalem and Jaffa worry about things like chlorinating water or building toilets. *Halutzim* had to do just as well as the Arabs and under the same conditions.

Defying the *halutzim*, Dr. Shapiro put in a filtration plant to purify the water at Migdal. The workers boycotted it, and kept taking their water from the lake. The foreman told his men: "The Arabs don't drink antiseptic water. We've got to live as they do." And to Shapiro he said, "You're wasting our time, Doctor."

It was a point of view, but that was all. What the men realized only later was that the mortality rate among the Arabs was fan-tastically high and only their enormous birth rate saved them from extinction. As they would later find out, the Arabs were glad to accept aid from the Hadassah teams.

What Dr. Shapiro could not do, nature did. Soon, a typhoid epidemic struck with terrible swiftness and stopped work in the labor camps. Common sense finally won, and in answer to an urgent appeal, Hadassah set up a thirty-eight-bed field hospital at Migdal.

But there was a point beyond which one could not reasonably ask a pioneer to go. He would now grudgingly agree to take a shot in the arm, but to demand that he eat oatmeal for breakfast? "What are you giving us?" the Russian Jew with the heavy beard demanded. He held a bowl of brown porridge in his hand, but looked at it as though it were poisoned mud.

The pretty young nutritionist, Yehudit Aaronson (later to become Mrs. Alex Dushkin) fresh from the United States, stammered, "You *must* eat it. You and all the other men are eating the wrong kind of food. You need a good diet to keep you going." She had put the bowls of steaming, enriched oatmeal on the mess tables as a surprise one morning, and watched from the kitchen as one worker after the other, stared at it, sniffed it, and passed it down to the end of the table where the bowls were now piled, untouched. The Russian glowered at Yehudit, "All our lives we men have done without this. We like herring and we will continue to eat herring. Don't throw this stuff at us again."

Yehudit was one of the few graduate Jewish nutritionists of her time. Highly successful in her field, she became a staff dietician of the American Red Cross and agreed to serve with AZMU at Henrietta Szold's request. In fact, she accompanied Henrietta to Palestine early in 1920. The Unit's new medical director, Isadore Rubinow, who had arrived in Jerusalem after the war, had cabled an urgent plea for a nutrition expert, because there was not one qualified dietician in the country at the time.

Soon after their arrival, Henrietta, Yehudit, and Rubinow had toured Galilee, and Yehudit agreed to try to help out with the nutrition problems at Migdal. No one spoke to her when she arrived. On her own she went to the kitchen and began peeling onions.

At the end of work on the second night, Jennie Landsberg, who was in charge of the kitchen, took Yehudit aside.

"You must be wondering why we ignore you," said Jennie. "Try to understand. We could not tell our people we were bringing in a nutritionist. As it is, you are suspect. You come from America where everything must be sterile and everyone must be healthy or life just cannot go on. But here, these people are followers of Tolstoy. They deny the importance of the body. To them the power of the spirit, of ideals, is everything. Remember that. I know you mean well. But go slowly."

Yehudit did not realize how slow. She tried introducing oatmeal and that was already a bust. So, she tried a bit of psychology, by working right along with them. She began by doing a hated job—washing pebbles out of the rice. Eight girls normally spent a full day at it and bitching because they were not out on the road working with the men. The water for rinsing the rice was carried in buckets from the lake. After a few days on the job, Yehudit suggested that she might save the campers the bother of rice-washing if they could get her a donkey and the use of a tinsmith for one day. They were all for this, and in no time Yehudit had an ass and an artisan. Outside the kitchen wall she built a heap of stones. On the stones she placed a barrel to which the tinsmith attached a pipe. The pipe led into the kitchen through an opening made in the wall. A spigot was fitted to the end of the pipe. Yehudit hired a boy to take the donkey with the barrels to fill them. The result was running water. It cut the rice-washing crew in half. Yehudit won points and now could move on.

The basic diet in the camp was bully beef, herring, mushy rice, and jam. The heavily spiced, British army tinned beef and the salty herring burned the scurvied men's bleeding, spongy gums. The bread was badly baked. Actually, as Yehudit found out, it was cooked. Yehudit solved this problem by making friends with a British officer who gave her a field oven from military stores in Affula. Better bread won her additional merit.

Slowly, at spaced intervals, she introduced peanuts, fresh vegetables, and dried milk to the tables. The supplies had to come all the way from Haifa and for that purpose a marketing agency was set up by Yitzhak Sadeh, who became famous as commander-in-chief of the Haganah in 1945, while the marketing agency that he set up later became Hamashbir Hamerkazi, the Histadrut's giant retail outlet. From vegetables, Yehudit went on to a highly nutritious, somewhat sophisticated dessert which she convinced the men was a delicacy from America. The dessert was Jell-O, and it was sent over to Palestine by the Zionist leader, Justice Louis Brandeis.

Yehudit was now at Migdal nearly six weeks and she was ready for her greatest triumph. One day, a delicious pudding reached the tables. It was dark brown in color and it was served in bowls. By now, the men had learned to trust Yehudit, and they dug in. After the first mouthfull, there was some hesitation, but a burly, bearded Russian Jew shouted, "All right men! This we eat for the sake of *Havera* Yehudit!" And with true Tolstoyan sacrifice they licked their bowls clean of pudding-disguised oatmeal. That night Yehudit held a party for some of the men and women, and she served herring. By now, all the malnutrition symptoms had disappeared.

Yehudit's oatmeal victory was more far-reaching than she had expected. By the time she left the camp, six weeks after her arrival, the leaders of the women's liberation movement at Migdal were convinced that their rightful place was in the kitchen. It happened that when one of the camp's fifty girls was found to have a defective heart she was forced off the road. "Well, food conquered our health problems, so it certainly isn't a disgrace to cook," she rationalized to the other girls. In a noble act of comradeship they all decided to join a permanent corps of cooks.

Malaria was a more difficult problem to beat. The answer of the pioneers was to take quinine, but the bitter pill was only a repressant. When the pill was not taken, the symptoms surfaced. The only effective control was to drain the swamps and to rid the country of its mosquito-breeding grounds. Malaria was endemic; it fevered the cities as well as the farms. The work against the blight in the urban areas was the exclusive domain of the Mandatory government's health department, which began to function in the latter part of 1920. At first, Hadassah was forbidden to do any sanitary work in the cities and towns, most probably for political reasons. Recent arrival Henrietta Szold was furious: "The prohibition would be just and proper provided the Government fulfilled its functions. It has a corps of Arabs, low-class inspectors, who are charged with practicing graft. They sell the petrol entrusted to them for [pouring into] wells, cisterns, and puddles, and accept *baksheesh* [bribery] from householders who desire not to have to drink petrolized water."

The Mandate government, under its first high commissioner, Sir Herbert Samuel, soon saw the error, and authorized Hadassah's sanitary engineer Louis Cantor to direct squads of inspectors in an all-embracing antimalaria campaign. Sir Herbert probably reasoned that Hadassah was, after all, killing mosquitoes that were biting both Arabs and Jews, and probably an occasional Englishman. Cantor's efforts were long remembered by all sections of the community. He introduced toilets and garbage disposal units in Arab villages. He drew up the first plan for draining quarters in Jerusalem that were avenues of running sewage. He gave the first course of instruction to Palestine's plumbers ("installators," as they are still known in Hebrew). And what some distinguished Zionist leaders always remembered him for was the hot shower installation that he introduced into the Hotel de France, Hadassah's headquarters. It soon became a regular Friday afternoon rite for the captains of the *yishuv* to wash themselves down under Lou Cantor's showers.

By 1921, Hadassah-directed teams under Dr. Israel "Kleeg" Kligler neutralized the anopheles in the rural areas. The breakthrough came when Justice Brandeis provided $10,000 for experimental work in malaria control. Kligler's teams found that, countrywide, 25 per cent of the Jewish and 50 per cent of the Arab populations were chronic malaria sufferers. With methods proven in Panama during the construction of the canal, new cases were reduced by 90 per cent. Sanitary inspectors stood guard over swamp areas during the breeding season. They forced quinine down the gullets of Arabs and Jews alike. They even went as far as to repair dripping faucets in town, village, and camp. By the end of 1921, the nation's worst pest holes had been eradicated. At one cooperative farm near Migdal, all but two of the eighty workers suffered at least two malarial attacks in the summer before the work was begun. By the beginning of 1922, only five cases were reported in the same area. Henrietta Szold was ecstatic: "The men sleep in the open without nets and remain unstung! It's a miracle."

Not everyone was so happy about the results. The government's health department chief, Colonel George Heron, was a physician of questionable sympathies. He had been transferred to the Colonial Office from the army when the military administration made way for the civilian Mandate administration in 1920. On one occasion he was asked to approve a big antimalaria project and to provide a token sum toward the expenses as a demonstration of British concern. When the project landed on his desk, he demanded, "Who owns the land?" His subordinate replied, "The Palestine Jewish Colonization Association, sir." Replied Heron, "Then, damn it, let them pay for it." After all, the mosquitoes were carousing on private land.

It was not until 1931 that the Mandate government finally agreed to pay the bill for killing mosquitoes, public or private. Hadassah had turned over the responsibility for malaria control to Sir Herbert Samuel in 1922, after showing the way, but the men who fought the good fight under British supervision were either former members of the Unit or trained by it. And the Jewish Joint Distribution Committee financed the work until 1931.

Hadassah's experience in the marshes of Galilee led to its participation in healing the land with reclamation projects. In 1926, Hadassah undertook major support of the Jewish National Fund, one of the earliest Zionist organizations which was designed to buy, afforest, and rehabilitate broad stretches of the Land of Israel for settlement. Hadassah would perennially be the largest single contributor to JNF and by its fund-raising would help drain the Huleh swamps (Lake Huleh has in fact been drained off the map of Israel), in 1930 would redeem over 4,000 acres of the Haifa Bay area, and—the largest of all projects—would rehabilitate 10,000 acres in Galilee in 1953 providing areas for ten new villages.

Relations between the Zionists and the colonial administration were testy. The fact that Sir Herbert Samuel was a Jew and pro-Zionist made little difference to Colonial Office bureaucrats, many of whom, like Heron, had transferred from the army or the Occupied Enemy Territory Administration to what they hoped would be adventurous, well-paid, easy jobs in Palestine. Many had served in Cairo and knew how to "handle" Arabs. Jews, ideologically motivated and anxious to establish a state, were another cup of tea.

In Haifa, for example, the anti-Zionist military governor had remarked that the overcrowded and unsanitary conditions in which Jewish immigrants were living endangered the health of the Arab population. This, despite a dispensary that was being run for Jews and Arabs alike by Hadassah.

In reply to the military governor's challenge, Hadassah rushed its public health officer, Joseph Shapiro, into the port town. His survey concluded, even to the satisfaction of the British governor, that the Arabs were less likely to fall ill from the Jews than from the drinking water which they were taking from shallow wells or from the garbage they was spilling into the streets or from the sewage that was running by their houses or from the open barrels of water which they used to wash clothes—and breed mosquitoes. Shapiro proved that the health and sanitation conditions of the Jews were just as good, and in many cases better, than that of their Arab neighbors.

Shapiro's biggest challenge was the common louse. By mid-1920 immigrants were entering Haifa and Jaffa ports en masse and were bringing with them an unprecedented plague of East European lice. Disinfestation of their bodies was not much of a problem since there was plenty of chlorine at hand. The problem was how to deal with the clothes. The British had invented an apparatus called a Serbian Barrel to sterilize clothes, but it was not yet available in Palestine. Shapiro improvised by taking empty alcohol barrels and making them air-tight. He then fitted them out with false bottoms which were filled with water. Placed over a fire, the barrels became giant pressure cookers. In a short time the clothes placed in the Shapiro Barrels, as they became known throughout the country, were free of lice.

By mid-1922, Hadassah asked the Mandate government to take over rural sanitation along with malaria control. In any case, inspection of newcomers ceased to be a great problem since immigration had been curbed. Thus relieved of preventive medical work Hadassah could expand its medical services throughout the country. From the Jordan to the Mediterranean, from Galilee to Judea, a string of sixty Hadassah clinics soon functioned in towns and villages. Clinics serviced nearly all the moshavim, or cooperative villages. In 1931, the rural medical service was turned over to Kupat Holim Amamit, a private sick fund founded by Hadassah which thrives today. Throughout the 1920's the Hadassah horse-and-buggy doctors and nurses who traveled the dirt paths into remote settlements were familiar and welcomed figures. At the beginning of the 1930's they were coming under different auspices, but that did not alter the fact that Hadassah was the first to send them on their appointed rounds. Henrietta Szold gave them the ultimate tribute when she said, "The itinerant doctors had become the lineal successor to the priest in the camps of ancient Israel."

Few people living today have a full understanding of the extent to which Hadassah—young, poor, and inexperienced—fashioned the future of the *yishuv*'s medical history in the third decade of the century. When Americans were only beginning to dream of national health insurance, Hadassah in Palestine was forcing an amalgamation of the sick funds that were started by the two existing labor parties. Both parties were serving as contractors on the road-building and swamp-cleaning projects in Galilee, and each demanded separate field hospital services from Hadassah. The Unit's acting director at the time was Henrietta Szold. She put her foot down and issued an ultimatum that the two would amalgamate or else. That decided the issue. The result was Kupat Holim, of the

Histadrut, Israel's Federation of Labor. Until 1931, Hadassah institutions took on all Kupat Holim cases free of charge. With financial help from Hadassah, Kupat Holim built its first hospital in the Emek Jezreel in 1929. A second, Beilinson, was constructed in Petah Tikva seven years later. These two institutions took considerable pressure off Hadassah and permitted Hadassah to reach for new horizons.

Just as in Galilee Hadassah pioneers were being told they were wasting time, so in Jerusalem they were being similarly rebuffed. But as in Galilee the Americans refused to accept "no" for an answer, so in the Holy City they persisted until the population accepted them. Often they had to use bizarre stratagems. No single Hadassah worker was more persevering than a dynamic mite of a public health nurse by the name of Bertha Landsman. To this day, her charges vividly remember how in the summer of 1921 she issued orders in the cadence of a top sergeant doing battle against a dangerous enemy. "If they don't let you in the front door go in the back door. And if they don't let you in the back door, go through the window. But get in!" It was a battle cry no one would expect could possibly emerge from a pink-cheeked, blue-eyed Bertha, who was anything but big.

In some ways Bertha's story was much like that of Shulamit Yedid-Halevy Cantor. At about the same time that Shulamit was threatening her father that she would run away from Beirut to go to nursing school, Bertha was doing the same: She told her father in no uncertain terms that nursing was definitely for her, and if she could not study in her native New York City, she would flee to Washington, D. C. The poor man agreed, providing she remained close to home. So Bertha trained at Mt. Lebanon Hospital, in New York, the source of many of AZMU's first nurses. After graduation she served in mother and infant welfare stations established by philanthropist Nathan Straus in New York City's underprivileged neighborhoods. But her heart was in Palestine, and in 1921 she followed it there. To the newcomer, Eretz Israel has always been seductively rich in challenges; Henrietta Szold would say, "Where everything is needed, everything needs to be done." Bertha looked at the needs and saw that in Jaffa–Tel Aviv four out of every ten babies never celebrated their first birthday. In Haifa, the mortality rate was 30 per cent, and in Jerusalem

20 per cent. To keep babies alive, then, was her challenge. She reached into her experience and pulled out a plan to adapt the Straus mother and infant stations to Palestine. She organized a platoon of nurses, opened the first center in the ancient walled city of Jerusalem, and then went out to drag in the reluctant mothers. In the beginning, the male members of the Jewish families beat off the nurses, even bodily. Most of the nurses did not wear marriage bands, so they would be taunted with: "Hah! You are not even married, and you—you are going to tell us how to take care of our babies!"

The unfortunate nurses were caught in a crossfire. From one flank they were being driven on by Bertha's exhortations; from the other they were being pushed away by irate husbands. At times they took Bertha's orders literally and climbed through back windows to plead, to cajole, to tempt mothers to come to the stations. Inside, they found dark, dank rooms where babies lay bundled like mummies, their hands and feet tightly tied "to give them good postures." The infants looked more like packages ready for mailing than human beings ready for living. Their eyes were watery from the smoke of charcoal cooking fires. Windows were kept closed even in temperate weather because the families believed it was the only way to keep out unseen germs—and the evil spirit. For extra protection, a *hamsa* (a brass hand) was hung in every room. Flies and vermin plagued the tots, but they were disregarded because they were "too small" to do harm. When mothers had insufficient milk to nurse, they gave the infants unpasteurized goat's milk.

Bertha broke the opposition. She began by offering free layettes and pasteurized formula milk to parents on condition they give birth in Rothschild Hospital. Once the mothers were in the hospital Bertha would say to each one, "Bring your babies to our station regularly and I promise you they will live to bless you with many grandchildren."

The Drop of Milk (Tipat Halav) station, as it was known, had a kitchen and two rooms. Each day in the kitchen hermetically sealed vats of milk would be lifted onto a three-headed kerosene stove. When the milk reached close to boiling point, the vat would be hurriedly shifted into a bathtub filled with ice where it would be quickly cooled. The result was the first pasteurized milk in all of Palestine, probably in the Middle East. Nurses and volunteers, headed by the wife of the director of customs, Mrs. Harold Solomon, would then prepare formulas, fill bottles, and wait for the mothers to appear. Those who came for the first time would receive a tin container free of charge to carry the bottles home. The word quickly passed from mouth to mouth in the Jewish quarter of the Old City that Hadassah was giving out a new type of milk; milk that did not turn rancid quickly. This appealed to mothers and their numbers at the Drop of Milk station grew. Some began coming from quarters outside the walled city, but many were still hesitant.

Bertha was impatient. If mothers did not come for milk, she would see to it that the milk was taken to them. And so was established the Donkey Milk Express. The bottles, each labeled with the baby's name, were packed in ice and put on a donkey cart whose sides carried the name "Tipat Halav" in Hebrew, Arabic, and English. Each weekday morning, the Donkey Milk Express began its journey from the David Street station, joined the raucous traffic of horses, camels, carriages, and tin-lizzies on its life-giving mission to the Rothschild Hospital, which was the New City's milk distribution point. There, volunteer women of the Hebrew Women's Federation (Histadrut Nashim Ivriot) handed the sterilized bottles to waiting mothers.

So popular was the Donkey Milk Express and its cargo that housewives from Western countries who had no infants clamored for pasteurized milk. One well-to-do American mother once approached Bertha to provide her with pasteurized milk because her daughter disliked drinking boiled milk. Bertha's reply was in character: "Of course we will provide you with our product. Just send someone each morning to pick up a pint. And send along 50 cents for each bottle." Hadassah's Robin Hood explained that she was charging the outlandish price to help cover the cost of the milk for several children whose parents could not pay one cent. Actually few got it free. Except for the destitute, mothers were required to pay something, even though it be a pittance. Bertha intended to drive home the lesson that mothers and fathers must care for their own children; that charity should not replace responsibility. Bertha and her nurses struggled with this problem as they had struggled to get the mothers to visit the station in the first place. Mostly, the fathers were the ones who objected. For this kind of luxury they expected the Americans or Europeans to pay. Mothers cried on Bertha's slim shoulders begging her to help convince their husbands. For those who did have more generous spouses Bertha would keep precise accounts of the mils the women paid and each Saturday would remain at home making out individual receipts which they could show their husbands. At times, exhausted, Bertha was tempted to give up the idea, be done with the accountancy, and hand out the milk free. Then one day a pretty young Orthodox mother came to her, smiling coyly, and told a story that convinced Bertha the battle was won.

The mother had always complained that she could not get milk money from her stubborn husband. This day she showed up with the coins clenched in her fist and a promise that she would no longer have to plead for milk money.

Bertha was surprised. "How did you do it?" she asked.

The mother's cheeks turned pink and she dropped her eyes. She wanted to talk to Bertha privately. They stepped aside and the mother whispered, "It was very hard, but my husband does not like sleeping on the floor."

Bertha's eyes opened wide with an unspoken question.

"It was the day I was supposed to go to the *mikveh* [ritual bath]. I absolutely *refused* to go until he gave me the money for milk. He won't refuse again," she said with a twinkle.

Forty years later, Bertha recalled the story and said that it was the turning point in her personal battle. Never again did she waver.

Soon, the milk program was running smoothly. Bertha now felt sufficiently sure of herself to move into related fields. She sent her nurses into homes to advise mothers how to prepare cereal, how to refrigerate, how to nurse. And by mid-1923 they were all going through the front door. At the station, Bertha insisted that babies be weighed regularly. Some mothers objected because they said it would invite the evil eye, so they fed their children before they took them to the station and then insisted that there was no need to weigh them. The nurses overcame that obstacle by forcing the mothers to leave the children at the center for three hours before going ahead with a test feeding and a weighing-in. Periodically, the children were examined and fortunately for everyone concerned, Jerusalem's first pediatrician was Helena Kagan, whose understanding and kindliness earned her the respect and gratitude of generations of parents. On July 31, 1958, Mayor

Gershon Agron and the city fathers bestowed upon Dr. Kagan the coveted Freedom of Jerusalem, the first woman to be so honored.

So popular was the station after a time that the non-Jewish mothers in the neighborhood began to ask for aid. Everyone was accepted, Jew and non-Jew alike. In 1923, with a gift from Nathan Straus, another station was opened in the lower Musrara Quarter near Damascus Gate where the population was predominantly Arab. Even during the bitter Arab riots, a Jewish and an Arab physician would remain on duty at the station. Veteran nurses in Jerusalem still remember with a smile the diminutive Dr. Abu Saud, who had to stand on a bench to examine the taller children's eyes and throats, and whose favorite—and effective—treatments for many common ailments were barley water or castor oil. The nurses, too, courageously carried on through the bloodletting, keeping to their rounds in both Arab and Jewish quarters.

One of those nurses was Hanna Elkayam who was sent into the village of Siloam (Silwan), in the southern environs of Jerusalem, to open a station. The village was mainly Arab, but about one hundred Yemenite Jewish families lived there peacefully. From 1925, Hanna lived in Siloam and served the community as nurse, confidante, pharmacist, social worker. All problems came to Hanna for resolution: how much to spend on a bar mitzvah party, what clothes to buy for the children, how to reunite a separated couple. Hanna was the mother of the village.

One night the leading Sheikh of Siloam, Haj Ghuslan, did Hanna the unique honor of calling upon her. After the usual formalities were ended, he asked her whether she would go to his house to deliver his wife's child. Not a little tremulous, Hanna agreed. She found the woman in difficult labor, but Hanna delivered the baby after a few tense hours. As the Sheikh's son uttered its first cry, the grandmother threatened the nurse, "That child you have brought into the world will grow up one day to throw a rock at you at the Wall." But Sheikh Ghuslan never forgot Hanna's kindness. During the riots of 1929 he placed guards over the property of all the Jews of the village and nothing was stolen or touched during their temporary absence.

The lone milk station that was opened by Bertha Landsman in 1921 had by the end of the decade multiplied to twenty-two, not counting numerous substations throughout the country. One result was that the Mandate government's slow-moving health department was obliged to emulate Hadassah and opened its first infant welfare center for Arabs in 1925, and by the end of the decade it had fourteen going. The idea spread beyond the borders of Palestine. In Cairo, WIZO (Women's International Zionist Organization) asked for the loan of a Hadassah-trained nurse to run a center. Nurses from Iraq were sent to Jerusalem to observe Hadassah's work and returned to Baghdad to organize similar operations. A center on the Hadassah pattern was likewise opened in Amman.

Fruits of the infant welfare work were quick and sweet. Mortality dropped dramatically. In 1922, 144 Jewish children out of every 1,000 throughout the country died before their first birthdays. By 1930, the rate had dropped by more than half to 69. Unfortunately, the net was not so large that it could provide blanket coverage for the Arab communities. Although Hadassah served both sections of the population, its work was done primarily in predominantly Jewish areas, so that in the same period infant mortality rates of the Arab community rose by 3 per cent. Had the welfare stations not been in operation, however, there is little question that the Arab rate would have climbed more rapidly than it did.

By the end of the decade Hadassah closed the Drop of Milk kitchens. In nine years the Jewish population had accepted as a matter of course the necessity of proper milk preparation. But the name endured, and to this day a mother of Jerusalem going to an infant welfare station will refer to it as Tipat Halav.

The pulse of every undertaking in preventive medicine and in education initiated by Hadassah in Palestine came from the heartbeat of the child. The generation of Moshe Dayan and Yigal Allon was now in its infancy, and Hadassah was doing its best to protect and nurture it. When AZMU arrived in Palestine trachoma afflicted the eyes of upwards of forty of every one hundred Jewish school children. A similar number had scalp and skin ailments. Home inspection was tried, but Hadassah soon learned that the most efficient place to attack these maladies was through strict control in the schools where one child was more apt to infect another. No agencies existed to carry out inspections in schools in 1918 and 1919. So, as Henrietta Szold reported back to New York in finger-snapping prose, "A school Hygiene Department was organized."

To beat trachoma, Hadassah doctors and inspectors spread

throughout the country. Itinerant opthalmologists made regular calls at remote settlements. One of the first eye specialists who traveled the trachoma circuit on donkey back was Haim Yassky, now on the threshold of a brilliant career that would end in tragedy. Hadassah took responsibility for children in the regular school system but also went into the homes of youngsters who studied at private schools. At one time thirty specially trained nurses were treating children under doctors' supervision. The results were spectacular. By 1930, the problem was practically beaten; by 1938 only four out of every one hundred children had the disease, even though immigration from Near East countries constantly brought new sources of infection. By comparison, both the Arab community and the Mandate government neglected trachoma with the result that sixty-five out of every one hundred Arab children still had the disease in 1938, the year it had practically vanished among Jewish pupils.

Hadassah's service to Jewish pupils was the most comprehensive in the world. At the start of each term the child was weighed, measured, tested for tuberculosis, examined for defective eyesight and hearing. He was periodically vaccinated and inoculated. A child absent from school for more than two days was visited at home by a school nurse, and he was cured of any ailment before he was permitted to continue study. In an average year 80 per cent of all Jewish public school pupils received some kind of medical help.

Under the energetic direction of department chief Mordecai Brachyahu, pioneering work was carried out in mental hygiene. Kindergarten teachers reported emotionally unstable or mentally backward children to Dr. Brachyahu, who ran guidance clinics in Jerusalem and Tel Aviv.

At the end of the first ten years—by which time Straus Health Centers provided the roof for all of Hadassah's preventive medical work—the School Hygiene Department was supervising more than 250 schools in 8 urban areas and 64 rural settlements. Altogether, 25,000 children were being examined yearly. And in that decade Hadassah dispensed to school pupils alone more than 10 million individual treatments.

By 1927, Hadassah wove its network of infant welfare stations and school hygiene services into a countrywide child welfare program that was years ahead of its time. By the latter part of the 1920's Hadassah was not only bringing children into the world,

feeding them, and making them disease resistant, but it was also
attempting to supervise their recreation. This came about after
the first playground in Palestine was opened in 1925 at the edge
of the Jewish Quarter inside the walled city of Jerusalem. The
money for the playground came from a $100,000 fund set up by
Bertha Guggenheimer, of Lynchburg, Virginia, aunt of former
Hadassah President Irma Lindheim. Until the lot was opened the
slum children's favorite games were playing cards, throwing dice,
or scrounging in ash cans. In February, 1928, the trustees of the
fund under which the playground was established turned over
responsibility to Hadassah. A teacher in the Old City, Rachel
Shwarz, wife of a noted Jerusalem attorney, who was also the
mother-in-law of two famous Israelis, Moshe Dayan and Ezer
Weizman, was placed in charge. She moved to a larger area outside the city walls, and brought in a Hadassah doctor to examine
all the children who registered to play. The playground was
beautifully equipped. It even had showers, and therein lay the
cause of dissension among the Arab parents. The following account was left by Eva Dushkin, who was sent to Jerusalem by the
Guggenheimer family to observe the work:

> When a rumor went around that showers were being installed,
> the Arabs in the neighborhood were very indignant. They never
> saw anything like it and could not imagine that a shower could
> be taken inside a room. They thought that showers were taken
> in open public places and I was called by several of the Arabs in
> the neighborhood, particularly the Moslems, and asked to under-
> stand that they would not stand for any such immorality. They
> did not propose to have their several wives look through the win-
> dow and see little boys and girls bathing nude in the street. When
> they were given to understand that these showers would be
> taken on the inside of four walls with a roof over their heads,
> they consented to hold back their anger for the opening day.
> Since then, there have been constant streams of Arab visitors who
> come and see and stand back with great admiration and awe
> over the fact that children may come and bathe at leisure without
> being forced to either pay for the water or bring it themselves.

The playground project was so successful that it quickly spread
to all parts of the country. But when a plot was opened in the
Mahane Yehuda Quarter of the new city of Jerusalem, opposite
the Etz Hayim Yeshiva, the principal of the school was enraged.
He complained bitterly that his children were not paying attention

to their Torah and Talmud lessons, and instead were gazing out the windows at the boys and girls playing below. Repeatedly he implored Rachel Shwarz to close the field, using the argument that it was sinful according to Jewish law to permit boys and girls to romp together. The principal was all the more disturbed because his own granddaughter was playing there. Rachel stubbornly stood her ground, countering with the argument that his pupils might study better if they had time off daily to kick a ball around. But he would not be moved and he applied to the Jerusalem rabbinical court to issue a summons calling on Rachel to give good reason why the playground should not be closed.

Rachel had no choice but to appeal to the rabbinical eminence of the day, Chief Rabbi Abraham Isaac Halevy Kook. Rachel stood before the saintly mortal and pleaded, "Our children have a natural instinct to play. How can a rabbi deny it to them?"

"My daughter," he said reassuringly without committing himself on the issue, "go back to your work and all will be well."

Objections evaporated as fog before the sun. The summons was withdrawn, the playground flourished, and municipal authorities all over the country made increasing demands on Hadassah's experience in helping establish them. But a last bailiwick of opposition remained; oddly, in the kibbutzim. There, members argued that children already had sufficient open spaces in which to run free, and that in any case land was much too scarce to use for swings and ball games. Hadassah reasoned that playgrounds were more than sites for idle frolicking; when run Hadassah's way with properly trained staffs, they were educational instruments that sharpened leadership qualities and molded good bodies and minds. Irma Lindheim finally broke the ice with the first kibbutz playground at Mishmar Haemek, located at the entrance to the Jezreel Valley, where she established her home after giving up the presidency of Hadassah in 1928.

By 1950, nearly fifty playgrounds had been set up by Hadassah while numerous others profited from Hadassah expertise. In that year all the grounds were turned over to the Israeli government.

The British authorities looked upon the project with benevolent grace. In 1934 they even went as far as to turn over to Hadassah a one-half acre plot in Jerusalem and then at the end of the year cited that act of charity in a report to the League of Nations as a major contribution to the Jewish population of Palestine.

8.

Butter for the Parsnips

ONE miserably cold day in December, 1922, a tall, gaunt figure with sad, bespectacled eyes and a finely-trimmed goatee stood before Henrietta Szold in her Jerusalem office. He was beloved in the city as a teacher and principal of a girls' school in the Old City.

"Not a day goes by," sighed Yeshaya Press, "that one of our children does not faint in the classroom. They come to school with nothing in their stomachs. When they go home, they are lucky if they find bread and a few vegetables to eat. I have found some of them raiding garbage pails. How can I expect them to do their lessons? Can't your American organization help us get some warm food into their bellies?"

Press would not admit it, but Henrietta knew that his teachers were just as hungry as the pupils, and there were instances where they had collapsed as well. Palestine was then paralyzed by an economic collapse. The country was not paying its way. Imports far outpaced exports. There was little industry and many of the plants that had opened soon went bankrupt for lack of working capital. Fifty years later in Jerusalem, Prime Minister Golda Meir would smilingly recall those days to an economic conference of millionaires: "I remember when I first came in 1921. The only 'heavy' industry was chocolate. But the chocolate it produced was full of sand, and when I asked why, I was told that sand was the country's only natural resource."

So poor was the country that in the struggling kibbutzim and villages farmers had nothing more to eat than the vegetables they grew. Their patron, the World Zionist Organization, was having trouble finding money to carry both them and the Unit over their initial period of development. AZMU got some support, as we have seen, from the non-Zionist Joint Distribution Committee, the Rothschilds, and from the young Hadassah organization in the United States. Partly because of a severe economic depression membership in Hadassah in 1921 was little more than 10,000 and so was not big enough to bear singlehandedly the burgeoning burdens of the pioneers in Palestine. Hadassah's weakness was also partly organizational. From 1918 to 1921, it was affiliated and subordinate to the male-dominated Federation of American Zionists. Full independence came only in 1933 when Hadassah stopped paying affiliation dues to the Federation's successor, the Zionist Organization of America. Growth was slowed down as well by the intellectual and political climate in the United States. The Jewish masses, engrossed in sopping up American culture, were practically untouched by Zionism. After some initial enthusiasm over the Balfour Declaration, apathy quickly set in when the British pledge failed to produce instantly a Jewish nation. Hadassah's problem was a small reflection of the general American lack of interest in the Zionist movement. In the early 1920's the largest fund raiser on the American scene was the Joint Distribution Committee which, in the main, channeled funds to the poverty-stricken Jewish communities in Europe. So it was that Palestine's requirements far exceeded Zionism's ability to meet them. In Jerusalem, Zionist headquarters was so badly off that electricity and telephone services were shut down periodically for nonpayment of bills. The Zionist Organization cut its budget for Hadassah's work by two-thirds and thus forced it to the brink of bankruptcy. Grocery bills piled up. Suppliers of pharmaceuticals pounded on Henrietta Szold's desk. Hadassah employees went for months without salaries and, at one point, were paid in linen. Medical Director Rubinow had to close a clinic in the Old City and the hospital in Tiberias and reduce the number of beds in the Tel Aviv hospital. The pressure was so great that Rubinow repeatedly threatened to quit. Into Henrietta's lap fell the whole sorry mess. She was then sixty-two years' old and ailing. She knew very well that the only logical thing to do would be to disband

the Unit but, she rationalized, even that was impossible because
there was no money to pay off the doctors. She wrote her sister,
Rachel, "If the Unit and I survive the winter, it will be a miracle."

Early in October, 1922, Henrietta Szold desperately fought to
keep the Unit alive by calling on Baron Rothschild in Paris. As she
walked past great works of art in his ornate mansion in the Rue
du Faubourg Saint-Honore, she daydreamed that all the old man
would have to do to save the Unit would be to say: "Over there
is a little thing of the school of Leonardo da Vinci—take it." But
he did not say it. Rather, he used the occasion to berate American
Jews in general and Zionists in particular for not supporting what
they started. The only constructive part of their meeting was the
lavish praise that the baron voiced for Hadassah's work. Bitterly,
she later commented, "I have heard that too often now to be
flattered. Fine words butter no parsnips and keep no hospitals
going."

The baron's advice to Henrietta was to go to America to raise
the money. She would have done so even though she detested the
idea, but poor Rubinow in Jerusalem had frantically cabled he was
about to leave for good. From the baron's she returned to her
hotel, and nursing a bad cold, she consoled herself by dining on a
bag of roasted chestnuts. She wrote home, "French laundresses are
artists and must be paid like prima donnas, and colds consume
handkerchiefs."

Henrietta was not back in Jerusalem very long when an old
friend, having heard of her distress, cabled $20,000. The money
was from Nathan Straus, but much as it was appreciated, the
dollars covered only one-fourth of the Unit's debts. The problem
now was whether to use it to pay salaries or to pay the baker or
the drug manufacturers. "I know the agony of an honest bankruptcy," Henrietta said. "Hour by hour I sit in the office and
count and calculate." Happily, the Unit's administrative staff and
"even a few of the doctors" were prepared to sacrifice. They were
ready to forego their back pay to allow the work to continue,
accepting Henrietta's promise that one day they would receive
their money in full.

It was at that hour in the gray fortunes of the Unit that
Yeshaya Press stood before Henrietta Szold. She told him that
she had no money to buy even a piece of chalk, but ever opti-
mistic she repeated to him her overworked slogan, "Where every-

thing is needed, everything needs to be done. And it will be done."
Press walked out of her office empty-handed buoyed by Henrietta's faith that help would come. Shortly after that, an American tourist, Rabbi Maurice Harris, of New York, burst into Henrietta's office. He introduced himself as a religious educator. He said he was appalled to see how badly nourished the school children of Jerusalem were. As it happened, the rabbi went on, he had brought a small sum of Hanukkah money with him, contributed by his school, and he thought that Miss Szold could put it to use to feed the unfortunate pupils. It was not nearly enough to help everyone, but what would Miss Szold think if he started a campaign in the United States to provide luncheons for Jerusalem's needy pupils? Would Miss Szold ask Hadassah in New York to help him?

Henrietta could hardly encourage Rabbi Harris to return soon enough. And Yeshaya Press was, of course, the first to be told. Rabbi Harris did go back and together with Leon Lang organized a school luncheon program committee on which Hadassah was represented. Very soon thereafter the project was transferred to Hadassah. At first, appeals for lunch money were made almost exclusively to pupils of religious schools throughout the United States. The slogan was simple: "Give a penny so a child in Jerusalem can eat." Pennies rolled in by the basketsful. Children sold brochures on Palestine to raise money. Hadassah women organized thrift luncheons whereby they would cook and serve the same meal that was served to the Jerusalem pupils. But they would charge each guest from five to ten times more than the cost of the meal given in Palestine. A typical lunch was oatmeal, soup, cole slaw, and date and raisin compote. On Fridays the children got free cocoa and bread at 10:00 A.M. recess because mothers gave them no solid food for breakfast in anticipation of the Sabbath evening meal. With a healthy donation from Hadassah the first hot lunches were served in Yeshaya Press' school in September, 1923. A small kitchen and dining room were equipped. At first, eighty girls could afford the one-half piaster (2.5 cents) for a meal. When the Hadassah committee under Nellie Straus Mochenson saw other girls standing "in tears at the door of the dining room looking on the feast," it was decided to include every child in the school. No one but Press knew who paid and who did not. But that was only the beginning of the story. It was Henrietta's policy that no

project would be an end in itself. Each endeavor must serve far
wider, educational aims. A cook was hired to supervise the six
weekly meals, but the pupils in the higher grades were required to
prepare them. They were taught not only how to cook but how
to serve and clean up, and most important, the fundamentals of
nutrition. Henrietta's ultimate goal was to introduce domestic science into the school curriculum. But in 1923 as the luncheon
program started that goal was remote. Among the girls of Press'
school there were some who were not accustomed to sitting on a
chair or at a table to eat. Before they could be taught how to plan
a balanced meal, they had to be taught how to use a knife and
fork. At the end of the first year Henrietta reported, "Eventually
the school luncheon program will be the means of teaching the
food values of the rich variety of cereals and vegetables obtainable
in Palestine which are largely disregarded now, particularly by
the newer arrivals."

Teaching dietetics was not exactly new. Yehudit Aaronson
Dushkin introduced the idea in the labor camps of Galilee. Student
nurses in Jerusalem took cooking lessons for three hours every
morning in a converted stable at Rothschild Hospital. The cadet
nurses liked their lessons on the whole, and the more proficient
were chosen to cook part of the luncheons served to the 120
patients and 105 staff members in the basement dining hall—
originally built as a mammoth cistern.

Hard times in Palestine grew harder in 1927 and 1928 and the
penny luncheons were extended to kindergarten children, but even
they did not get away with merely filling their little stomachs.
The five-year-olds were also taught how to use cutlery, how to
set a table, and how to ask politely for the bread plate. By the turn
of the decade, one thousand children were being fed from eight
centrally located kitchens in Jerusalem, Haifa, Safad, and Tiberias.
So extensive had the project grown that Hadassah set up a Nutrition Department in the newly opened Straus Health Center in
Jerusalem.

In charge was a Dutch-born nutritionist, Sara Bavli, who
opened the first course to train domestic science teachers in December, 1930. As the teachers became available, the luncheon
programs broadened. By the time Israel was founded in 1948,
28,000 children were being fed daily in 300 schools, and when
Israel was ten years old, the number increased to 130,000 children.

That was more than 25 per cent of the entire school population of the country. By now the government itself was carrying most of the budget, and the parents were only paying 10 per cent of the bill. Meantime, Mrs. Bavli had, in 1953, opened up a College of Nutrition and Home Economics in Jerusalem.

What had started out as a frantic measure to ease the hunger pangs of a few score children (and teachers) in the Old City of Jerusalem had within twenty-five years grown into a ramified educational effort. Girls were being taught more than nutrition. Their courses included everything from child development and child guidance to interior decorating and stain removal. Hadassah's School Luncheon Committee made inroads into the kibbutzim where the science of food preparation was generally ignored in favor of the business of food production. Teachers in a number of kibbutzim asked Hadassah to set up cooking lessons even though kibbutz parents oddly enough objected. After an experimental lesson in one collective succeeded, the idea caught on and many set up kitchen committees. Hadassah knew it had succeeded when one kibbutz finally put hated spinach on the menu in the children's dining room. The kids ate it because they themselves had prepared it.

9.

The Blood of August

TIRED and tense close to midnight on Friday, August 23, 1929, the administrative director of Hadassah Hospital in Jerusalem, Reuven Katznelson, scrawled a cable to Hadassah in New York: "WE HAVE ELEVEN DEAD AND TWENTY-FIVE WOUNDED. ARABS ATTACKING SEVERAL JEWISH HOSPITALS."

On Saturday night, August 24, he wired:

ANOTHER SEVEN DEAD AND EIGHT OF YESTERDAY'S WOUNDED HAVE DIED ALSO. MORE THAN THIRTY WOUNDED. THE ARABS ARE ATTACKING MEKOR HAIM, TALPIOT, AND MOTZA. NEW SURGERY DEPARTMENTS HAVE BEEN OPENED. WE ARE CALLING ALL DOCTORS WE CAN. BABIES HOME HAS BEEN TRANSFERRED INTO TOWN. NEED MONEY BADLY.

That was only the beginning. Arab rioting lasted eight days, spanned the whole of settled Palestine from Safad in Galilee to Hebron, city of the Patriarchs, south of Jerusalem. The violence was the bloodiest since the end of the World War: Arabs killed 133 Jews and wounded 330; British police killed 110 Arabs and wounded 232, and the Jews killed 6 Arabs. The riots illuminated the inadequacies of the British police and the need for a better Jewish system of defense. Zionist leaders in Jerusalem took immediate remedial measures that transformed the underground Haganah, forerunner of the Israel Defense Forces, into a skilled fighting unit.

The Arab riots of 1929 were the fruit of a quarter of a century of political struggle and intrigue. Throughout, Hadassah had a unique role to play, particularly during the height of the bloodletting. And everything that Hadassah accomplished in the Land of Israel from the arrival of the two nurses in 1913 seemed in retrospect to have been fated as preparation for those eight bloody days in August, 1929.

The seeds of the riots, which were a turning point in Middle East history, were watered by the turbulent political crosscurrents of the late nineteenth and early twentieth centuries. Jewish nationalism in the form of Herzlian Zionism, dramatized by the formation of a political movement at the Zionist Congress in Basel in 1897, was only a hop, skip, and jump ahead of a similar movement then forming in the Arab world. Herzl was dead only a year and the Zionist platform was just beginning to sweep over the Jewish communities of Europe when the first serious call was heard for Arab secession from the Ottoman Empire. In 1905, a Christian Arab publisher, Neguib Zaouri envisioned an Arab empire stretching "from the Tigris and the Euphrates to the Suez Isthmus and from the Mediterranean to the Arabian Sea." Interestingly, he excluded Egypt from his Arab nation because, as he wrote, "The Egyptians do not belong to the Arab race; they are of the African Berber family."

During World War I, the British and French secretly arranged in the Sykes-Picot agreement to divide the spoils of war and to establish two protectorates over lands the Ottoman Empire had held for four centuries: the French were to have Syria and Lebanon and the British would control Iraq and Palestine. No provision was made for Jewish autonomy.

The British high commissioner in Cairo was goading the Bedouin of the Arabian peninsula to join the war on the side of the Allies. Sir Henry McMahon made contact with Sharif Hussein Ibn Ali of Mecca. In his letters from Cairo, McMahon pledged British support for the Sharif's dream to place the Arab world under one caliphate.

By June, 1916, Hussein got the Arab revolt under way against the Turks. Lawrence of Arabia, a British agent who was assigned to assist Hussein's forces, glamorized the revolt. But as things turned out the Arab contribution to the over-all war effort was not so effective as either the British or the Arabs had hoped it would be. Sharif Hussein planned a bold strategy. He intended to drive straight north and capture Syria. Once that was done he would install the commander of his troops, his son Feisal, as the king of a united Arab monarchy in Damascus, and the power behind the throne would remain in Mecca with the Sharif himself.

While this scheme was being hatched, the noted chemist Chaim Weizmann, unaware of the Sykes-Picot agreement, was organizing a Zionist machine whose purpose was to encourage the British government to establish a Jewish nation in Palestine once the Turks had been defeated.

Feisal's forces, together with the British, did not reach Damascus until October, 1918, and did not take all of Syria until a fortnight before World War I had ended. What the Arabs tried to do in battle, Weizmann had already succeeded in doing on paper. He had helped the British war effort by inventing a cheap method to produce explosives, and he had convinced the British to support the establishment of a national home for Jews in Palestine. The Balfour Declaration was issued on November 2, 1917, a month before General Allenby reached Jerusalem and nearly a year before Feisal got to Damascus. Arabia was stunned by the Zionist victory. The British tried to allay Arab fears and at the same time urged them to fight on by promising, in June, 1918, to work for Arab independence as well.

Little more than a month after World War I ended on November 11, 1918, the Allies solemnly gathered in Versailles for the peace conference. Zionist and Arab leaders were present too, among them Chaim Weizmann and Emir Feisal. The two were no strangers to each other. In June, 1918, they met in Feisal's tent on the shores of the Gulf of Aqaba in an attempt to pave a path to Arab and Jewish co-existence. Later that year they met again in London where, with the assistance of T. E. Lawrence, they drafted an accord which was to have tied the destiny of their two peoples. But the agreement came to nothing. Poor Feisal fell victim to British-French power politics and the extremists among his own people. The latter pressed him to lead a revolt against the French who had taken over from the British in Syria. He was forced to renege on his pledges to Weizmann, and from Damascus he began to mouth vicious anti-Zionist propaganda.

Feisal was at the mercy of an extremist group called the General Syrian Congress. The congress was created by Arab nationalists in July, 1919, with the aim of creating an independent Syria that would include Lebanon and Palestine. Once the French took over Syria and Lebanon, as laid down by Sykes and Picot, the congress shifted to violence. On March 1, 1920, it instigated an attack on two Jewish farm settlements in Galilee—at Tel Hai and at Metulla—in which seven pioneers died, including the noted Russian-born Zionist, Captain Joseph Trumpeldor. One week later, the congress crowned Feisal king of United Syria. Arab bands roamed Galilee. At Passover time, April 4 and 5, Arab mobs ran amok in Jerusalem, killing six Jews and wounding 211.

The Allies' counterattack was a death blow to the congress. Toward the end of April, the Allied powers met a few miles east of Monaco in the Italian town of San Remo. They had still not concluded a treaty with Turkey, and since the situation in the Middle East was fast deteriorating, they gathered at San Remo to work out a permanent settlement for the peoples of the area. Three mandates were set up: two went to Britain to administer Palestine and Iraq, and one went to France to govern Syria and Lebanon. Most important for the Zionist cause was the rider on the Palestine mandate that obligated the British to implement the provisions of the Balfour Declaration.

Little more than two months after the San Remo conference ended, the French sent King Feisal packing into comfortable exile (on the shores of Lake Maggiore, Italy) and brought independent United Syria to an ignominious and abrupt end. In that same month of July, the British appointed a prominent, pro-Zionist Jew, Sir Herbert Samuel, to be the first high commissioner of the Mandate government of Palestine.

As Jewish and pro-Zionist as Sir Herbert may have been, he was still committed to British colonial policy. Then, the policy was called "the equality of obligation." In our day, it might be known as "evenhandedness." Eight months after he took office, in the worst decision of his career, Sir Herbert appointed Haj Amin Husseini to be Grand Mufti of Jerusalem. The wily Husseini was a rabid anti-Zionist and was one of the leaders of the Passover riots in Jerusalem. Sir Herbert mistakenly believed that the Arabs would now be satisfied.

In March, 1921, Winston Churchill appeared on the scene. He

was now colonial secretary, and as such he was responsible for the Mandate. New to the area's problems, he was determined to clean up the mess that had been created by contradictory British promises to Jews and Arabs. His ultimate aim was so to pacify the area that he could remove all British military forces. In his view the Arabs were the injured party, and in characteristic Churchillian style he moved boldly. He called Emir Feisal out of Italian exile and rigged an election that made him king of Iraq. Churchill then sliced off that portion of Palestine that lay east of the Jordan River, including the hills of Moab from where Moses saw the Land of Israel, and put Feisal's brother, Abdullah, on a separate throne. Abdullah was to rule an area to be called Trans-Jordan, later to be renamed the Hashemite Kingdom of Jordan.

The idea of a United Syria was shattered. Arab nationalists despaired of uniting their peoples under one flag. So they turned their energies to, and found unity in, fighting Zionism in Palestine. To Churchill's credit, he did not renege on promises to Zionists even while he championed the cause of Arab independence. When a delegation of Moslem and Christian Arabs asked him in Jerusalem to rescind the Balfour Declaration and to stop Jewish immigration, Churchill replied, "That is not in my power and it is not my wish."

Zionist leaders did not kick up much dust at Churchill's handing half of Palestine to Abdullah. Only at the end of the decade, when a British Labor government would turn against the Zionists, would Revisionist Vladimir Zev Jabotinsky cry out that the Jordan River passed through the middle of the Land of Israel. In retrospect, Churchill did not succeed, but unlike others who tried to solve the problem of Palestine, he executed his failure with brilliance and with flair. He did not achieve a rapprochement between Zionists and Arabs. He fractured the idea of a single Arab state, apportioning slices to the favorite sons of Sharif Hussein, who would shortly be overthrown in Arabia by Ibn Saud. The result was that Arab nationalists remained dissatisfied and the Jews grew apprehensive.

Churchill was gone from the scene little more than a month when violence again erupted. In Tel Aviv, now twelve years old, members of the socialist Zionist Ahdut Avodah party held a May Day parade. A rival parade was staged at the same place by the Trotskyite party. The two met head on with banners flying. Being an all-Jewish riot, there were no serious casualties. Arabs, watching from Jaffa, picked up arms, and while the Jews were scuffling, went on a rampage of killing. Martial law was declared, but the "disturbances" continued sporadically for a full week. The Arabs had been provoked with stories that atheist, Bolshevik immigrant Jews who recently arrived in Palestine were going to raze the mosques.

The first Arab target was an immigrant hostel in Jaffa. Twelve men and one woman who just arrived from Russia were hacked to pieces. The Arabs raced on toward the center of Tel Aviv where they were held off by Jewish veterans of the World War. It was the first successful defense of the all-Jewish city. But farther north, Petah Tikva was sacked by hundreds of angry Arab peasants. Hadera, Kfar Saba, and Rehovot were invested by Arabs who destroyed crops and vineyards, and made off with farm equipment and livestock. Henrietta Szold happened to be having lunch in Jaffa on the day of the riot. Halfway through the meal she rushed to the Hadassah dispensary. The three hundred dead and wounded lined the floors and crowded neighboring buildings. She immediately phoned to Jerusalem for additional medical personnel and supplies. Then she went about talking to eyewitnesses and residents. Her conclusion was that the riot far from being spontaneous had been well-planned.

Faint-hearted Herbert Samuel tried appeasement again, this time by suspending Jewish immigration. It was another major *faux pas*, for the Jewish community of Palestine never trusted him wholeheartedly after that. In London, attempting to mediate the problem, the Colonial Office met separately with a Moslem-Christian Arab delegation and with Zionists. The talks which began in 1922 went on for a year, but the Arabs would not accept anything remotely like the Balfour Declaration, and the Jews would not accept anything that diluted it. Winston Churchill tried to mollify both groups by issuing a White Paper in which he defined the meaning of the declaration as giving the Jews a national home in Palestine but not over all of Palestine. The policy was a forerunner of partition. He candied the pill for the Jews by adding that they were in the Holy Land by right and not on sufferance. Weizmann wisely convinced his colleagues to accept the White Paper, although with some reservations. The Arabs rejected Churchill's formulation totally and also rejected a plan to set up a legislative assembly in Palestine in which they would hold a majority.

The immediate effect of all the Arab "no's" was to hamstring some of their firmest supporters in England. And the outcome in 1923 was a decision by the British that effective administration of the Mandate was feasible only if the Balfour Declaration and the Zionist cause were given full support. The deadlock between Arabs and Jews had become so hardened during the discussions that the British even considered giving up the Mandate altogether. What won the day for holding on to Palestine was the argument that the area might be needed at some future time to protect the Suez Canal.

A lull of almost five years dominated Palestine affairs afterward. Strangely, Zionism suffered thereby despite some progress. In Palestine, Hebrew was fast catching on. The Histadrut had taken roots as a powerful trade union, and out of the road-building projects in the north had sprung the first major construction company, Solel Boneh. But the kibbutzim were still struggling. Land was hard to come by, and Arab landowners demanded steep prices; even when a transaction was completed Mandatory officials often interfered. The brightest star of the mid-1920's was the opening of the Hebrew University on Mt. Scopus in Jerusalem. Arthur Balfour, architect of the controversial declaration, was present. Wherever the white-haired, white-moustached diplomat traveled, cheers rang out—but only from the Jews. Arabs prepared plots, but either through good security or bad planning he escaped harm.

Quietly, Haj Amin el-Husseini, the Grand Mufti, organized his forces against the Zionist settlers. On the surface it almost seemed that co-existence between Arabs and Jews was possible, so much so that Zionist land developer Arthur Ruppin founded an organization called Brith Shalom (Peace Covenant). This group, in which Henrietta Szold and Hebrew University Chancellor Judah Magnes were active, foresaw a bi-national state in Palestine where Jews and Arabs would enjoy equal rights and equal duties. Chaim Weizmann himself was likewise lulled into thinking that peace was really possible with the Arabs. At the Fourteenth Zionist Congress held in Vienna in 1925 he said: "Palestine must be built up without violating the legitimate interests of the Arabs—not a hair of their heads shall be touched. . . . Palestine is not Rhodesia."

The tranquility that enveloped the land can be explained in a number of ways. In these years a general malaise gripped the Zionist movement. The Arabs, seeing that the idea of a national home was not taking hold among Jewish masses, decided to wait patiently until Zionism collapsed from a process of natural degeneration. There was good reason to believe this might happen. In the years following the setting up of the Mandate, American and European Zionists fought bitterly over two contradictory philosophies. The prevailing feeling of most American Jews was to give priority to raising money for special projects in Palestine that would establish facts on which future political decisions could be based, while the Europeans saw Palestine as the last stop on the way home for millions of Jews living abroad in "exile." To the Americans, Palestine was more cause for the philanthropist and the investor; to the European, Palestine was the site for the fulfillment of age-old prayers to rebuild a Jewish commonwealth.

In the United States, Zionist ranks came under the strong influence of Louis Brandeis, a justice of the Supreme Court. Still, Weizmann and the Europeans had their supporters, most notably Louis Lipsky, a rebel within the establishment. The differences between the American and European approaches came to a head with the establishment by Weizmann of the Keren Hayesod (Foundation Fund) as the principal fund-raising arm of the World Zionist Organization. The Brandeis group insisted that money raised in America by the fund be used mainly for economic and industrial projects in Palestine. The Weizmann-Lipsky group urged that the money be used for settling immigrants on the land. These differences split the Federation of American Zionists. When Weizmann's view finally prevailed, the Brandeis group resigned from the American Zionist leadership. The dispute had a decisive effect on the future of Hadassah, most of whose leaders sided with Brandeis. The organization felt a growing need for complete autonomy, and at Hadassah's national convention in Pittsburgh, in 1921, delegates voted to break the amalgamation with the Federation of American Zionists, which it had voluntarily accepted three years earlier.

Because immigration to Palestine was less than a roaring success, the Arabs had good reason to suspect that Zionism was a flash in the pan. The Jewish multitudes in the Diaspora did not rush to enter the gates of the Holy Land. Palestine's only good year was 1925 when about 35,000 Jews immigrated, most of them prodded by a depression and raging anti-Semitism in Poland. Toward the end of the decade the numbers fell to a point where by 1929 more Jews were leaving the country than settling in it. Palestine was not particularly attractive to many Jews. A devastating earthquake struck in July, 1927. A severe financial crisis hit the Jewish economy; Tel Aviv, the much-touted all-Jewish city, was bankrupt.

Fortunately for Palestine the British appointed a fine high commissioner, Field Marshal Lord Plumer, one of the most brilliant officers of World War I. He replaced Herbert Samuel in August, 1925, and quickly built a reputation for fairness and firmness. He created an air of good will by reducing the security forces of the country, but Plumer's tenure was all too brief. He left in July, 1928, and about six weeks later the peace of Palestine was ended.

When the Jews did not sink from the weight of their woes, Arab patience ran out. Only a small spark was needed to set the two communities on fire, and that was provided by a British official. On the eve of Yom Kippur, in 1928, Jews gathered for Kol Nidre prayers at the Western Wall. Hemmed in by a warren of Arab hovels, only several hundred worshipers could crowd into the narrow alleyway in front of the Wall. But a few thousand always tried to crush in during the holy days. To separate men and women, the rabbi at the Wall put up a screen. Two pieces of flint could not have provided a sharper spark. Although the screen had been there on Rosh Hashanah, a British official now declared its presence to be a major violation of the status quo in Jerusalem.

On the morning of Yom Kippur, as the Jews were reciting the sacred Amidah prayer, British police arrived to remove the menacing divider. The aforewarned Arabs were right behind. Fortunately, no one was killed in the melee that followed, but the tempers of Jerusalem immediately began simmering.

A countdown on the inevitable blow-up began far from the scene in Zurich on July 28, 1929, when Zionists gathered for their Sixteenth Congress. There, Chaim Weizmann crowned seven years of labor by formally establishing the broadly based Jewish Agency, composed of both Zionists and non-Zionists. The establishment of the Agency was authorized by the Mandate, which was decided upon at San Remo and later ratified by the League of Nations. The Jewish Agency was the executive arm of the World Zionist Organization and was designed to work hand in hand with the British for the implementation of a Jewish national home. As it turned out, the Agency developed into a shadow government of the incipient state.

At that same Zurich congress, firebrand Vladimir Zev Jabotinsky spoke passionately about the borders of the national home. In a widely reported oration, he pronounced, "the Jordan River does not mark its frontier but flows through its center."

To the Arabs of Palestine the Zurich congress was clear evidence that the Zionists planned a takeover in Palestine. This, coming on top of all the frustrations that had built up since the World War, primed the bomb of mob violence.

One day in August a Jewish boy, who had run into an Arab courtyard after his ball, was knifed to death. Zionists turned his funeral into a protest march. Tishah Be-Av, the fast day when Jews mourn the destruction of the Temple, occurred shortly thereafter on Friday, August 22, and it was then that the Arabs struck.

Crowds gathered to worship at the Al Aqsa Mosque on the Temple Mount above the Western Wall. On this Moslem sabbath day the Grand Mufti, leader of the Supreme Moslem Council, chose to address the congregants. British police officers noticed that many of the worshipers were carrying weapons. When they made inquiries, the Grand Mufti assured them they only wanted to protect themselves from possible Jewish revenge for the murder of the boy. The assurance was accepted. Shortly after the noon hour, a single shout was heard. Then several. Someone began running in the direction of the Jewish Quarter opposite the Wall. The mob followed.

The Arabs' timing was good. British forces had been moved to Egypt, and only a few hundred policemen were available. The new high commissioner, Sir John Chancellor, who had been at his post eight months, was out of the country. All the important members of the Jewish Agency were abroad at the Zionist Congress. The violence spread like wildfire beyond Jerusalem. Jewish settlements were laid waste, wholesale murder and pillage struck Safad, Tel Aviv, Haifa, and Hebron. In the course of eight days 820 Jews and Arabs were either killed or wounded.

Hadassah in Jerusalem faced its own crisis. Henrietta Szold was attending the Zionist Congress. Director Ephraim Michael Bluestone had resigned, and the responsibilities for supervising the medical services were left in the hands of the one-time itinerant ophthalmologist Haim Yassky. Administration was under Reuven Katznelson. Yassky, too, was in Europe. When the storm struck, it was Katznelson aided by Chief Nurse Bertha Landsman and Mrs. Katznelson who ran the show. Fortunately, they had prepared for trouble. A week before the riots began, fifty extra surgical beds were made ready in Hadassah-Rothschild Hospital. In the Old City, an emergency first-aid station was opened. The spanking new Straus Health Center was set to house and feed refugees; it finally catered to 3,700.

Newspapers ceased to publish, so Hadassah became an information center for the outside world simply because it alone had telephone contact with its units throughout the country and knew better than anybody what was happening. For eight days in August, Hadassah in Jerusalem filled the role of an operations center. Telegrams arriving from abroad asking for information about relatives were delivered to Hadassah. Medical communiques were issued not by the Mandate's department of health but by Hadassah.

The man who controlled communications was Haim Shalom Halevy, who began at Hadassah in 1927 as the keeper of statistics and went on later to develop the first modern hospital record department in the Middle East. He noted at the time:

> I slept with the phone at my ear so that I could answer a ring in the middle of the night. It was the only telephone with connections to all parts of the country.
>
> On Saturday night, Hadassah had 13 victims in the mortuary. Katznelson said that we must make arrangements to bury them today because tomorrow it might be necessary to bury other patients—it might even be necessary to bury them in the courtyard.
>
> The young boys from the Haganah and others refused to go to the Jewish cemetery on the Mt. of Olives. They said they

were ready to face any danger to protect the living but not to bury the dead. After a lot of discussion the Burial Society agreed to take the bodies and we had two laymen along besides myself. I went as Hadassah's representative. We were ten in that party. We had assured ourselves of a *minyan*.

Edward Joseph, a massive man with massive hands, arrived in Palestine from his native New Zealand in 1928. He had fought at Gallipoli in 1915, studied medicine, and came to Israel after three years at Rochester's Mayo Clinic. A follower of Jabotinsky, Dr. Joseph was convinced that Israel was the place for him after he read a boast of the Grand Mufti of Jerusalem, "The Jews want to make a National Home in Palestine. We Arabs will turn it into a Jewish national graveyard." He arrived at Hadassah to find himself in charge of the small surgery unit. The chief was on three months' leave. Sooner than he expected, he was saving riot victims, working day and night in the stifling August heat, bare to the waist.

> They suffered mostly dagger wounds. We had no antibiotics. Surgical treatment was rather primitive. If there was active bleeding into the lung, we would go in and try to find the source and control it. Otherwise we would let things alone. If there was too much blood accumulated in the pleural space pressing on the lung, we would withdraw it with needles and hope it would stop. If it didn't stop, we would have to go in and try to suture the blood vessel.
>
> We had no plasma but I remember introducing blood transfusions. That was the citrate method. Problem was we had no saline for the people. We used the saline as an anti-shock treatment but even so everybody got reactions. Today it is routine. Nobody gets a reaction. In those days it was so dangerous we were afraid to use it.
>
> During the riots the hopsital was fired at by Arabs passing in the streets, but no one was hurt. We had no security. So, our orthopedic surgeon, Dr. Treu, and I decided to barricade the hospital to keep out the invaders. Treu was a little man but very courageous. He would venture out into the night to call on his patients. I warned him against it. He held up a huge Arab key and said, "This is enough for me. If anyone comes near me, I'll slug him with this."

In Jerusalem, Hadassah was not the only hospital that took in

the wounded. But in other cities Hadassah was the sole source
of medical care and supply.

News of the riots in Jerusalem reached Tel Aviv on the afternoon of August 23. Immediately, twelve girls at Hadassah prepared
bandages. Weekend leave was canceled for everyone. On August
25, three operating tables were ready with a surgical team for
each. First-aid corpsmen stood alert at the hospital doors with
stretchers. Jewish policemen were given 300 bandages cut from
diapers. By noon, the first 16 wounded, attacked near a mosque,
were brought in. Their names were posted outside the hospital.
The hospital could not get to its laundry so improvised one in the
yard. The municipality was in charge of the 700 refugees who
sought shelter in the Ahad Ha'am School, but in fact Hadassah
nurses looked after them.

In Haifa, Hadassah took in all wounded from Galilee. Expecting riots to break out, Hadassah prepared the Technion (Israel
Institute of Technology) to take in refugees. August 26 was the
worst day. Arabs used firearms as well as knives, stones, and clubs.
Thirty-eight wounded flooded the hospital. Medical personnel
accompanied by British escorts went into the thick of the fighting
to drag out the victims, among them Arabs whom the British
authorities asked Hadassah to treat. By nightfall of August 26,
3,000 Jews were evacuated from their homes by the British.

The Galilee town of Safad was alerted by Jerusalem on the
23rd. Next morning, to the roll of drums, Arabs gathered at the
mosque. At noon they raced from the mosque screaming hysteri-
cally and throwing stones at Jews. They did not move into the
Jewish Quarter that day and only one person was hurt: an Arab
had been hit on the head by a stone thrown by another Arab.
He was treated at Hadassah. The situation remained tense until
August 29 when at the hour for the afternoon prayer, they attacked the Sephardi Quarter, started fires that kept the city illuminated all night, killed twenty, and destroyed over one hundred
Jewish dwellings. The first wounded was an Arab policeman. The
first dead was a Hadassah worker, Yitzhak Maman. (A second
victim was Hadassah physician Haim Israeli who died defending
his home in Be'er Tuvia.) Three hundred refugees filled the Safad
hospital. On September 2, Dr. Yassky, home from Europe, organized relief work and ordered expansion of medical facilities
in the town.

When we arrived [reported Dr. Yassky] many of the ruins were still smoking and it was impossible to attempt to remove corpses. The stench was unbearable. Whole streets were razed as though they had been bombarded and the city presents a picture of desolation and suffering that cannot be described. Things happened there during the riots that do not bear the telling. The people are in a state of extreme hysteria. The city and the roads leading to it present a picture of war times—armored cars, automobiles with armed escorts bringing medical supplies from Haifa and returning with refugees.

The most macabre orgy of killing took place in Hebron where Jews had lived for centuries side by side with their Moslem neighbors. Life with the Arabs was amicable, although the Jews there were always second-class citizens: no Jew was permitted into the tombs of the Patriarchs because a grand mosque had been built over them. For the seven hundred Jews of Hebron it was sufficient to be able to live and to study the Law close by. Haganah men were sent to the yeshiva, but they were summarily dismissed by the rabbis who said that their presence in the town was a provocation.

On August 24, the Sabbath, armed Arabs reached Hebron. Arab policemen watched them race through the town, enter an inn where Jews had taken refuge, and hack twenty-three to death. The mob then marched to the yeshiva where about forty Jews were massacred. Their bodies were butchered as though they were cattle.

Not long after the riot in Hebron, the former president of Hadassah, Irma Lindheim (1926–1928), who had moved with her family to Palestine, visited the scene.

Manya Shochat and I went to Hebron with the chief of police, Fred Partridge. We visited the yeshiva. The moment Manya entered she said it was a pogrom, because in a pogrom they always ripped open the mattresses to look for money and broke the windows and mirrors. We walked on feathers and glass, a most Godawful combination. Blood had soaked everything. From there we went to the Hadassah clinic. The place was a shambles. Every wall was down. Every floor was up. Every test tube was smashed. Hadassah had a first-class clinic and it was smashed completely. Why? Because the Arabs wanted nothing of the world that Jews represented. Hadassah had done a wonderful job in Hebron, did more than any other group to build real Arab-Jewish friendship. Miss Szold did it consciously.

In 1929, Hadassah was in its eighteenth year. One Hadassah eyewitness to the riots, an American tourist from Pittsburgh, returned home a month later and reported the words of an unidentified Haifa resident, "If Hadassah had done nothing else in the land during its years here, this one week of its activities would be worth all the money it has spent."

All the services which were started up to that time suddenly integrated into a smooth-functioning lifesaving machine. Refugees were shepherded to the new Straus Health Center, opened less than four months earlier to house Hadassah's preventive health work. The homeless were fed by the school luncheon service. Meals were cooked and diets prepared by Hadassah's nutritionists. Tots were cared for in the infant welfare stations. Even the school playground project became vital as it set up special recreation activities for children who were separated from parents.

Chaim Weizmann later wrote "if the riots were intended, whatever their effect on our nerves, to overthrow the structure of the National Home, they came too late. We had built too solidly and too well."

The British government fumed and fumbled in the years that followed the disturbances. High Commissioner Chancellor issued a caustic statement blaming the Arabs for "savage murders." But for balance—and to soften Arab protest—he announced that a commission would investigate "Arab and Jewish responsibility." The commission, headed by jurist Sir Walter Shaw, concluded that the attack on the Jews had not been premeditated. This august commission was immediately followed by another, chaired by Sir John Hope Simpson. His task was to investigate land sales to Jews. He concluded that Palestine could economically hold only 100,000 more immigrants—Jews and Arabs.

On October 21, 1930, the colonial secretary, socialist leader Sydney Webb, as Lord Passfield, issued a White Paper, based on the reports of the commissions. The White Paper in effect restricted Jewish immigration into Palestine and land sales to Jews.

One outcome of the riots was to rally Jewry behind the Zionists, and the Zionists made the most of it. In the United States,

Hadassah joined the men's Zionist organizations in a political demonstration. Hadassah's President was then Zip Szold, Savannah-born wife of attorney Robert Szold, cousin of Henrietta.

> We went to Washington [says Zip Szold] with Israel Goldstein as our spokesman. We wanted our Government to stop the riots in Palestine. I don't believe we were very effective but we did speak to many Congressmen, Senators and one or two Cabinet members. This was probably the first time that Hadassah had taken part in a political act.

Arab extremists emerged from the crisis stronger than ever. The Grand Mufti lost his battle to throttle the Zionist effort in Palestine, but he became a national hero nevertheless because he had won strong British support for the cause of Arab nationalism.

As Palestine entered the 1930's, the stage was set for a drama in which three motifs would play simultaneously: Arab against Jew, Jew against Arab, and both against the British. These were cruel years. America was agonizing in economic depression. Germany was watering the weeds of Hitlerism. Russia was turning into Animal Farm.

In Palestine, oddly, economic recovery was quicker than almost anyplace else in the world. Investment in Zionist projects ran relatively high. Construction picked up and despite the restrictions, Jewish immigration was heavy. There would be a brief eruption of violence in 1933 as the Arabs, having failed to frustrate the Zionists, would suddenly turn against the British. In 1936, the Grand Mufti would try for three years to rid the country of the infidel Jew and would make a pact with Hitler toward that end.

In the new storm that was gathering, Hadassah would brave the winds along with the rest of the *yishuv* and emerge from the decade strengthened many times over, for it was in these years that membership would mushroom, new and vigorous leadership would rise, and genuine independence would send Hadassah into a Zionist orbit of its own. In short, Hadassah was on its way to becoming the most forceful single Zionist organization in the world. All this could be traced in part to Hadassah's decision to save children from the inferno of Nazi Europe.

10.

The Contract

ONE cold February afternoon in 1932, Recha Freier was musing in the study of her home near Berlin's Alexanderplatz. She was the wife of a prominent Orthodox rabbi, the mother of three sons, and an author of fairy and folk tales for children, a task that helped her escape the wretched world that was crumbling around her. Here in Germany, the Weimar Republic of Chancellor Heinrich Bruening was collapsing under the twin sledgehammer blows of an economic blizzard and Hitler's hypnotizing cry for a new order. Across the frontiers dictator Benito Mussolini held Italy in the vise of Fascism, and was about to undertake a reckless escapade into Africa. Fickle France's Third Republic was changing governments as fast as fashions. England languished under an austerity economy led by ailing Prime Minister Ramsay MacDonald. Across the seas, mighty America agonized under a depression that put millions of men out of work, and militaristic Japan, having subdued Manchuria, began its imperial march into China. What then was there for a poetic soul like Recha to do but to write and dream and call up memories

> of my early childhood in Norden on the North sea at the turn of the century . . . of Sabbath afternoon strolls into town with the family and of one special Sabbath when we come upon a white paper with a black border posted on a gate . . . we stop to read it. I am only four and cannot understand but I hear what the

others are saying. They say the sign reads ENTRANCE FOR-
BIDDEN TO DOGS AND JEWS. Soon we move to another
town and there I am the only Jewish girl in the class and the
pupils ridicule me when I say that my religion does not permit
me to ride on the Sabbath . . . how homesick I am for a town
I can really call home. In my childhood I know of the Land of
Israel but I believe that it is unreachable because it is in heaven.

A knock on the door roused Recha. Her caller was a pale, thin
sixteen-year-old boy who introduced himself as Nathan Höxter,
son of the late Rabbi Höxter.

"Why have you come to me?" Recha asked.

"I thought that you might be able to help us."

"Us?"

"Yes, my five friends and me. We are members of the Brit
Ha-Olim, a group of Zionists. Our problem is that we have been
thrown out of our jobs. They said they no longer want Jews.
Maybe we can find work in the mines in the Rhineland. We don't
know where to turn."

"Bring your friends to me and let us discuss it. We will work
something out," replied Recha.

Next day she ran to the office of the Jewish Labor Exchange
of the Zionist movement. Yes, the secretary knew the problem, but
insisted with a shrug that it was only temporary. With Norden
strongly in her mind she could not accept his assurance. She sat
at night in her study and pondered:

How I always dreamed of an exodus of Jewish youth to Palestine! But this was only a dream that was never practical. Maybe,
just maybe, now is the time. How helpless that boy made me
feel. And how joyous, too. This certainly must be the hour. I
must dream no longer. I must make reality my partner. Palestine
is their home. They must go to it. It is my home too.

Recha called on Enzo Sereni, an Italian-born Zionist living in
Palestine, who was in Germany as the representative of a kibbutz
movement. Later, during World War II, Sereni was killed by the
Nazis after he parachuted into Italy to organize underground
rescue operations. She explained to him that she would like to
organize large groups of German youth to live in the kibbutzim.
Sereni fairly jumped out of his chair as she spoke.

"Do it. Do it at once and you will revolutionize the entire German Zionist movement," Sereni exclaimed.

When Nathan Höxter returned with his five friends, Recha said, "I will not help you go to the mines. There is no future for Jewish youth in Germany. Eretz Israel is your home. You must go there. You can work in a kibbutz. And if you so decide I shall help you."

The boys immediately agreed. At Sereni's suggestion, Recha wrote the Histadrut in Tel Aviv for assistance to arrange places in kibbutzim. The Histadrut was encouraging; but Berlin's established Zionist leadership was not. When Recha called on Zionist leaders, they dismissed the idea. Several told her to send the boys to German farms where, as one advised, "They'll really learn to work and to spend money properly."

In the spring of 1932, Recha was ready to give up the idea when the Histadrut's education and cultural chairman in Tel Aviv, Yaacov Sandbank, wrote that three agricultural settlements, Geva, Ein Harod, and Nahalal, were ready to accept the boys. Recha went back to the German Zionist Organization, to WIZO (Women's International Zionist Organization), and to EZRA, a Jewish agricultural society. All rebuffed her.

"In the kibbutzim they will become Communists."

"You cannot separate adolescents from their parents."

"The kibbutzim are not kosher."

Only young Zionists showed enthusiasm. "In them I kindled a spark that burst into a flame," Recha later recalled. After she spoke to teenagers in Jewish schools, they rushed to her to register for Palestine. The excitement of the youth moved Georg Landauer, a member of the Zionist Executive in Berlin, to agree reluctantly to Recha's plan on the condition that the Va'ad Leumi (National Council of Jews in Palestine) arrange for the care of the young immigrants. The head of the Social Welfare Department of Va'ad Leumi was then Henrietta Szold. Recha wrote Henrietta. Henrietta replied that no funds were available in Palestine for the poor children already there; a large influx of parentless children from Germany might strain the limited resources of the *yishuv*. The memory of Norden and the exuberance of the youth around her pushed Recha on.

In June, 1932, Recha, still unable to mobilize sufficient aid, had a visitor from Palestine. He was Siegfried Lehmann, founder of the Ben Shemen youth village. He liked Recha's idea and was ready to arrange twelve entry permits for her boys if they would agree to study farming with him. Recha's ideal was the kibbutz, but she agreed. Forty teen-agers met with her and twelve were chosen. She now worked feverishly to raise money for their care at Ben Shemen. Recha fought stiff opposition from parents and peers. But she had a few friends who helped. One raised 4,000 marks by pawning her jewelry.

On October 12, 1932, the first group of boys left Berlin by train en route to Ben Shemen. When Nathan Höxter and his friends landed in Jaffa on December 2, they became the vanguard of the mass movement of children who traveled to Palestine under the banner of an organization, unique in history, that was soon to be known in Germany by its bilingual name *Jugendaliyah,* or Youth Aliyah.

Great movements, like great rivers, rise from many tributaries. In the latter half of the nineteenth century liberal Jewish community leaders in pogrom-mad Russia tried to form save-our-children organizations. They too met heavy opposition. Opponents argued that children must remain with parents. In 1870, Carl Netter, a learned and wealthy Strasbourg merchant who championed rights for Jews in France, opened a farm school called Mikve Israel outside Jaffe. Netter moved to Mikve Israel with a group of Polish orphans. Shortly thereafter, Israel Belkind, a leader of the Bilu, the earliest of Zionist agricultural colonists, tried to set up several schools for orphans of Russian pogroms. He attempted one at Shefeya, but it failed because he could not raise sufficient money. In Baltimore, in 1917, Hadassah's own Alice Seligsberg stated publicly that the only solution for Europe's Jewish orphans was to open schools for them in Palestine. Later, as adviser to Junior Hadassah, she made a success of Meier Shefeya Youth Village. In 1927 Siegfried Lehmann established a "Youth Republic" (a kind of Boys' Town) at Ben Shemen, amidst the gnarled olive groves near Lydda, and took in a group of orphans of the Russian revolution from Kovno, Lithuania. Lehmann saw the possibility of expanding Ben Shemen in 1932 with young German immigrants. And so he called on the visionary Recha Freier in Berlin.

Among the Jewish youth of Berlin, Recha became known as "the dreaming woman." She did not mind and she would say, "I happen to come from the world of fairy tales. There as you know, everything is anonymous. So I would like to remain anonymous, too. It's the youth, not me, that wants help. I only want to turn dreams and fairy tales into reality."

Recha spoke incessantly, at times obsessively, about sending ten thousand German youth to Palestine. This only enhanced her image as a dreamer, for even her closest colleagues thought in terms of fifty or sixty. Time and genocide would vindicate her.

Early in January, 1933, the Histadrut's Sandbank wrote Recha that she must come to Tel Aviv if she wanted to further her cause. In that same month Henrietta Szold had decided to retire. It wasn't the first time. In 1931 she returned to Palestine from the United States only at the urgent insistence of *yishuv* leaders to organize the haphazard social service of the incipient Jewish nation. Now, she had written to her sister Bertha that she wanted at last to finish out her years with her family in Baltimore.

Back in Berlin, Recha prepared to go to Palestine. On the last day of January she gathered together in the office of a notary, Hugo Fuerth, seven young Zionist leaders, some of whom were not yet twenty-one. They called themselves the Aid Committee for Jewish Youth, carefully avoiding any hint that their real purpose was emigration to Palestine. But among themselves they referred to the project as *Jugendaliyah*, Youth Aliyah. At nightfall they left Fuerth's office, and as they turned into Berlin's broad Unter den Linden boulevard, they saw masses of jack-booted Brownshirts marching in a mammoth torchlight parade in celebration of the coming to power, earlier that day, of Adolf Hitler.

Persecution of the Jews became a major function of the new German government, and even in that day of primitive international communication it was not long before the Jews of Palestine felt the foul winds blowing in from Europe. By April, 1933, Berlin decreed a boycott on all Jewish enterprises but then at the last minute canceled it when Mussolini convinced Hitler the time was not ripe. Chaim Arlosoroff, head of the Political Department of the Jewish Agency in Jerusalem, went to Berlin to try to convince the German Zionist organizations to prepare for the emigration of Jews to Palestine. They knew he was right. The Zionist opponents of Youth Aliyah made a quick turnabout and formed one joint committee to prepare youth and to raise money.

Henrietta Szold's personal plans were now complete. She invited sister Bertha to Palestine to show her all the sights, after which they would return home together; for Henrietta, home was still America. But the Jewish leadership in Palestine pressured Henrietta to give up the notion of retirement. They were now forming a committee to do something about German-Jewish refugees and they insisted that she head it. Bertha went home alone.

Recha was now in Tel Aviv. At the end of May she attended a Histadrut rally at the Jascha Heifetz Hall where a large audience heard labor and kibbutz leaders call for the immigration of German youth. One even mentioned the number ten thousand. The meeting passed a resolution opening the settlements to the youth. After the rally, Recha rode to Jerusalem where she had her first meeting with Henrietta Szold. No two more dissimilar personalities ever faced each other. Recha failed to convince Henrietta that it was urgent to flood the gates of Palestine now with German youth; Henrietta could not convince Recha that the *yishuv* was not prepared for mass immigration. What, asked Henrietta, would happen to German youth left unattended on the wharves of Jaffa and Haifa unless homes were waiting for them? In the back of Recha's mind was the frightening torchlight parade on the evil night of January 31 and all that it portended. Henrietta was concerned that the kibbutzim were simply not prepared to cope with German teen-agers.

Recha went home that summer only slightly encouraged by Palestine's noted land developer and pioneer of the kibbutz idea, Arthur Ruppin. He promised to try to convince Henrietta of the worth of Recha's idea. In Berlin, Recha pestered Zionist groups to organize training camps for the youth. Already entire German-Jewish families were beginning to leave. In 1932, total Jewish immigration into Palestine was 9,553. In 1933, the year Hitler came to power, immigration of Jews into Palestine was 30,327, two-thirds of whom were Germans. But Recha was interested in the youth and especially in those whose foolish parents had faith that Hitler was a passing fantasy.

In Jerusalem, the committee that Henrietta headed had no guidelines. Housing was short. So many refugees had already arrived that they bedded down underneath the sky on Tel Aviv's beaches. That made Henrietta all the more dubious about the idea of encouraging large numbers of German youth to immigrate. Then, the kibbutzim agreed to accept one thousand children.

Recha was jubilant. Henrietta insisted on inspecting kibbutz housing facilities. Finding they were not up to her high standard, she
suggested a compromise whereby some youth would be put into
homes and boarding schools, while others would go to the settlements. But when she went to the British authorities for certificates,
they refused, saying that the facilities for none of these were
ready. Immigration in those days was limited to capitalists (those
with the equivalent of $5,000) and to those youth for whom two
years' sustenance was available. Henrietta personally urged the
settlements to begin building for the youth she knew would
come.

The Eighteenth World Zionist Congress met in free but
threatened Prague on August 21, 1933. While Hitler's shadow
grew darker over Germany, the political debate at the congress
was marred by the deep rift between the Labor and extremist
Revisionist parties. But the Congress did take up the German
question and established what became known popularly as the
"German Bureau" under the chairmanship in London of Chaim
Weizmann. Henrietta did not attend the congress, but Arthur
Ruppin, who chaired the Jerusalem section of the German Bureau,
implored her to take over as head of a new *ad hoc* office of the
Jewish Agency to be devoted to Youth Aliyah affairs. That
October, at a worldwide meeting in London of Jewish organizations called to declare a boycott on all German goods, she heard
more of the disaster that was overtaking the Jews of Germany, so
off she sped to Berlin. In the German capital she deliberated day
and night with Zionist leaders. She expressed dismay at the lack
of understanding they had for life in Palestine and at the absence
of an organized effort to raise funds and prepare youth for their
new life. If ever she had any doubts that the youth must leave
they were now dispelled. Before departing she succeeded in ar-
ranging for the early "conditioning" and transfer of sixty-three
boys and girls aged fifteen to seventeen under the leadership of
Hanoch Reinhold. Henrietta did not meet Recha Freier in Berlin,
and Recha resented it. But Henrietta did appreciate Recha's role.
At the Nineteenth World Zionist Congress held in Lucerne in
1935 Henrietta Szold said: "I would like to say a word of thanks
to the organizer of this movement [Youth Aliyah], Mrs. Recha
Freier. It was she who conceived the ingenious idea and carried it
through despite all difficulties and obstacles. We are grateful that

she held with such devotion to her idea, which in the beginning found little support." Recha reached Palestine only in 1941 after a harrowing journey through East Europe.

By the time Henrietta returned to Palestine the British government offered Youth Aliyah 350 permits for German-Jewish children. Immediately, she left for Kibbutz Ein Harod where she personally whipped the kibbutzniks into frenzied building of housing for the expected newcomers.

In mid-February 1934, the winter's worst gale hit the shores of Palestine. On the high seas opposite Jaffa was the S.S. *Martha Washington*. On February 18 she tried to drop anchor off Jaffa, but the weather was so bad she headed north to the recently opened port of Haifa. There, on Monday, February 19, the first organized group of Youth Aliyah children walked down the gangplank—exactly two years after Recha Freier brought up the idea in her meeting with Nathan Höxter in her Berlin apartment. Henrietta smiled as she watched the well turned-out youngsters from Germany standing on the quay with their mandolins and their skis and rucksacks on their backs. Some had brought along bicycles and even flagpoles. No one seemed to mind the pelting rain. Henrietta greeted each child by name. It was a custom she was to follow for the rest of her days. She escorted them to Ein Harod, spent the first day with them, even joined them in a hora in the kibbutz dining hall.

From that day on Henrietta's life was taken up with the affairs of Youth Aliyah. All the tremendous vitality that she could mobilize went into raising funds, supervising training, struggling for permits. By the end of 1934 a dozen groups consisting of about five hundred arrived and Henrietta wrote: "This great constructive movement has only begun. Five hundred young people is not more than 5 per cent of the number that should be drawn out of Germany into the productive, promising life of Palestine."

Her toughest problem was money. It always was. But money now meant young lives. On her way back from Berlin in November, 1933, she wrote, "If only there were funds . . . the Joint Distribution Committee has practically nothing to give." Raising cash in Palestine was difficult. Henrietta went to one wealthy landowner in Jerusalem and came away, after much pleading, with a paltry fifty pounds. In one letter home she wrote, "The public does not like the German Jews." Cash was being collected in

Germany by a joint committee, the Arbeitsgemeinschaft. But the
first appreciable sum that came into the organization's coffers
grew out of a pageant, "The Romance of a People," that was produced at the Century of Progress Fair in Chicago by Meyer
Weisgal. The pageant took place on Jewish Day, July 3, 1933,
before 130,000 people jammed into Soldiers Field. At Weisgal's
insistence Chaim Weizmann traveled eight thousand miles to make
this appearance. Weizmann's speech was good for the unheard-of
sum of $100,000. He received $25,000 on the spot for refugee
relief. The remaining $75,000 was presented a few months later by
Weisgal in London to the director of the German Bureau, Martin
Rosenbluth, with the words, "Here is money you can use for
Youth Aliyah. Now you're in business."

In its infancy Youth Aliyah was thwarted by the harsh
immigration restrictions of the Palestine government, by the in-
decisiveness of world Jewry, and by a dearth of funds. The free
world had not only been put off balance by Hitler but had been
impoverished by a financial crisis. In the United States, wellsprings
of philanthropy were dry. All the while young German Jews
waited. Separated from the European scene by two thousand miles
of ocean, the people of the United States were not adequately
aware of the significance of Hitler's rise to power. Even in England, ever so much closer to the whirlwind, Winston Churchill
was jeered for demanding national preparedness. How much more
so those few voices who shouted into the wind in faroff America.
But voices there were, few but powerful, like that of Stephen
Wise, who warned that Hitler was not a temporary aberration.

In New York City during 1934 there was a woman who in
some respects was the counterpart of Recha Freier. Tamar de Sola
Pool, Hadassah's national president from 1939 to 1943, was also a
visionary and a treasurehouse of madcap ideas. But she had charm
and she had megatons of energy. And no matter what the opposition, Tamar had an abundance of resilience that kept her always
afloat. She was then president of the New York City chapter of
Hadassah. With her husband, the courtly Rabbi David de Sola
Pool, she had been abroad many times. She knew Palestine well.
Now she was back from her most recent trip with a bug in her
head that Hadassah must enter, as she put it, "immigration work."
Tamar sensed that an immigration project was essential to main-

tain a high level of involvement in Hadassah at the grass roots. Many of the board agreed, but the responsibility was a tremendous one and the leadership, while moving in that direction, decided to move cautiously. Many years later, Tamar would remark with justification, "The National Board had no confidence in me. They thought I was scatter-brained, that I was not a good organizer. But I must admit I do have a talent for creative thinking."

Hadassah was then in the midst of a devolutionary program, which in simple terms meant that it was transferring some of its responsibilities in Palestine. In line with the principle laid down by Henrietta Szold, Hadassah turned over its projects to municipal or other local public authorities as soon as they were ready to maintain them. The transfer of hospitals, preventive medical stations, school hygiene programs, and tuberculosis care outside Jerusalem was hastened in the early 1930's because of the financial squeeze caused by the depression, and because of Hadassah's eagerness to move ahead on Mt. Scopus with the construction of the most modern medical center in the Middle East. In October, 1934, Henrietta Szold laid the cornerstone of that center. Hadassah was then 50,000-strong, but board member Judith Epstein, a great champion of the center, would later recall: "We suddenly found that our world could not be bound by Palestine and the medical work we were doing. Nobody saw clearly in 1934 in what direction an expanded program would go."

To find new direction and purpose Hadassah President Rose Jacobs left for Palestine in the summer of 1935 on a mission for the National Board. An intimate friend of Henrietta Szold, Rose Jacobs was a powerhouse of energy armed with an iron will. Some found her schoolmarmish and criticized her for expecting to be followed blindly into the unknown. But few faulted Rose Jacobs on her decisiveness. During Henrietta's presidency, Rose often served for long periods as acting president. She wore Henrietta's mantle and had her confidence.

In Palestine, Rose Jacobs pondered two non-medical projects for Hadassah, Youth Aliyah and vocational education. She drove herself to exhaustion in the two months she spent there. Henrietta was her mentor, but did not suggest that Hadassah assume the responsibility of funding Youth Aliyah. What Rose saw confirmed Tamar de Sola Pool's earlier observations.

Youth Aliyah was first on my list. . . . When one follows the
youth groups from the port of entry in Palestine into the settlements [Rose wrote from Palestine], one is prone to forget that
what one sees is connected with a desperate situation in Germany
and that their being in Palestine is the challenge of a tragic
dilemma. Youth Aliyah looks like the beginning of a movement,
initiated by German youth, to save itself from destruction. It may
be faced with the despair of homelessness.

She wrote vividly of meeting the ships bringing Youth Aliyah
children, of following them together with Henrietta to the kibbutzim. Rose reported that in Merhavia one frightened youth fresh
from Berlin suggested that the windows be closed so that their
conversations would not be overheard. In a kibbutz near Haifa,
the children arrived with books by Schiller, Goethe, and Heine.
The kibbutz children jeered when they saw the German writings.
Reported Rose:

I shall never forget Miss Szold. She turned to the German
children and said, "It is wonderful what you have brought; you
have brought prize possessions from Germany which Germany
itself does not value. Don't forget the cultural things, the fine
part of Germany that you have learned. Try to forget the other
things." The children of the kibbutz bowed their heads, ashamed.
Thus did Henrietta Szold lay the basis for mutual respect in the
relationship of German and Palestinian youth.

Rose also saw the need for vocational training and wrote a
report on it, although she leaned toward Youth Aliyah. But she
planned to take both back to New York and let the National
Board decide. In August, Henrietta and Rose traveled to Lucerne,
Switzerland, where the Nineteenth Zionist Congress convened.
Chaim Weizmann returned to the presidency after four years out
of office and Henrietta reported on two years of Youth Aliyah.
To a hushed hall she said:

Before I left Palestine last week I took a trip through all the
kvutzot where our young boys and girls are placed, in order to
see at close hand the full extent of my responsibility. I was
gripped by the thought of the children whom we have lost during the course of generations. I thought of the children who
were sent to the Island of St. Thomas by the Inquisition, of the
cantonists in Russia, of Edgar Mortara in Italy, and I thought also

of the crimes we are committing against our own children—that we have not gathered the funds which Palestine needs to solve the most important problem—the problem of the Jewish child.

Seventy-five-year-old Henrietta was the star attraction of the congress. Rose Jacobs was as proud as though she were Henrietta's own daughter. There was no longer any doubt that the National Board would accept Youth Aliyah as its own ward in America. Attending the congress, too, was Georg Landauer, director of the German Settlement Bureau in Jerusalem. With Henrietta's acquiescence, Rose and Georg drew up a confidential letter on August 27, 1935, which spelled out the terms under which Hadassah would be the sole agency for Youth Aliyah in the United States. The five-paragraph statement, addressed to Rose as president of Hadassah and signed by Georg, specified that Hadassah would be sole representative of Youth Aliyah in the United States for an experimental two years during which Hadassah undertook to cover the expenses of 100 German and Polish youths at the rate of $500.00 each, a total of $60,000. It stipulated that if the Hadassah convention due to meet in November declined or reduced the number from 100, the Arbeitsgemeinschaft in Berlin would carry out its own campaign in the United States. But if the convention did accept, then "no organization for Youth Aliyah shall be established in America."

It would be difficult to find in the annals of American Zionist history a document that raised more dust than that one. Both Georg and Rose were vaguely aware that they had overstepped the limits of their authority. The Zionist Congress had just passed a resolution prohibiting separate fund-raising appeals apart from those which were already established. Yet Georg Landauer committed the Zionist Organization to doing just that, and he was to suffer great embarrassment for his sin. With Henrietta's support, Rose was confident, but she certainly had gone far beyond her terms of reference.

By the end of September, Rose was back in New York. She immediately convened a meeting of the National Board. "The saving of European Jewry is the crying need of the hour," she said with deep emotion. "Hadassah is that channel through which the appeal for the rescue of our youth can be made effective. We can help convert the Youth Aliyah project into a great movement." With the still secret contract in hand, Rose obtained the board's unanimous consent to accept Youth Aliyah as Hadassah's newest major project. No sooner was the meeting over than Rose rushed off to Atlanta to be at the bedside of her ailing father. Acting for her, Judith Epstein wrote Landauer in Jerusalem of the board's unanimous acceptance and of its intention to recommend it to the convention opening in Cleveland on November 28. No one was more jubilant than irrepressible Tamar de Sola Pool. She wrote a letter to Henrietta in Jerusalem saying how happy she was that Hadassah had accepted Youth Aliyah, and said that she was sure that Hadassah would raise at least $100,000, not $60,000. (As a matter of record, Hadassah raised $250,766.76 in the first two years.)

On October 29, one month before the convention was to meet to approve the Youth Aliyah project, the Jewish Agency Executive in Jerusalem annulled the Landauer-Jacobs contract.

Louis Lipsky, the chairman of the board of the American Palestine Campaign, had not heard of the agreement until October 11—a full six weeks after it had been signed. He immediately wrote indignantly to Rose Jacobs that a separate campaign for Youth Aliyah run by Hadassah would "inevitably lead to the disintegration of the Zionist Movement in the United States." The gladiator of American Zionism was wounded in the heel. There were good reasons for his concern. Organized Jewish philanthropy for domestic and overseas causes was in turmoil. Part of the trouble was that there were simply too many mouths to feed and there was too little to go around. After the depression of 1929 hit America, the American Palestine Campaign joined the Joint Distribution Committe (for all non-Palestine causes) to form the Allied Jewish Appeal. But that mixed marriage went on the rocks after the first year. Zionists and non-Zionists found it impossible at that time to work together. Then in 1934, they tried again— this time under the family name United Jewish Appeal. That marriage lasted two years, but at the end of the 1935 campaign the JDC asked for a divorce. Lipsky, as head of the American Palestine Campaign, was terribly concerned. He found sympathy and relief at the Zionist Congress in Lucerne where delegates urged consolidation and unity in Zionist ranks, especially in fund-raising. Toward that end, the American Palestine Committee joined with the land reclamation and land purchasing agency of the Zionist movement, the Jewish National Fund, in what was then called the

United Palestine Appeal. Now, in the latter part of 1935, Hadassah was about to fall out of line. Lipsky would not suffer this breach of Zionist discipline and there then began what became known as the "battle of the cables."

Lipsky began the offensive from his headquarters in New York on October 22 when he cabled "strong protests" to the Jewish Agency Executive in Jerusalem. He insisted that "a coordinated front for Palestine fund-raising was imperative." Otherwise, "the entire Zionist program is menaced."

On October 27, in a stormy meeting with Hadassah, Lipsky insisted that Hadassah forego its exclusive rights. Later, Lipsky reported on the Hadassah leaders' reaction in what must have been the understatement of any year, "They remained unimpressed." He added, in a fit of self-righteousness, "They thought as always only of their own Hadassah fund-raising without seeming to care for one moment what the effect would be on the rest of fund-raising in America. They would hear of no arrangement other than the one which they *think* [Lipsky's underlining] they have concluded with Landauer." Immediately after the meeting broke up, Lipsky protested against the Jewish Agency Executive's entering into the contract "without our consultation, communication or advice." There, he obviously had a point, and it was a point that stuck.

Two days later, on October 29, the Zionist Executive met in Jerusalem. Treasurer Eliezer Kaplan was in the chair. Among the other eight present were Moshe Shertok, Jewish National Fund President Menachem Ussishkin, David Werner Senator, Rabbi Yehuda Leib Fishman, and Georg Landauer. On the agenda was an urgent item: "Special Campaigns."

Kaplan had before him Lipsky's cable of protest. Obviously angry, Kaplan eyed Landauer and said that it was obvious that American Jews would not contribute twice in the same year to a Zionist appeal. Therefore, the congress had wisely forbidden separate fund campaigns. Landauer asked for the floor. He took a practical line: Youth Aliyah needed about $200,000 for those children already registered to emigrate from Germany and Poland. "The Keren Hayesod [fund-raising arm of the World Zionist Organization] simply cannot provide that kind of money for Youth Aliyah," Landauer said. "The Joint Distribution Committee is propagandizing for the children to be sent to America. They will not provide funds for them to come to Israel. The question is

where the money is to come from. Without America we simply
cannot do it. Hadassah has informed us that it has the capability
to carry out a separate campaign and has guaranteed to care for
100 children. I would favor a United Zionist Campaign if it would
guarantee to raise the money Hadassah is willing to raise. But if
it won't, then I suggest that Hadassah do it."

Landauer was outnumbered. Ussishkin, a double-fisted stalwart
of classic Zionism, expressed astonishment that Landauer should
have dared to violate discipline by signing the agreement with
Hadassah. To have been so harshly attacked by a veteran of the
movement must have been the ultimate hurt for well-meaning
Landauer. The stern-eyed Rabbi Fishman, supporting Ussishkin
and Kaplan, said that unity of the Jewish people and its campaigns
overrode all other considerations.

The balanced, precise Shertok came mercifully to Landauer's
support. "The money must be found," he said. "Separate appeals
have been made for this purpose elsewhere. In any case, Hadassah
conducts campaigns for other projects and I see no sin committed
if this year it includes Youth Aliyah in its general appeal." Senator
supported Shertok. But they were in the minority. Zionist discipline
was all-important. In deference to Shertok, Kaplan was a trifle
more plastic at the end of the debate, saying that Hadassah could
go ahead and raise funds for Youth Aliyah but only within the
framework of the over-all united appeal in America. In effect,
however, he abrogated the contract. His strictly conservative stand
won a majority.

But in an attempt to forestall a fraternal war in the American
Zionist camp, Kaplan instructed his colleague stationed in London,
affable Berl Locker, to hurry to the United States. The cable he
received would have floored a giant, and Berl stood just over five
feet: "bring back an agreement between Hadassah and the American Palestine Campaign that will satisfy the just demands of Hadassah, that will assure the participation of the American Palestine
Campaign, and will safeguard the interests of Keren Hayesod."

On October 30, Kaplan ordered Lipsky to go ahead with his
plans for a united Palestine drive and to "include youth immigration in the slogan." Kaplan also cabled Hadassah an official repudiation of the Landauer-Jacobs contract. The Hadassah board went
into emergency session. On Friday, November 1, it drafted a cable
to the Jewish Agency that matched Kaplan's slap with one of its

own: "Repudiation of the contract would hurt the Youth Aliyah project and Hadassah's effectiveness in Palestine."

Hadassah's cable went on to explain cogently that its way of running a campaign—on a year-round, day-to-day basis—was much more effective than the one-shot drives run for a short period by the united campaign. And then the cable ended: "Your failure to honor the contract will stunt Youth Aliyah's future development in America and force Hadassah to adopt a substitute specific project."

With that cable Hadassah, perhaps unknowingly, entered the major league of Zionist politics. It had challenged the Jewish Agency, and therefore the World Zionist Organization, as well as the organized, male-dominated Zionist Organization of America. Hadassah, now twenty-one years old, had come of age with a flair.

Two days later, Kaplan in Jerusalem cabled Lipsky in New York: "Hadassah has cabled a demand for revision on the basis of the agreement with Rothenberg in Lucerne."

This cable referred to an oral agreement made at the Zionist Congress between Rose Jacobs and Morris Rothenberg, President of the ZOA, to permit Hadassah to run the Youth Aliyah campaign.

That same day a livid Lipsky replied: "Neither Rothenberg nor myself in Lucerne knew of Hadassah's intention of taking exclusive possession of children's aliyah in America. Would not have agreed then. Cannot agree now."

The Hadassah board exploded at that and went on preparing its campaign to sell Youth Aliyah to its membership which by now had reached 60,000. The American Palestine Campaign people were becoming edgy. Executive Director Robert Silverman cabled Jerusalem on November 13, only two weeks before the Hadassah convention: "Despite Jewish Agency Executive rescinding exclusive contract, Hadassah insists continuing the children's campaign, threatening a serious conflict."

On that same day Silverman fired off a second cable to Jerusalem, having just learned that Rose Jacobs had outflanked him on another front: "Hadassah expecting to bring Miss Szold to America for children's campaign. She should be advised not to project herself into this conflict."

Hadassah received support from outside the Zionist fold. Maurice Hexter, non-Zionist member of the Jewish Agency Executive and key figure in American-Jewish philanthropic work, cabled the Jewish Agency: "Your decision concerning Youth Aliyah will repeat the civil war reminiscent of 1921.* Strongly urge revision in favor af Hadassah."

If there was one thing on which both Hadassah and the Lipsky-Rothenberg-Silverman group agreed, it was that the presence of Berl Locker in America was pointless. On November 18, ten days before the Hadassah convention, Silverman cabled Jerusalem to that effect and then added in anger: "Urge Executive ignore Hexter cable supporting Hadassah." The next day Hadassah's cable message was firm: "Useless send Locker. Insist Executive honor contract."

That same day, the Agency Executive wired Hadassah in tough no-nonsense language. Obviously, the leaders of the movement had had their fill! "Executive anxious to settle conflict by agreement without resorting to the imposition of our decision. Therefore deputizing Locker with the approval of Szold and Halprin for mediation with instructions to safeguard the interests of Hadassah, Ampalc, and the integrity of the Zionist Organization."

Into the war of the cables there now entered a gun of heavy caliber. David Ben-Gurion, as chairman of the Zionist Executive, thought the situation sufficiently serious to force a solution. His message was addressed personally to Rose Jacobs: "Conflict liable to endanger the integrity of the Zionist Organization. Object to the intervention of non-Zionists in internal Zionist affairs. After consultation with Szold, advise settlement by agreement through the intervention of Locker as an impartial deputy."

Ben-Gurion's reference to "non-Zionists" was to Hexter and others such as the Arbeitsgemeinschaft who were solidly behind Hadassah. The final cable that arrived on that climactic November 19 was from Henrietta Szold and Rose Halprin, then Hadassah board representative in Jerusalem, and was addressed to Rose Jacobs: "We've been shown your cable to the Executive. Advise acceptance of the intervention of Locker whatever else you may do."

That settled it. Locker left on November 20 and arrived six days later in time for the opening of the Cleveland convention. The Hadassah board carried the fight from New York to Cleveland. The members had been in continual negotiations with Lipsky

---

* This was a reference to the bitter battle between the Weizmann-Lipsky and Brandeis forces over the aims of American Zionism.

and Rothenberg; they even carried the debate to an all-night beanery opposite Hadassah's New York office at 111 Fifth Avenue. In Cleveland, the sessions between the nationwide board and Locker went on throughout the night before the convention formally opened. He pleaded with Hadassah leaders to let go of their exclusive rights to Youth Aliyah. They held like tiger cats, and then informed Locker that the entire issue would be put before the delegates. Forlorn, frustrated, alone on foreign soil, Locker retired for what was left of the night.

On the following day Rose Jacobs addressed the delegates at a session lasting from 10:00 P.M to 2:00 A.M. Marian Greenberg followed with an exposé of the cable war, the acid messages, the acrimonious negotiations. The delegates gave both women an ovation. With that, Locker knew his mission was lost. He gallantly seconded Rose Jacobs' resolution affirming Hadassah's role as the sole agency in America for Youth Aliyah.

Recalling the convention fight, Rose said in 1957,

> Berl was no match for our women, who proved they could stay up all night, if necessary, to win their right to a project. . . . In the end everything worked out beautifully. Youth Aliyah was a great success, the United Palestine Appeal was not destroyed, a Jewish State came into being and Hadassah gave Lipsky a citation.

In January, 1936, a peace-making formula was worked out whereby Hadassah could begin its Trojan toil in earnest and still satisfy the needs of the United Palestine Appeal and the Jewish Agency Executive in Jerusalem. Hadassah agreed, in exchange for its exclusive rights, to confine its campaign to women (a pledge made to be broken) and to credit the Palestine Appeal with the money it raised. Thus, the UPA reported that during its first drive from January 1 to October 15, 1936 it raised $1,779,454, *including* the $125,000 raised by Hadassah for Youth Aliyah.

Even before the formula was worked out, the dynamo began to hum. In December, Henrietta Szold, who had fought gamely for Hadassah in Jerusalem, arrived to a hero's welcome. The night was cold and wet when her ship tied up at Hoboken, but reporters were there for interviews. She was rushed to a newsreel studio for a statement that appeared on screens across the nation. Later, Mayor Fiorello LaGuardia handed her the key to New York City. She spoke at a mass rally. "I come to you not only from Palestine, but from Germany, Austria and Holland," she began. There was hardly a dry eye in the crowd when she finished. Her trip netted thousands of dollars for Youth Aliyah. She was the pampered guest at the luxurious home of Mrs. Felix Warburg, where the first National Youth Aliyah Committee was set up.

Hadassah's "massed motherhood," as Marian Greenberg phrased it, fought for the children with every trick and gimmick it could devise, approached Zionist and non-Zionist, Christian as well as Jew, to fulfill its contract. Thousands of Hadassah workers were in the field rousing America to the need. They mobilized the most prominent women in America, among them the wives of Secretary of the Treasury Morgenthau, Senator Robert Wagner, Supreme Court Justice Louis Brandeis, Governor Herbert Lehman. Elinor Morgenthau, a close friend of Eleanor Roosevelt, brought Youth Aliyah to the attention of the First Lady. Later at a meeting in the Blue Room of the White House with Hadassah representatives, Mrs. Roosevelt accepted an honorary post with Youth Aliyah and on the death of South African Field General Jan Smuts [*] became the second World Patron of Youth Aliyah.

Of all the star-studded names that went on the official letterhead and on the posters, none worked more conscientiously for Youth Aliyah than Eddie Cantor, the comedian. He was brought into the act by Tamar de Sola Pool who, with the campaign now officially on, went into a state of perpetual motion. In February, she raced off to the Hollywood Beach Hotel in Florida where Eddie was staying. In her hand she held an article written by the right-wing columnist Westbrook Pegler, in which he denounced Hitler's war on children. Eddie was having his breakfast when Tamar bounced in. She showed him the article and asked him to work for Youth Aliyah. "For this cause," the pop-eyed father of five girls said, "I'm ready to give my life." One month later, in March, 1936, when Hadassah ran the first donor lunch in New York for Youth Aliyah, Eddie appeared. He surprised everyone with the announcement that he had already collected $44,000— in those days a considerable sum.

In Madison, Wisconsin, the local Hadassah president, Mrs. Herman Mack, found that it was too much to ask the members to raise $360 each to take care of a child in Palestine. For some, that

[*] Smuts accepted the titular post of World Patron at the behest of an active Youth Aliyah worker, Vera Weizmann, a leader of WIZO and first First Lady of Israel. Following Mrs. Roosevelt's death, the title went to Baroness Alix de Rothschild.

was four month's salary. She got the idea of holding a *minyan:* ten women would gather weekly or monthly for teas or parlor meetings and each would ante-up a few dollars until the $360 sum was reached. The *minyan* idea spread throughout the country.

Junior Hadassah, Hadassah's young adult group which was organized in 1920, carried out its own campaign. At their convention in Washington, in December, 1936, one thousand delegates pledged to expand the children's village of Meier Shefeya to care for 150 young refugees. Junior Hadassah had adopted the village in 1925 and retained the responsibility for financing it until 1957 when Hadassah merged the Juniors and Young Judea into a single youth organization called Hashachar (The Dawn).

Hadassah used German refugees for nationwide speaking tours. Among them were three members of the Warburg families: Ilse, Ingrid, and Gisela; and Yettka Levy-Stein. Speakers were advised not to talk at rallies about the atrocities taking place in Germany because the Nazis were listening. The Gestapo grilled Ilse's father-in-law after an American newspaper wrote a story about her under the headline, "Blonde Victim of Nazi Persecution Refuses to Acknowledge Atrocities."

In Palestine, Henrietta was unbelievably active. Nearly eighty years old, Henrietta awoke at 5:00 A.M. every morning and after her usual calisthenics, dived headlong into a long day on behalf of Youth Aliyah. In June, 1936, she wrote Rose Jacobs, "Three days a week I get to bed at two and rise at five; the rest of the week I have from four to five hours' sleep, including the nap. I never, never relax. I never read unless it is a memo. I am inhuman."

The Arab riots of 1936–1939 had already broken out. Typically, the British government searched for a way to ease tension and started by handing out fewer immigration certificates to Jews. In December, 1936, Henrietta appeared before a royal commission, set up to hear Arab and Jewish grievances, but when she appealed for more certificates for Youth Aliyah she was told, "We have heard all that before." When she persisted, again she was cut off. The situation looked desperate. In October, 1937, Henrietta attended Hadassah's Jubilee Convention in Atlantic City. The convention elected Judith Epstein president. Retiring Rose Jacobs then became the first woman to be named a member of the Jewish Agency Executive. With more than 2,500 delegates present, it was the largest Zionist gathering to be held in the United States up to that time. Henrietta told the delegates, "My office is the center of a cobweb; threads run out of Germany to the youth in Palestine."

On March 10, 1938, the British government suddenly changed course and notified the Jewish Agency that it was establishing a new category of immigrant—students. Certificates would be unlimited on condition that housing was made available for the students. On the following day, March 11, Germany marched into Vienna and annexed Austria. Two hundred thousand Jews sought to leave. Most wanted to go to Palestine, but in Palestine there were places—in the kibbutzim primarily—for only one thousand youths. In New York, Youth Aliyah Chairman Marian Greenberg called a meeting at the home of Mrs. Roger Straus. An emergency committee of one thousand was organized with the aim of raising enough money to pay for one thousand youths in Palestine by September 30, 1938.

Responding to urgent pleas by Hadassah to step up his work, Eddie Cantor cabled Hadassah, "Except for Sundays and Mondays, Hadassah's time is my time." He was Youth Aliyah's single biggest money raiser. Eleanor Roosevelt came to Hadassah's aid with endorsements of the rescue movement in her "My Day" column. When the September 30 dateline arrived, 903 of the 1,000 were already in Palestine, and the remainder were on the way. Hadassah had managed to triple its Youth Aliyah income in that period.

1939 was a year of frantic effort. Hadassah dramatized the appeal by organizing meetings featuring noted British women, among them the wives of Foreign Secretary Lord Halifax and the Marquis of Reading. They told poignant stories of refugees arriving in England. In Washington, Hadassah board member Denise Tourover pounded the sidewalks between the White House and Congress, even appealed to foreign diplomats to bring pressure on the Germans on behalf of Youth Aliyah. In June, Marian Greenberg flew to England to meet leaders of the Arbeitsgemeinschaft at a Youth Aliyah conference; the previous year the Berlin office of Youth Aliyah was closed by the Nazis, and headquarters were now located in London.

On September 1, the Luftwaffe bombed Warsaw. Two days later Britain and France declared war on Nazi Germany. Trapped behind the iron gates now closing on the Continent were nine million Jews.

The war marked the end of Youth Aliyah's first phase. Between

February 1934 and September 1939, Youth Aliyah rescued 4,886 children. By the close of the war 7,446 children would be moved to Palestine from Europe by Youth Aliyah. The total saved from Nazi Europe would thus number 12,332, which does not include about 4,000 more children from Asian and African countries. But at least two million young Jews were killed in Hitler's death camps.

Rose Jacobs was not the only one to evaluate Youth Aliyah as a success. Eleanor Roosevelt said, "I have always felt that Youth Aliyah is one of the most creative accomplishments in history and that its importance is reaching far beyond the borders of Israel." On its twenty-fifth anniversary, in 1959, Youth Aliyah won the coveted Israel Prize for "rescuing nearly 80,000 children and youngsters." Education Minister Zalman Aranne said, "There seems to be no similar exodus of children and youngsters of this scope in the annals of mankind." As the fourth decade of the organization's work closes, it can be justly proud of its rehabilitation work; 150,000 young people have benefited from its pathfinding in education and human reconstruction. It has earned its acclaim.

That having been noted, the time has come to take a retrospective look at the early years and the rescue program of Youth Aliyah. The question whether Youth Aliyah could have saved more children from Europe during the Hitler period has for years remained unasked and unanswered. There can never be a satisfying reply. When the Hitlerite phenomenon appeared on the scene, nearly everyone was unprepared and there was a willingness to dally and to rationalize. Pogroms had been common in Europe. They were understood to be temporary storms, usually limited to specific periods of time and locales. Nothing in living experience prepared the world for the commission of evil on so vast a scale and in such broad dimensions as that which Hitler unleashed on one single, defenseless people.

The few years that it took for normally sensitive Jewry to interpret in full the signals emanating from Berlin were precious years lost; precious time that only now can be counted in numbers of dead. It was not until 1943 when the war was half over that the Jewish Agency Executive accepted full authority and established the Department for Child and Youth Immigration.

Henrietta Szold was a woman of impeccable character and boundless energy. She was, as David Ben-Gurion has said, the most outstanding Jewish woman of the twentieth century. Yet when she was asked to manage the affairs of Youth Aliyah, she was a mortal in her seventies. She did the work that should have been done by a legion of imaginative younger men and women. She applied to the rescue operation good principles. Her demand for perfection provided those who did escape assurance of proper housing, proper education, proper upbringing. Henrietta met every single ward that came off the boat. But the tragic fact is that in light of the history that followed, Jewish steps toward rescue were a classic World War II case of "too little and too late."

And what of the British? A nation that had the courage to snatch 360,000 men from the bombed beaches of Dunkirk in eight days grudgingly permitted Henrietta Szold to save less than 5 per cent of that number in eleven years because of its morbid fear of Arab retribution. As Josef Mengele decided the fate of a Jew at Auschwitz with the wave of his hand to right or to left, so a British civil servant in Jerusalem decided the fate of a Jew destined for Auschwitz by saying yes or no to the request for a permit. But the lack of permits cannot completely absolve world Jewry for dragging its feet. In March, 1938, the Mandate government announced a policy of "unrestricted" certificates for a new classification of youth—the student. Henrietta wrote in despair, "Unrestricted! On second thought—restricted not by Government, but by our limitations; available places and available funds."

And what of American Jewry? They held the richest pocketbook in the Jewish world. Millions of dollars were urgently needed from them but only thousands were given—sometimes with hesitancy. Such was the temper of American Jewry that in December, 1936, when Hadassah petitioned the British to grant Youth Aliyah permits for young Jews from Poland, in addition to those from Germany, protests were heard. At best, American Jews were out of touch with the scene in Germany. The American Jewish Committee's *Historical Review* for 1936–1937 noted a tone of disconcern in words that today are chilling:

> For the first time since the Spring of 1933, when the present regime in Germany began, there were indications that although it is continuing to follow with lively attention the events of Jewish interest abroad, the Jewish community of the United States is again beginning to give the major part of its thought to domestic needs.

Hadassah never claimed perpetual command of Youth Aliyah in America. When, finally, Jewish Agency leaders thought of *aliyah* of youth in terms of 50,000 rather than 10,000 and budgets soared beyond the capacity of one organization, Hadassah took the initiative in relinquishing its monopoly. On November 29, 1943, Henrietta together with Kaplan and Landauer confirmed (in a cable, of course) that a coordinating committee suggested by Hadassah, would now operate to collect money in America. Joining Hadassah in the fund-raising effort on an equal footing were the United Palestine Appeal, Mizrachi Women, and Pioneer Women. Hadassah was permitted to retain the title of official agent for Youth Aliyah in America.

Hadassah's noteworthy deed in the early years of the Hitlerite menace was to awaken masses of Americans to the need of Europe's children. No other organization was sufficiently broad-based or more intrinsically suited to the task. There are no measurements to judge the accomplishment in human terms. As regards money, the results achieved were impressive. The original contracted sum of $60,000 in two years was actually quadrupled. In the first eight years, Hadassah alone covered 75 per cent of Youth Aliyah's requirements. At the beginning of 1960 when Hadassah's accumulated contribution was close to $40 million (by the end of 1972 Hadassah's total outlay for Youth Aliyah was $65 million), Israel's director of Youth Aliyah Moshe Kol said, "Were it not for Hadassah, Youth Aliyah would have ceased to exist." By the same token Hadassah's good work for Youth Aliyah carried America's woman Zionist organization to full flower and maturity. Within one year after assuming responsibility, Hadassah's chapters soared from 272 to 375. Said Judith Epstein, "Youth Aliyah was a great turning point in Hadassah's development." Gisela Warburg Wyzanski, a "lonely refugee" from Germany in 1938 and Hadassah's energetic Youth Aliyah chairman from 1940 to 1945, said, "It forged the maternal tie between Hadassah and Israel." Henrietta's successor as mother of Youth Aliyah was Bertha Schoolman. To her, "Youth Aliyah remains the humanizing force on the American scene for our Hadassah work."

A two-year obligation became a lifelong partnership. The contract was fulfilled.

1934. *Above:* Henrietta Szold, first director of Youth Aliyah, greets the first arrivals from Nazi Europe. These teen-agers were from middle-class German homes and had prepared for aliyah through a pioneer program.

1943. *Below, left:* These malnourished and dwarfed "Teheran children" arrived in Palestine in 1943 after wandering across war-torn Europe.

1959. *Below, right:* Eleanor Roosevelt, world patron of Youth Aliyah, during one of several visits to a children's village.

Top: 1948. Militia guards Rothschild-Hadassah University Hospital and Henrietta Szold School of Nursing on Mt. Scopus. This picture was taken just before War of Independence. Magnificent buildings and landscaping were later vandalized and fell into disrepair.

Middle: April 13, 1948. Hadassah convoy with supplies and medical personnel is ambushed at Shiekh Jarrah Quarter on road to Mt. Scopus hospital. Seventy-six doctors, nurses, and staff are killed, including Dr. Haim Yassky, HMO Director General. During War of Independence access was cut off by Jordan and hospital wasn't returned to Hadassah until 1967 after the Six-Day War.

Bottom: 1949. Even before Hadassah sets up 100-bed emergency hospital in Rosh Ha'ayin for Yemenite immigrants, nurses visit in tent cities, where babies were flown in dehydrated and dying of malnutrition.

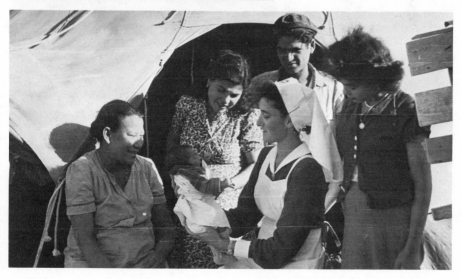

Left: 1949. Despite the loss of Scopus, Hadassah moved into five scattered buildings in Old Jerusalem and first class of Hebrew University-Hadassah Medical School opened. First class of 70 veterans are still in uniform.

Below: May 17, 1949. James G. McDonald, first American ambassador to Israel, and David Ben Gurion, first prime minister of the new state, at dedication of the Medical School, held in the Municipal Gardens of Old Jerusalem.

Above: 1960. Harassah moved into its magnificent new medical center perched on the Judaean Hills in Ein Karem in Western Jerusalem.

Below: Marc Chagall, at left, studies installation of his famed 12 windows in the hospital synagogue with center's architect, Joseph Neufeld.

Etta L. Rosensohn, ninth national president of Hadassah, at the groundbreaking of the new medical center at Ein Karem in 1952 with Prime Minister Ben-Gurion, who had suggested that site in Western Jerusalem, predicting that "the city would grow out to Hadassah."

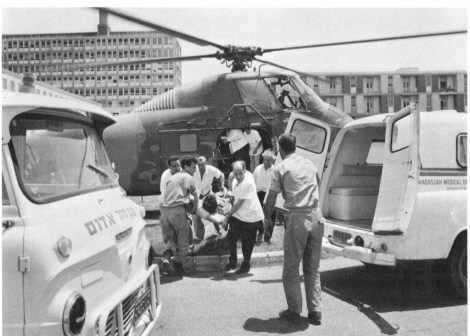

1967. Helicopters bring soldiers to Hadassah from the front during the Six-Day War. During subsequent Palestinian uprisings in Jordan, terrorists asked to be taken to Hadassah, where they knew that friend and foe would be treated alike.

11.

Nails on the Road

AFTER the Arab excesses of 1929, with few exceptions Palestine enjoyed seven years of truce. Then, in 1936, began the worst bloodletting of the century.

Exasperated by the flood of Jewish immigrants and frustrated because the British had not blocked the tide, extremist Arab nationalists demanded armed action. More moderate Arab leaders, meanwhile, were engaged in confidential but futile talks with David Ben-Gurion and other Zionists to seek an understanding. In one such conversation in August, 1934, Ben-Gurion was asked to agree to restrict immigration so that in ten years the Jewish population would not top one million. Ben-Gurion replied negatively, even though the Jews in Palestine then numbered only 400,000. By 1936, Arab right-wingers had gained the upper hand, their three demands being: stop Jewish immigration, stop land sales to Jews, make Palestine an Arab state now.

The British tried to coax both sides to accept a single, bi-national state and invited Arab leaders to confer on the subject. When the divided Arabs failed to agree on the make-up of their delegation, the British finally despaired of the proposal. That undermined the moderates further and by mid-April the Arab fanatics, riding high in the saddle, flashed the signal for a rebellion that flared intermittently until the eve of World War II and ended in a major, if shortlived, political victory for the Arab nationalist cause.

It was the evening of April 15, 1936, outside Nablus, the eye of the Arab nationalist hurricane. Ten trucks and cars were stalled in front of a barrier of barrels and rocks. An eyewitness recalled:

> We were proceeding from Haifa to Tel Aviv. Yehoshua Napchi, of Tel Aviv, stopped his car. Two Arabs appeared from the side of the road. They took Napchi to a lorry standing in front of us and they shot him, but he was only wounded. The shots killed Israel Khazan, 61, a Salonica Jew who was taking a load of chickens to the poultry market. They also wounded Zvi Tannenburg. A bullet went through his spine and he died later. One Jew identified himself as a German, and he was not touched.

The leader of the gang was a feared highwayman, Sheikh Izz e-Din, who had marauded in the Samarian hills for years. Now he was mixing business with politics. He informed his victims before he shot them, "I am taking your money to buy arms for the holy cause."

Friday, April 17, was a day of public bereavement for the *yishuv*. Thousands attended Khazan's funeral, and Tel Aviv Mayor Israel Rokach addressed the mourners, "Our innocent brother was murdered by people who wish to frighten us and stop our work. But the world will know that terrorist acts will not stop our work."

Someone in the assembly cried, "Revenge!"

Rokach replied: "Our revenge will be in creative work!" The policy of the *yishuv* throughout the riots was to be one of *havlaga* (self-restraint).

But the Jewish crowd marched to Magen David Square where they scuffled with British police. Flying stones, the traditional weapon in Palestine since the days of David, injured a few constables who finally dispersed the demonstrators with shots in the air.

Arab violence mounted by geometric proportions. A false rumor spread in Arab Jaffa that Tel Aviv Jews had murdered several Arabs. Arab gangs, some dressed in Boy Scout uniforms, smashed, knifed, and clubbed their way through the Jewish Quarter on the border between the twin cities. Elsewhere, Jewish

movie houses, clinics, and shops were broken into and their occupants shot. Arab protest took many forms. At Kibbutz Ein
Harod Arabs uprooted five hundred citrus trees. Houses, barns,
machinery, and forests were burned down. Arabs returned eight
times to burn groves near Mishmar Ha-emek. A children's home
was set afire but doused before the one hundred infants were
singed. Crude bombs were thrown in marketplaces. Snipers shot
at cars on the road and at Jewish pedestrians. The terrorists poured
lysol and kerosene on vegetables being delivered by Arab peasants
to Jewish markets. Henrietta Szold commented wryly in a letter
in the summer of 1936, "It is interesting that the typhoid record
for these months is the best yet. The elimination of vegetables
raised by Arabs in Palestine with their use of sewage for fertilizer
has in turn eliminated typhoid." By the end of April, half of
Jaffa's 18,000 Jews were refugees in Tel Aviv. Refugees filled
synagogues in Jerusalem and Tiberias. As a result of the general
strike called by the Supreme Arab Council, hundreds of Jews were
unemployed because they feared to cross picket lines. No accurate
count of the losses can be made, but the toll between April and
October of 1936 is estimated at 700 persons dead, thousands
wounded, 2,000 Jewish communities attacked, 100,000 trees destroyed, and $15 million in property damaged.

In an attempt to tame the tempest, the British dispatched an
army to Palestine and promised to establish a Royal Commission
that would probe the causes of the disturbances. After a long hot
summer, the Arabs finally called off the strike in October and in
November a six-member commission arrived.

The people of Palestine were cynical about commissions.
Moderates on both sides of the fence were doubtful that any third
force could possibly solve Palestine's problems; left alone Arabs
and Jews might possibly work out a modus vivendi whether
through arms or negotiations. But this was never to be; foreign
noses would always be stuck, and stung, in the Palestine beehive.
Even so, this latest commission, led by Lord Peel, managed to
raise faint hopes that Jews, Arabs, and British could together
pave a new road to peace. In the end, the Peel Commission failed
in its immediate mission, but it did succeed in introducing a new
concept in the tiresome search for a settlement. From the commission's sessions came the first concrete proposal to carve a Jewish

and an Arab state out of Palestine. It was an idea that would be realized precisely eleven years later.

On their arrival in Jerusalem on November 11, 1936, the commission members checked into the five-year-old King David Hotel and then drove straight to the British War Cemetery on Mt. Scopus for Armistice Day services. In Jerusalem, the Anglican bishop and even the chief rabbi of the non-Zionist Agudat Israel issued appeals to pray for the success of the commission. But the Grand Mufti of Jerusalem did not consider such an appeal appropriate. The Arab leadership decided on a boycott and dramatized it in a bizarre fashion. On the day after their arrival in Jerusalem the commission members were the guests of high commissioner Sir Arthur Wauchope at a gala reception held at the official residence on the Hill of Evil Counsel. On the way one car after another was put out of action. The Arabs had strewn nails on the road. Lord Peel got through unscathed, but one of his colleagues was immobilized three times by flats.

The Peel Commission opened its hearings in the rococo ballroom of the Palace Hotel on November 16. Sir Arthur was the first of the many witnesses who would testify in sixty-six sessions over the coming two months and two days. The third witness was of special interest to Hadassah. He was Colonel George Heron, the director of Palestine's medical services, who told the commission: "The Arabs must rely on Government health services whereas the Jews have their own organizations." He noted that the government spent £180,000 a year on health work, while Jewish organizations spent nearly twice that much. "On the Jewish side there are very complete medical services," he stated. And he boasted that Palestine had one physician for every six hundred persons, compared to one for every eight hundred in the United States. That was one of the highest—if not the highest— ratio in the world. Nearly all the doctors were Jews, many of them newcomers.

The most poignant moment in the commission's hearings was the appearance of Chaim Weizmann. Speaking in deep, measured tones, he traveled the history, hopes, and fortunes of the Jewish people for more than two hours. He spoke prophetically and tragically of Jews in Europe "pent up in places where they are not wanted, and for whom the world is divided into places where they cannot live and places which they may not enter." He flayed at the bugaboo of Palestine's "absorptive capacity"—the specious argument used by anti-Zionists to keep Jews out—when he recalled that Lord Passfield had once told him, "But Dr. Weizmann do you realize that there is not room to swing a cat in Palestine?" Weizmann could now tell the commission, "Many a cat has been swung since then, and the population of Palestine has increased since that talk with Lord Passfield by something like 200,000." The Zionists weighed in with forty more witnesses, among them David Ben-Gurion and Henrietta Szold. So strong was the evidence on behalf of a Jewish state that the Arabs broke their boycott and testified. The Grand Mufti came first with a counterbalancing review of Arab history, hopes, and broken promises, and of fears that the Jews were immigrating with the intention of reconstructing the Temple on the mount where now stood two of Islam's most sacred shrines. Fourteen more Arab leaders followed, and finally on January 19, 1937, the commission members started for home to determine the fate of Palestine.

Of all the sessions, the most fateful was a closed meeting with Chaim Weizmann on January 8. One member of the group, Oxford University historian Reginald Coupland, asked Weizmann to comment on the possibility of partitioning Palestine into independent states. Within the British government the idea of establishing a Swiss-like cantonal system under a British federal government was being mooted at the time, but this was the first occasion that the idea of two independent states was broached officially to the Zionist leadership. Weizmann thought to himself that he had finally arrived at the threshold of the Jewish state. He spoke with high enthusiasm to intimates; he was aware that the road ahead was burdened with obstacles, but he intuitively realized that somewhere at the end of the maze partition was the only way out. Aloud, he asked the members of the commission for time to consult his colleagues. The story is told—although it may be apocryphal—that a few days later Weizmann met secretly with Professor Coupland in the cooperative farm village of Nahalal. There they stooped over maps to try to determine rational borders for the two new states. And when they emerged from their meeting place in a wooden shack Weizmann exclaimed to a group of inquisitive Jewish farmers, "Today, here in this place, we have laid the foundation of the Jewish state!"

Lord Peel published his report in July, 1937, and died days

later. He complimented the Zionists for their constructive work in Palestine and presciently noted that "there is no common ground" between Jews and Arabs. "Neither Arab nor Jew," he wrote, "has any sense of service to a *single* state." Thus, partition was the only solution, because it alone would allow for the parallel development of national goals and cultures. Having come to that sensible conclusion, and having noted that the country's 400,000 Jews made up 40 per cent of the population, the commission went on to recommend the creation of a Jewish state with only 20 per cent of the territory. The much larger Arab state was to be united with Trans-Jordan. Jerusalem was to remain British—a captivating jewel in the imperial crown. These recommendations appeared in a White Paper issued by the British government almost simultaneously with the appearance of the Peel report.

The White Paper of 1937 angered the British administrators in Palestine who wanted to retain more control over the land and its people through a federated system. The Arabs, horrified at the prospect that Jews were about to be given a plot of the Arab domain, reached again for their guns. The Jewish leadership, meeting at the Twentieth Zionist Congress on August 3, fought bitterly over the Peel report. The partition principle itself was acceptable to most, but the size of the state proposed by Peel was not. Favoring the map were Weizmann, Ben-Gurion, and most Palestinian Jewish leaders. Opposed were the Americans led by Stephen Wise and Robert Szold, who were supported by Hadassah. Among the militant "maximalists," surprisingly, was Henrietta Szold who opposed Peel partly because he severed Jerusalem from the Jewish body. "How can one be with a Jewish state from which Jerusalem is excised," she wrote. "I don't like it." In whole or in part, neither did most Zionists.

Those in favor, however, made a strong argument that any small bit of sovereign territory was welcome now to provide a haven for masses of European refugees who had nowhere to go. "Territorial adjustments" could be made later, Weizmann said. "The Negev will not run away." The opponents argued that a state the size suggested by Peel was not viable. One speaker ridiculed the proposed state's dimensions: "We will call the new Jewish state 'England' because it is so small." The opponents' argument was that the Arabs would not resist the temptation to declare war on the state; it would be quickly overrun thus destroying forever the dream of Jewish national renascence.

In the end, the congress rejected Peel's proposals. The overwhelming majority of Hadassah's eighteen delegates, who were elected as a separate political entity for the first time, rejected partition on any terms. This stand was confirmed by a large vote at the Hadassah convention in Atlantic City two months later. But the congress, having in mind the refugees and the first practical offer of Jewish sovereignty, did not close the door completely. It accepted the partition principle as a basis for further negotiation. As it turned out, the fight was academic since the Arabs were not ready to tolerate the most microscopic Jewish state in Palestine and the British were in no mood to buck Arab opposition. Predictably, the Arab response to Peel was murder. After a congress of four hundred Arabs held at Bloudan, Syria, rejected the surrender of even an inch of Palestine to the Jews, they cranked up the rebellion. In October, one of the first victims was the popular district commissioner in Nazareth. That was enough to tame the British lion, and in November the government pacified the Arabs by declaring that it was not bound to partition. Then within three months the government formed a new commission, presided over by old India hand Sir John Woodhead. He was assigned the task of drawing up new partition borders. Woodhead presented two maps, both of which whittled down Peel's Jewish state to 400 square miles—the size of Hong Kong—or twenty times smaller than the state that came into being in 1948. No Jew could possibly have accepted such "a useless little ghetto," as it was described by historian Christopher Sykes. In the face of this new absurdity the British, in November, 1938, froze the idea altogether, announced that it was renewing its hold on the Mandate, called the Jews and Arabs to attend a negotiating confrence in London, and warned them that if they did not reach a settlement one would be imposed.

It was now February, 1939. The mood of western Europe was appeasement. In March, Prime Minister Neville Chamberlain would talk of "peace in our time" as Hitler devoured Czechoslovakia. The Arab delegation arrived at St. James Palace in London for talks and promptly announced their refusal to sit in the same room with the Jews. As a consequence, Prime Minister Chamber-

lain ordered two ceremonial openings for the conference, and for
his pains gave the same speech twice. The St. James negotiations
were still-born: the Jews said that the Peel report was their basic
minimum; the Arabs pushed their demands to stop immigration,
stop land sales, and declare an Arab state in all of Palestine. True
to their ultimatum, the British tried to enforce a solution. Weizmann had some forewarning of what was coming after a long
conversation with Lord Halifax, the foreign secretary, who suggested to Weizmann that he forget about the creation of an independent state. "Renounce your rights under the Mandate," Halifax
advised. On May 17, 1939, the Chamberlain government issued a
White Paper that will live in infamy in Zionist annals. On the same
day the Nazis took Prague. With only four months to go before
war would trap millions of Jews inside Hitler's bastion, the White
Paper decreed a drastic reduction of Jewish immigration into
Palestine (only 15,000 yearly for five years). It placed heavy
restrictions on land sales to Jews. And it called for the establishment of a bi-national state within ten years. The limitation on
immigration made it certain that the Arabs would rule Palestine.
But even this proposal was utterly rejected by the Arabs: they
now demanded a state immediately, an absolute stop to immigration, and a review of the status of all Jews who emigrated to
Palestine since 1918.

Nullification! That word became the branding iron of enraged
Zionist leaders, for with the White Paper of 1939 the British
government had nullified the Balfour Declaration. By their in-
transigence the Arabs had won a major political victory.

Dejected, disheartened, Chaim Weizmann could only call the
White Paper exactly what it was—"a sellout." But it was for a
younger man of action, David Ben-Gurion, to utter a popular reply. As chairman of the Jewish Agency he characteristically set a
course of defiance: "This cruel blow will not subdue the Jewish
people." But after the war against Hitler began, it did present a
dilemma. Should Jews in Palestine fight a weakened, pre-occupied
Britain for a Jewish state, or should they join Britain to fight the
greater evil, Hitler. Ben-Gurion's reply was Solomonic. At a
public gathering he declared the words that would be quoted for
generations to come: "We will fight together with Great Britain
in this war as if there is no White Paper, and we will fight the
White Paper as if there is no war."

Ben-Gurion sensed that the British had papered over the Balfour Declaration for reasons of expediency. With war imminent Britain could not anger millions of Arabs into firing up the revolt again. But Ben-Gurion knew also that the Jews would pay a heavy price for that expediency: the lives of those masses who could not pass the locked gates of Palestine. For Ben-Gurion, there were now two supreme tasks: to build a Jewish army that would help fight Hitler and to build an organization that would bring in Europe's refugees despite the British lion and the German were-wolf.

Now, Jews were facing their darkest hour. Everyone seemed to be against them—Germans, British, Arabs. An unholy combination of forces had dashed their sweetest dreams. The Jews of Palestine steeled to meet all comers.

Dark as the hour was, the *yishuv* did not give up faith. The Jews of Palestine continued to build, to train, and to prepare. The concrete mixers churned and the hammers swung. Morale lifted considerably only eight days before the White Paper was issued when Hadassah opened for all creeds the Middle East's most modern healing, research, and medical education center. The glistening hospital on Mt. Scopus in Jerusalem dominated much of the city. Not overlooked at the time was that this accomplishment of Zionist endeavor should stand on the site from which the Roman Emperor Titus launched his attack on the Holy City nearly 1,900 years before.

12.

"We Will Build!"

FOR several days in October, 1934, sound engineers of the Palestine Broadcasting System bustled in the turret office of the Hebrew University's chancellor on Mt. Scopus. They had a thousand problems. Not the least of them were the heavy echoes in the room and the field mice that nibbled away at the tangles of wire lying twisted on the floor. In preparation was the first live broadcast from the Middle East to New York through relay stations in Cairo and London. From the Manhattan studios of the National Broadcasting Company, the program was to be transmitted from coast to coast, and piped specially into the grand ballroom of the Wardman Park Hotel in Washington, D.C., where fifteen hundred Hadassah delegates were convened for their national convention.

H-Hour was four o'clock in the afternoon on Mt. Scopus, nine o'clock in the morning in Washington. The date was Tuesday, October 16, 1934. Seated uncomfortably in the office of Judah Magnes with a grand view of ancient Jerusalem were Henrietta Szold, Nahum Sokolow, Menahem Ussishkin, Hadassah Director Haim Yassky, and Magnes. Ceremonies on Mt. Scopus, attended by five hundred, were already over. In the Washington auditorium the delegates had been long in their seats; some had gone without breakfast to make sure they were close to the loudspeakers. Across the hall was a banner: "We Will Build."

A few minutes after nine, Rose Jacobs read a cable from Jerusalem into a battery of NBC microphones that relayed the proceedings over a national hookup. The cable described the ceremonies that had just taken place on Mt. Scopus. At 9:28 a crackle of static filled the hall. The first words were those of Magnes' assistant, Julian Meltzer: "This is Jerusalem calling from the Hebrew University on Mt. Scopus."

Then came Nahum Sokolow's voice: "world Jewry celebrates . . ." The static allowed only a few words to get through. Magnes was heard to say, "it is but a few minutes' walk to the laboratories of the Hebrew University . . ." Third was Henrietta. The delegates were on the edge of their seats: "we celebrate today the culmination of an idea . . . the healing of my people." Dr. Yassky followed: "coordination and united effort will bridge the distance between us . . ." Radio was not sufficiently developed at that early stage for such broadcasts but that did not matter. The "Hadassah Newsletter" reporter wrote:

> The words are not clear. But that does not matter. Hadassah's founder is speaking to thousands of her colleagues and it was enough to hear her voice. On the platform and scattered throughout the hall are some who toiled with Miss Szold in the early days. Before them, in these seconds, must have flashed a quick kaleidoscope of those pioneer years. They could not restrain their tears. The audience is tense, electric, trying to catch every syllable. And when the 20-minute broadcast is ended the whole assembly rises to its feet, applauds, and cheers and breaks into singing Hatikva. Women weep for joy and kiss and embrace one another.

The same exuberance had burst forth at the Hadassah convention in Chicago the previous October when, the depression be damned, the delegates voted to raise $200,000 from Hadassah's 30,000 members to build a hospital in Jerusalem. But it was on October 15, 1934, in Washington, that Hadassah formally voted to join the American Jewish Physicians Committee to begin construction of a medical center on Mt. Scopus. With that act Hadassah unknowingly moved from an age of pioneering into an age of sophistication and voted itself a physical permanence in Palestine.

Hadassah gave full expression to the idea that all facets of

medicine—healing, teaching, and research—were inextricably
bound to the ultimate goals of the political Zionist movement.
The idea itself was not new. In 1920, the Zionist Organization in
London probed the possibility of establishing medical and scientific
institutes in Palestine. As a follow-up, Albert Einstein and Chaim
Weizmann on behalf of the Zionist Organization sailed to America
in 1921 to drum up support for the Hebrew University. While
there they inspired the founding of the American Jewish Physicians
Committee under Nathan Ratnoff. The committee raised $500,000
and in 1924 bought land on Mt. Scopus for a projected medical
school. Later, more land was to be donated by the JNF and Mary
Fels. In that same year—one year before the Hebrew University
was to open—the first medical institute in microbiology was begun
by Saul Adler, world-famous parisitologist.

In 1926, the malaria-fighter Israel Kligler, director of Hadassah laboratories and head of the university's Hygiene Department,
urged the establishment of a medical center in Jerusalem. Henrietta
Szold was four-square behind Kligler and drew in Chancellor
Magnes. The first formal discussion of the joint project was held
on April 23, 1927, with the American Jewish Physicians Committee acting as marriage-broker.

The medical center proposal took seven years to blossom and
another five years to ripen. Countless meetings were held in New
York and Jerusalem to clear the many obstacles posed by financing,
planning, and division of authority. One roadblock was Hadassah's
budget. In 1930 it was cut for the first time owing to the depression. But on the other hand, with immigration beginning to soar
in the new decade, hospitals rapidly became inadequate. At times,
some departments of Hadassah's 150-bed institution were running
to 120 per cent of capacity. Magnes spoke of the eighty-year-old
Rothschild building as "that rickety, dangerous structure." Finally
in 1934, Hadassah and the Hebrew University reached a sensible
agreement on the running of the medical center: the former
would oversee its medical work while the latter would supervise
its teaching aspects. A monumental debate, however, broke out
over the site of the center. Magnes insisted that a medical center
should be located close to a university, and he maintained that
the only plausible site was Mt. Scopus. The university was in
general agreement on that point. But Hadassah was split. Dr.
Ephraim Bluestone, who resigned as director in 1928, but con-

tinued as chief consultant in New York, fought a mighty battle to put the center where potential patients could get to it quickly. Bluestone claimed at the time that it was folly to site a vulnerable medical complex where it would be isolated from the rest of the Jewish population and surrounded by hostile Arab quarters and villages. To arguments that Scopus had the most beautiful view in the Jerusalem area, he answered, "It is more important for a patient to see a doctor than to see the landscape. Never place an obstacle between the patient and his doctor, and remember that distance is an obstacle."

Magnes rebutted, somewhat illogically, that Montefiore Hospital in New York, of which Bluestone was then director, was far from the center of the people it served. What Magnes overlooked was that the Indians had for several hundred years ceased to be a danger to New York City. The primary difference between the two men was in outlook: Magnes, a pacifist and humanitarian, believed with all his heart that Jews and Arabs would soon live in peace and then could jointly enjoy the fruits of the university and center. He felt the medical center would hasten the peace process. Bluestone, a coldly analytical scientist and realist, was just as sure that the medical center would be a sitting duck for vengeful Arabs.

Bluestone received backing from many Hadassah physicians and leaders, some of whom were hoping that the center could be placed in what is today the heart of residential Jewish Jerusalem —in the Rehavia Quarter. Inter alia they also objected to the building of the center close by the World War I cemetery on Scopus. For political reasons the Jewish Agency sided with the university. It was interested in building up Scopus so that Jewish Jerusalem could then "reach out" to the ridge and encompass the neighboring Arabs.

Hadassah failed to support its chief consultant. Instead it sought more advice and sent off to Palestine the director of New York's Hospital for Joint Diseases, Jacob Golub, and Dr. Nathan Ratnoff to examine all the possibilities. Hadassah agreed in advance that their decision on siting the center would be irrevocable. On July 23, 1934, Golub and Ratnoff cabled: "CONCLUSIVELY DETERMINED SCOPUS MOST SUITABLE SITE." Looking back many years later, Golub wrote that the clinching argument for Scopus was the fact that a medical school would one day be established there and it was only logical that it should be near the university. Even as late as 1947, Golub could write: "The hilly landscape of Mt. Scopus will increasingly become a university and hospital campus for students and faculty."

But Golub wrote too soon. Within one year a convoy of physicians, nurses, teachers, and workers of Hadassah and the university would be ambushed by Arabs while passing through the Sheikh Jarrah Quarter of Jerusalem on its way up to Scopus, and most would perish. Not long after the ambush, Scopus was abandoned for nineteen years, and for most of that time Jerusalem was to be without proper hospital and university facilities. It was a crippling blow and a mighty expensive price to pay.

What went wrong? "Two mistakes were made," says former President Rose Halprin, who went to Jerusalem as Hadassah's liaison in 1934, "The minute that our hospital went up, there should have been a Jewish community started near Scopus. That was our mistake. The second error was that of the Jewish Agency. They should, as they promised, have built settlements to close the gaps in the road."

In mid-1935, Golub reported to Hadassah that during the first half of the decade the number of physicians in the Jewish population had doubled. One out of every 225 Jews in the country was an M.D. Because of the immigration from Central Europe, there were proportionately four times more physicians in the Jewish area of Palestine than in the entire United States. Hadassah tried to cope with the problem, took in as many as thirty-five doctors at one time to prepare them for medical work in Palestine. But it soon realized that it must get on with the medical center if for no other reason than to build a bigger roof to house this great treasure of brain power.

They now had Ludwig Halberstaedter, from the University of Berlin, one of the world's greatest authorities in cancer therapy. Refugee Halbertstaedter arrived carrying one-fifth of a gram of radium, an enormous amount in those days, worth $15,000. With it he opened the first radium and X-ray institute in Palestine under Hadassah's auspices. So badly quartered was Hadassah at the time that the professor had to go to work with his precious radium in a converted stable. With him from Berlin came an equally noted cytologist, Leonid Doljansky. They worked in tandem, providing Palestine with its first effective treatment of cancer. Gynecologist Bernhard Zondek, a co-founder of the first quick, reliable test for pregnancy, known popularly as the A-Z test, was among the immigrants. Viennese surgeon Felix Mandel opened a second surgery department in Hadassah. Pediatrician Benno Gruenfelder and physiologist Ernst Wertheimer were familiar names in the Old World. But there were young men, too, who would soon make their mark. And most of them would work as volunteers. The volunteer doctor is a strange phenomenon in the annals of medicine, and in Palestine—rich in talent, poor in everything else—the profession was to bear the burden for years to come.

Some doctors had escaped Europe by the skin of their teeth. Aharon Yehuda Beller, born in a small town in Galicia, was twenty-four when he was arrested by the Nazis in Vienna. It was November, 1938. "The [Vienna] Rothschild Hospital was closed. I was taken. My head was shaved and I was put on a bus to Dachau. En route we were turned around. There were no places left for us in the death camp and for some unexplainable reason I was released." Via Rumania, Beller reached Palestine. "I started working under Dr. Joseph as a volunteer in the Department of Surgery. I was the seventeenth doctor—only one was paid. Dr. Yassky gave me a job as a translator. The German physicians had to lecture in Hebrew and they did not know the language so I translated their papers from German to Hebrew in Latin characters."

Professor Beller is now Hadassah's Chief Neurosurgeon.

Some became experts in other fields. Theodor David Ullmann was born in Germany in 1908:

> Following my graduation from medical school in Würzburg, I came to Palestine in 1934. At that time it was very difficult for a young medical man to practice medicine so I went to work in a paint factory in Haifa. Gradually I advanced in this factory to the position of manager. There was a time when I was more experienced in making paint than treating the sick.

Professor Ullmann, Hadassah's leading authority on kidney diseases, now heads the Nephrological Service.

Hanoch Milwidsky, born in Berlin, arrived in Palestine in 1932:

> I saw there were sufficient doctors here so I started working for a fruit jobber. I also knew some car mechanics and found that helpful. In those days it was more of a *mitzvah* to go into agriculture and the trades than take up a profession. But my father insisted I return to Germany to complete my medical studies. When the Nazis came, I went to Strasbourg because I did not want a diploma with a Nazi signature. Then I returned to work in the only Jewish hospital in Berlin. When the Germans got wind that I was also helping Jews leave the country illegally, I had to run away. In Jerusalem, there was no possibility of getting a job as a surgeon at Hadassah because the hospital was so small. I worked in pathology and as an anaesthetist. I started as a volunteer but later received a salary of £1 a month. Dr. Yehuda Bromberg, the Hospital's redheaded administrator, told us volunteers when we asked for a proper salary, "It is a buyers' market. I am an economist and I work according to market conditions. If I can get doctors like oranges why should I pay high salaries?"

Surgeon Milwidsky was the first to do a heart operation in Palestine. The operation, carried out against the opposition of hospital authorities, was successful. He was warned by senior hospital officials not to go through with it because it would reflect on the medical reputation of Israel. It did, but in a positive way. The elderly patient's stenotic valves had become obstructed by scar tissue due to rheumatic heart disease and his only chance to live was through the radical new surgery that Milwidsky learned under the tutelage of American heart surgeon Charles Bailey. Now this type of procedure is commonplace. Hanoch Milwidsky perished when a Swissair plane blew up in mid-air en route to Israel on February 21, 1970. The Arab Popular Front for the Liberation of Palestine proudly claimed responsibility.

Ino Sciaky was born in Salonika, spent his childhood in Turkey, and studied dentistry in Switzerland when his parents moved to Bulgaria:

> When I came to Israel as a tourist in 1937, I declared my desire to settle but the British refused me permission. They said I could remain only if I were a capitalist. I went to Egypt, borrowed

£1,000—the minimum needed to be regarded as a capitalist—sent it to Palestine and followed soon thereafter. After I was accepted as an immigrant, I returned the money to my cousin. I was then a bonafide capitalist but without capital.

Now professor of Oral Medicine, Dr. Sciaky was the first dean of the Hadassah–Hebrew University School of Dentistry.

One young doctor who had received his education in Odessa left for Palestine before winning his degree. The closest thing to medicine he could get from the British health authorities was the job of sanitation inspector in Tel Aviv, for which he received £6 monthly. That was in 1919. After tiring of running after garbage men, he left for Geneva with his wife to continue his studies in eye diseases and public health. In 1921, with his framed degree on the wall, he joined Hadassah in Haifa as an assistant in the eye department. Three years later he headed the Hadassah eye department in Tel Aviv. It was there that this six-foot idealist caught the eye of Henrietta Szold. "Trachoma in the villages and settlements is appalling," he insisted. "I want to go out there." She agreed. And the lanky eye doctor, often traveling bareback on a donkey, his shoes scraping the ground, went as far as the Galilee, treating and operating on Arab and Jew alike. By 1927, Haim Yassky was called to Jerusalem to take over the eye department.

After much soul-searching, Henrietta Szold named Yassky acting director of the Hadassah Medical Organization. In 1931, likewise after much soul-searching the Hadassah National Board made the post permanent. Haim Yassky held his post until he was murdered in the Scopus convoy on April 13, 1948.

Yassky did not rise easily to the custodianship of Hadassah medicine in Palestine because he was not an American. Understandably, the Hadassah board in New York kept its faith with American medicine and administration and from the beginning its man in Jerusalem was always an American citizen. In the early years of the twentieth century, American medicine was avant-garde, lacking the tradition of Vienna, Berlin, or Geneva. The New World's doctors were much more informal and its hospital administration was much less bureaucratic than that of the autocratic, status-conscious Old World. New Zealand surgeon Edward Joseph would soon find that "the German doctors considered themselves the top people. They looked upon American-trained physicians as being beneath contempt. A director coming from America would also be considered beneath contempt, and so there was always hostility between them." Russian-born Moshe Rachmilewitz, the noted heart specialist who arrived at Hadassah in 1931, was critical of "the German approach" even though he himself was trained in Germany. Not long after his arrival he went off to New York for eighteen months of advance study at Mt. Sinai Hospital where, he recalled later in life, "I was reborn medically. There had been a shifting of centers for me from the Continent to America." The American approach was direct, simple, natural. Status did not decide which medical opinion should be accepted. An opinion was judged solely on its merits. A young man was able to express himself—he was free to speak up. This was distinctly different from the European approach.

The clashes of approach, the babel of methods, the mixtures of nationalities had made it impossible for American directors to work in Jerusalem at anywhere near the efficiency they were accustomed to back home. Their problems were aggravated by Hadassah's requirement that policy and budget be controlled from New York. Thus decisions could not be made quickly. And where there were basic disagreements between these two ends of Hadassah's world, much time was lost as telegrams bounced back and forth over the oceans. In the end medical work was bound to suffer. Often, even Henrietta Szold found herself locking horns with Hadassah's centralized authority. The result was that, as she focused her interests more and more inwardly into local problems of social welfare, she began to urge Hadassah to become increasingly subservient to local Palestine Zionist authority. But Hadassah in New York understandably insisted on making its own policy to ensure maintenance of high American scientific standards in Palestine.

Henrietta's headaches with Hadassah directors began the moment she stepped into Jerusalem in 1920. The first formally appointed medical director, Dr. Rubinow, gave up after two attempts to juggle budgets and staff. Henrietta took over for a time, then asked Magnes to step in while she returned briefly to the United States. In November, 1923, Simon Meshullam Tannenbaum, of New York's Beth David Hospital, went to Jerusalem, but left again in October, 1924. Henrietta then asked Alexander Salkind, chief of the department of internal diseases, to assume charge, but he had to quit after falling ill. The search for a permanent director ended, so it was thought, with the appointment of the assistant director of Mt. Sinai Hospital, Ephraim Michael Bluestone. Young, talented, idealistic, firm Bluestone was regarded by the Hadassah board as the answer to any woman organization's prayer. He came from a well-known Zionist family, was graduated with distinction from Columbia University's College of Physicians and Surgeons, served overseas in an American base hospital during the war, and by the age of thirty-five had made a name in hospital administration in New York City. He signed on for three years; Hadassah felt he would remain longer. But Bluestone was back home in America little more than two years after he arrived in Jerusalem in March, 1926.

"Dr. Bluestone had a horrible time," according to one physician who served during the period. Henrietta Szold, who admired Bluestone's talent but found it difficult to work with him, once confided to Hadassah President Irma Lindheim, "I have been afraid of only two persons in my life. One was the maid that we had for very many years and the other is Bluestone." As strong-willed as Henrietta herself, Bluestone was hamstrung from the beginning—his sharp sense of humor, facile pen, ramrod sense of duty were to no avail. He had an early warning of what he might expect. On the ship to Palestine he met an elderly man who had taken ill. The doctor, loyal to his new employer, assured the gentleman that once he reached Jerusalem, he would see to it that the patient received perfect care. When they arrived in Jerusalem, little could be done for the old man because Hadassah's X-ray department was on strike. To Bluestone of Mt. Sinai this was anarchy. But that was only the start. Word had spread throughout the *yishuv* that the chief at Hadassah was receiving the absurdly high salary of $10,000 a year—about ten times the amount of a worker. This brought upon Bluestone the wrath of labor leaders as well as newspaper editors who singled him out in editorials. Doctors in Kupat Holim, the health fund of the budding Histadrut, which Hadassah supported financially for a number of years as it teetered on a cliff of bankruptcy, spread vicious rumors about Bluestone. The young doctor, unwilling to suffer this, considered returning to civilized New York. But Henrietta, joined by Rose Jacobs and Norwin Lindheim, urged him to remain.

Henrietta reported to the Hadassah board in June, 1926, only a few months after Bluestone's arrival, that he was commendably "guided purely by professional considerations." But there were other considerations too. Zionist ones. She noted that he objected to Hadassah's participation in running hospital facilities in Tel Aviv and Haifa. He was not attuned to the consensus technique of arriving at decisions, and he did not have time to train administrators. Bluestone complained that the *yishuv*'s National Health Committee was "a serious menace to the independence of Hadassah." Henrietta wrote to New York, "If that means detachment from the Zionist movement, I am personally not interested in medical work in Palestine." She was firm that Zionist necessity must transcend Hadassah's exclusive objectives. On that Bluestone and Henrietta split. He resigned in February, 1928.

This state of affairs could not last long. Henrietta concluded that Hadassah must have a director who was ready to cast his lot, physically and spiritually, with the *yishuv*. Bluestone was wise enough to concur. With Henrietta's acquiescence, he approached Haim Yassky. Yassky was reluctant but when Henrietta impressed upon him the importance of the task, he agreed. Bluestone left early in September, 1928, and continued a long association with Hadassah as a consultant, becoming the first chairman of Hadassah's Medical Reference Board.

Dr. Yassky found that he was not alone at the top. Hadassah retained him as acting medical director, because he was still in his early thirties and he had no formal training in administering a hospital. Reuven Katznelson was named as acting business director. As they shared a stormy stewardship, Henrietta sensed that one permanent Palestine director with over-all authority was the only answer to the Hadassah Medical Organization's problem:

> The time has come when the permanent Palestinian and not the elusive American should be considered for the directorship. We cannot go on paying salaries and we cannot go on paying apprenticeship monies to Americans who must adjust themselves, each one in succession, to the conditions of Palestinian life and who, no sooner adjusted, take flight. Whether we approve or disapprove of the conditions of Palestinian life, for better or worse, they are the conditions under which the country is being developed by the forces who are content to throw their lot in with the country.

In New York, Hadassah's board realized that a co-directorship could only be a stopgap solution. Finally, after several reappointments as acting director, Yassky was appointed director-general of the Hadassah Medical Organization in June, 1931. And in 1932 under the board's auspices he spent six months in the United States studying administration. On his return, he set his compass in the direction of Mt. Scopus. There he was to achieve his greatest dream and his tragic end. His objectives were high: "To create a medical institution whose fame will extend far beyond the boundaries of Palestine is our national and human duty." Without Yassky on the spot the Scopus institution would certainly not have been ready for World War II. He was the engine that kept the project moving forward. It was he who created a pre-medical faculty that was to be the forerunner of the medical school of which he dreamed but which never saw. Under his directorship new medical disciplines were introduced into Palestine—neurosurgery, occupational therapy, a medical record system. "The medical center," said Yassky's widow many years after his death, "was Dr. Yassky's entire life—his whole devotion."

After Mt. Scopus was finally agreed upon as the site of the center, Hadassah sent Dr. Golub on several trips abroad in connection with the plans. On one occasion he met in London with the German exiled architect Eric Mendelsohn who had taken up residence in Palestine and who was chosen to create the hospital complex on the stony ridge. Mendelsohn dreamed of the simple lines of Escorial and Assisi: "I want to create monumental austerity even though it will disappoint the layman who expects British baronial splendor or America's imposing verticals." He took as his guide the simple lines of the Arab village because he was seeking local harmony—of unornamental walls, of courtyards with fountains and pergolas. "This," he said, "must be built for the ages."

Mendelsohn had great problems in creating immortal architecture. For the location he was given a narrow, knifelike ridge about one mile long, rising 150 feet above the city of Jerusalem. To the east there was a deep descent toward the Dead Sea; to the west a slope into the Kidron Valley looking on to the site of the Temple where Moslems had built the dominating golden Dome of the Rock. He had cold, rainy, windy winters of four months to cope with and dry, cool summers of eight months with parchment-dry days of spring and autumn sandwiched in between. Mendelsohn laid out three three-story buildings in an east-west pattern: the hospital connected by his beloved pergolas to the Henrietta Szold Nursing School and, opposite, the Nathan Ratnoff building for post-graduate medical studies. Like the surrounding Arab villages, the architect kept the profiles low.

First earth for the hospital and nurses school was turned in mid-November, 1936. They were completed in September, 1938. Construction of the post-graduate institute began in January, 1937, and was finished in April, 1939. For the first time in Palestine's construction history, machine-cut white stone slabs were used to face the edifices rather than the traditional hand-fashioned stone. For greenery Hadassah planted a grove of 1,500 pine trees in honor of Henrietta. The total cost was over $1 million—the single most expensive project Hadassah had undertaken up to that time. Said Golub, "For the first time there will be an institution which combines teaching and research and the immediate care of the sick. The medical men of Palestine look forward to the new institution as a model not only for the medical work of that country but for the whole Near East."

On May 9, 1939, Chaim Weizmann rushed out of Palestine on an Ala Littoria plane from Haifa for London after hearing that in eight days the British White Paper was to nullify the Balfour Declaration. Berlin and Rome agreed on a pact that established the Axis, and Japan said it was willing to join. In Germany, a quarter of a million Jews were waiting for visas to leave: 90 per cent would never make it. On Mt. Scopus, Mendelsohn looked upon the completed work as though it were shangri-la and said to a colleague, "It has the serenity of the greatest spiritual creations in this part of the world." The dedication was modest: it had to be because of the security situation. Haim Yassky was the chairman of the ceremony. Rose Jacobs spoke on behalf of 82,000 Hadassah members in America. Dr. Magnes spoke for the American Jewish Physicians Committee. Henrietta Szold, now seventy-seven, opened the ceremonies, and accepted a silver key from Yassky. On the key was an inscription: "From Hadassah in Palestine to Hadassah in America with deep appreciation."

The ceremonies were hardly over when the move began from the old Rothschild Hospital on the Street of the Prophets in downtown Jerusalem. Even as trucks lumbered up to Mt. Scopus doubts still lingered about the site. "I remember the morning when we moved to Scopus," Dr. Moshe Rachmilewitz said later. "There was an explosion. There was shooting throughout Jerusalem. There had been much discussion whether it was advisable to move the hospital to Scopus. I was not clear in my own mind about it." The move went on nonetheless, and the old Rothschild building was put up for sale. Approval for the sale was given by the Rothschilds on condition that their family name be part of the new Scopus building. But the building was not sold and in the end was to serve Hadassah's educational needs for many years to come.

At first, Scopus had 200 beds, 50 more than its predecessor. By the Spring of 1940 the number was 300 and eventually it would have 500. Now the staff enjoyed modern lighting, central heating, an efficient phone and communications system. Nurses could effectively control an entire ward from their central stations. "It was a fine hospital from every point of view," said veteran surgeon Edward Joseph.

> The best in the Middle East. A very elaborate place. Of course, they made mistakes. For instance, the operating theaters had huge glass windows. The whole side was one field of glass. It looks very beautiful from the road but it was the unfortunate surgeon who had to operate there, for the sun came in after noontime making it difficult to work in that place. We tried not to operate in the afternoon. We used to sweat dreadfully. All the time our foreheads had to be wiped.

By May 14, the Hadassah Medical Organization's offices were on Scopus; and on Tuesday (a twice-blessed day, according to Jewish tradition), May 30, 1939, the hospital doors swung open for the public. Happily, the first case was maternity, and on that first day two babies were born. In all, 120 patients, aged 2 to 70, were moved up to Scopus. The first *brit milah* was held on the second day with Chief Rabbi Isaac Halevy Herzog officiating. The infant was named Meir in honor of the founder of the Rothschild family.

Little more than three months later, the world was at war. Palestine was soon isolated and threatened. Scopus was set for battle.

13.

A World Aflame

FIGHTING back the tears on that late August night in 1939, Chaim Weizmann bade the 1,500 delegates farewell knowing in his heart that by returning home many were going to their doom. Said Weizmann: "It would need the eloquence of a Jeremiah to picture the horrors of this new destruction of our people. We have none to comfort us." This was the end of the most melancholy Zionist Congress in the history of the movement—the Twenty-first or, as Weizmann had hopefully named it, the "Coming-of-Age Congress." In the midst of the sessions Berlin and Moscow announced their villainous pact. War was now certain. The general mood was one of frustration, helplessness. President Judith Epstein, heading the Hadassah delegation, observed, "The most horrible feeling in Geneva was that not a sound came out of the magnificent League of Nations building looking at us. I shall never forget the silence coming from those portals."

Most delegates were warned to leave Geneva immediately. Polish delegates were ordered to detour Germany through Yugoslavia and Hungary. German Zionists faced a horrible dilemma of remaining abroad and joining the underground or rejoining their families. Some Palestinian Jews brazenly crossed into Nazi Germany to try to organize escape routes. The delegates, having gone through the motions of condemning and rejecting the terms of the British White Paper, hurriedly turned out the lights and scattered.

Weizmann, who left for England a few hours before the ceremonial closing, embraced his old colleague, Menachem Ussishkin,
and despairingly whispered, "What kind of a world will it be
when we meet again, Menachem?" Ussishkin shook his head
gravely.

Back in London, Weizmann penned a letter to Neville Chamberlain politely asking the British government to permit Jewish
manpower and resources in Palestine to join the war effort.
Chamberlain demurred. Then, a few days later Hitler bombed
Warsaw. For the next six years most of the world was aflame.

Palestine at war became a menagerie of paradoxes. Cut off, the
country fell into economic chaos. Banks took a three-day holiday
to prevent a run. Prices skyrocketed. The depression hit so fast
and hard that Jews and Arabs cooperated economically to stave
off ruin. Hardest hit was citrus, Palestine's largest export, in which
both communities were engaged. As markets closed abroad, however, oranges soon came into demand locally as a source of acetone
for making smokeless gunpowder. Soon, Palestine regeared for a
war economy and emerged from its financial doldrums.

The *yishuv* was trapped into simultaneously helping the British
fight Hitler and fighting the British to save the refugees from
Europe. Throughout the war the Palestine administration successfully fought off attempts to create an independent Jewish army.
The British constantly obstructed Haganah men who trained to
meet a Nazi invasion, but at the same time British Intelligence used
Haganah men surreptitiously on dangerous missions behind enemy
lines. The Arab countries had alliances with Britain, but either
cooperated with the Nazis or remained neutral until victory was
almost in sight.

Amid these seething cross currents of conflicting interests, the
yishuv, which begged like a neglected child for British recognition,
struggled for its survival and for its goal of statehood. That it
finally achieved national status, considering the geometric odds
against it, is one of the most breathtaking dramas in the long history of this ancient land, and one in which Hadassah played a key
role.

As the war took its toll of European nations, Nazi Field Mar-
shal Erwin Rommel crunched steadily eastward across the North
African sands toward British Middle East Headquarters located in
Cairo. Anxiety gripped Palestine and the British army hurriedly

began training the Haganah's strike force, the Palmach, to make a last-ditch stand on Mt. Carmel which was to be a modern version of Massada. The fear was that if Rommel broke through to Cairo, the entire Middle East would fall under the sign of the swastika. In the summer of 1942 it seemed that the world's fate—which was actually more critically at stake at Stalingrad—depended on whether the British could hold Cairo. Weizmann saw the dangers as early as mid-1940, after the Italians joined the Axis, and so renewed his pleas in London for a Palestine Jewish Army. Winston Churchill, now prime minister, supported the proposal and in February, 1941, even arranged that Weizmann meet the intended commander of the Jewish force, General Leonard Hawes. In the end a combination of anti-Zionist British in Palestine and a dearth of supplies prevented the establishment of the army.

Palestine turned overnight into a war camp of Allied soldiers. In light of the peril the British put the country under virtual martial law. Anticipating the worst and hoping that the British would agree to the mobilizing of a Jewish army, the Jewish Agency opened its own national service register ten days after war began. Within two weeks, 135,000 men and women—about 20 per cent of the entire *yishuv*—had signed up. In Jerusalem, the recently vacated Rothschild-Hadassah Hospital served as registration headquarters. Haganah men began to drill but the British, fearful of Arab reaction, brought their heel down heavily and on one occasion arrested forty-three men eager to move against the Nazis.

But still the *yishuv* prepared; the Haganah secretly worked up contingency plans for partisan warfare should the British pull out. Blackouts, air-raid warnings and drills, food rationing and controlled prices were part of the scene. Forty-eight hours before fighting began in Poland, the nineteenth class of nurses and the first on Scopus was graduated. Dr. Yassky called it the "Disturbances Class" because the girls had studied through three years of Arab riot and terror. Even in August, 1939, three months after the Arabs had supposedly been tranquilized by the White Paper, eighty-seven persons died in riots. On Hitler's D-Day, Yassky cabled New York for emergency funds, and immediately the National Board sent a first-aid grant of $60,000. The role Hadassah was to play in the war was clear from a message sent to

Yassky by Tel Aviv Mayor Israel Rokach: "We turn to Hadassah in our need just as grown children turn to their mother when they are in distress."

Feverishly, the preparations to withstand an onslaught went on. Most feared was attack from the air. Patients and staffs were given air-raid drills. On Mt. Scopus a shelter was built with seven self-contained units for doctors, nurses, and patients. By setting up emergency beds Scopus was ready to care for five hundred patients. The twentieth class of nurses was put ahead by two months and all graduate nurses were called in for refresher courses. Over the Palestine Broadcasting System, Hadassah dieticians gave instructions on how best to use rationed foods. Yassky offered the British Medical Corps and the families of all men in uniform the full use of Scopus' facilities. Henrietta Szold cabled New York from Jerusalem: "CRY OF THE HOUR TO FEED HUNGRY CHILDREN." Hadassah put 25,000 children on an emergency feeding program in addition to serving 75,000 luncheons daily in 600 schools. And apart from free medical services for men and their families in uniform, refugees received free drugs and clothing.

The result was that Hadassah went on a full war footing at least two years before the United States itself. In an Order of the Day sent to the national membership, President Tamar de Sola Pool wrote: "Our front line of defense lies in Zion as in Britain." Hadassah's Palestine Chairman Rose Halprin announced at a press conference that "Britain, America and Palestine are one fighting front. . . . The 500,000 Jewish inhabitants of Palestine are banded together as one man to aid England and protect democracy. The aggressor stands for everything which, both as Americans and Jews, we abhor. By helping Palestine defend itself we are helping the Allies." Zionist objectives were thus immediately aimed at making Palestine part of Allied war aims. At the same time, Hadassah did not neglect homefront duties—selling War Bonds, mobilizing members for Civil Defense, volunteering for auxiliary services—and, for its work, won, in December, 1944, the big E (for Excellence) award from the U.S. government. Hadassah could make this contribution to the war effort because of its ability to meet crises as they arose. In responding to the government representative at the presentation ceremony, President Judith

Epstein said: "We are proud to receive this award; we would have been ashamed if we had failed to receive it."

As Britain's fortunes were running into bad luck on all war fronts, the Palestine administration reluctantly began putting uniforms on Jewish volunteers. A Palestine Battalion was organized under the Union Jack and by March, 1940, nearly 2,000 Jews were fighting. By June, 1941, the number reached 8,900, and already 1,000 were missing and 1,200 were Nazi prisoners in the Greek campaign. Jewish soldiers were fighting in Libya, Greece, and Syria. They served in the Royal Air Force. Haganah scouts opened the way for General Maitland Wilson's forces moving into Vichy-held Syria. On one such scouting mission Company Commander Moshe Dayan lost his left eye. Others parachuted into Europe on British intelligence missions. Bombs crashed into Palestine's cities. Haifa was hit most often from the air because it was a principal naval facility, but Tel Aviv suffered too. In September, 1940, one air attack took the lives of 122 persons in the all-Jewish city. While the Jews of Palestine were understandably jittery, the Arabs seemed sure of their future regardless of who won. In London, Weizmann heard that the Arabs of Palestine were preparing to divide the spoils once Hitler arrived. He noted in his memoirs, "Some of them are going about the streets of Tel Aviv and the colonies marking up the houses they expect to take over: one Arab, it was reported, has been killed in a quarrel over the loot assigned to him."

In June, 1942, in one of the major tank battles of World War II, Rommel shattered the British defense at Tobruk, Libya, and took 33,000 British prisoners, including Palestinians. The fateful breakthrough left Egypt wide open. Churchill sailed secretly to Washington for a conference with Roosevelt. There he received a letter from Weizmann offering to raise three divisions of 32,000 men and a force of 40,000 home guard. "If we go down in Palestine, we are entitled to go down fighting," he pleaded. That and the apparent hopelessness of the situation persuaded the British to enlarge the Palestine Battalion to a regiment of about two thousand men. It was still not a Jewish army and nothing that could stop the Nazis. But small as they were they acquitted themselves well enough to win Churchill's commendation.

For eight months before the fall of Tobruk, the transport

company of the Palestine Battalion kept the British at the front supplied, and after the defeat transferred a New Zealand division from Syria to Egypt in a record six days. The engineers kept the bombed roads and ports repaired, paved the way for the fateful battle at Alamein, where Rommel's advance faltered, one day's ride from Cairo. As the British moved westward after Rommel, the Palestine Regiment marched in the vanguard. In Tunis, where the chief rabbi welcomed the battalion as "messengers of peace," their commander, General Fred Kisch, a Jewish Agency Executive member in the 1920's who was now General Montgomery's chief engineer, was killed.

For the Allies in the Mediterranean area, the big headache was lack of supplies. Convoys had to pass mined waters, duck sorties of Axis bombers. Tens of thousands of tons of shipping went to the bottom. The civilian effort was likewise dependent on a constant supply of goods, medicines, and equipment from abroad. Some did get through the Mediterranean, others had to be re-routed around the Cape of Good Hope to Basra on the Persian Gulf, then by truck over the desert to Palestine—a voyage of 18,000 miles. Like clockwork, thirty tons of supplies were shipped every month from New York to Hadassah in Jerusalem. Along with the new wonder sulfa drugs came surgical instruments, serums and vaccines, cod liver oil, clothing and X-ray film. On one ship there was a twelve-ton steel elevator for the Scopus medical center's underground shelter and an incubator. More than one thousand sewing groups in the United States sent hundreds of thousands of clothing items.

As a result of the need to get these vast quantities of scarce supplies through war zones, Hadassah became a familiar figure in high places in Washington. In 1939, foreseeing the need, the National Board appointed one of its new members, New Orleans-born Denise Tourover, to represent the organization in the nation's capital. Having lived in Washington since 1920, Denise soon became as familiar as the Washington Monument to political leaders. She moved among them with easy informality but could, if need be, be as determined as a bulldozer in removing bureaucratic road-blocks. At the beginning of the war, it was relatively easy to get money and supplies abroad, since America was not at war. Because shipping was severely restricted the White House set up a special board—the President's Advisory Committee for Foreign Voluntary Aid—to approve good causes. Hadassah was a charter member and remains a member to this day.

"We had to clear everything with the Board of Economic Warfare," recalls Denise.

> To do that we had to have export licenses from Washington and import licenses from the British in Cairo. We did a great deal of work with both the British and the American boards. For example, if we needed quinine, which was in short supply, we would put our hands on the drug through various drug associations. Then we had to see the right people in the Board of Economic Warfare to get clearance. Very often we got the licenses, sometimes we did not. If after ten days we did not receive an affirmative reply from the British, we would assume the clearance was lost. We would send the article on and mark on the shipment CLEARANCE LOST. Somehow, they worked out the problem on the other side.
>
> It could be maddening work. I remember well a shipment of *milchig* and *fleishig* [dairy and meat] dishes which had to be sent. When all was cleared we found that 24 dozen cups were left behind. I had no chance to get clearance and I felt the best thing to do was to take the cups to the top of the White House and throw them one by one down into the street. But the man who was helping me insisted we could get clearance. We succeeded but only after a long struggle.

Denise had her own peculiar techniques in snipping red tape. It helped that she represented a volunteer, humanitarian organization. At the time Washington was crawling with war profiteers and "ten percenters"—agents making fortunes on 10 per cent commissions. In contrast, Hadassah was "clean," and not one major Hadassah item was refused by the board during the entire war.

Of all the war years none was more crucial for Zionism than 1942. Annihilation seemed constantly imminent. The scare of invasion did not pass until November, but there was much more to be dreaded than Rommel's tanks. On January 20, subordinates of Hitler, meeting at Wannsee near Berlin, adopted a program of systematic genocide, euphemistically calling it the "Final Solution." The decision that led to the extermination of six million Jews would not reach the ears of world Jewry until autumn.

Even without knowing the specifics of Wannsee, Chaim Weiz-

mann was sufficiently depressed at the turbulence thrashing at
world Jewry to call an extraordinary conference of Jewish leaders
in New York City in May. He felt that without a united front in
America—the only great bastion of free Jewry remaining—the
hobbled Zionist effort could collapse. The assembly of about 650
delegates, among them Tamar de Sola Pool and Bertha Schoolman
representing Hadassah, met at the Biltmore Hotel. Emerging from
the deliberations was the first clear call by Zionists for the establishment of an independent political state in Palestine as distinct
from the less precise "national home" of the Balfour Declaration.
The Biltmore Program also demanded unlimited Jewish immigration at a time when the British were limiting it to 15,000 a year.
Biltmore put the derelict Zionist movement on a firm course. But
it also served as the scene for a bitter fight between Chaim Weizmann and David Ben-Gurion. Shortly after the meeting ended,
Ben-Gurion, who was now the Jews' shadow prime minister in
Palestine, challenged Weizmann's leadership. At a painful meeting
in the private study of Rabbi Stephen Wise, chairman of the conference, Ben-Gurion accused Weizmann of depending wholly on
his own personal prestige to fulfill Zionist goals and by so doing
of failing to create a Jewish army. No one had ever addressed the
eminent Zionist in terms so brutal and so frank. Weizmann could
only reply that there was no answer to political assassination. Ben-
Gurion went on to claim credit for the Biltmore Program although
Weizmann had outlined its principles in an article in the January,
1942, issue of *Foreign Affairs*. Whatever the source, the Biltmore
Program was a Zionist milestone that brought the movement's
blurred aims into sharp focus.

In a negative sense Biltmore spotlighted the widening gap between Diaspora and Palestine Zionism. Weizmann believed that an
irreparable breach with Britain would be more injurious to the
Jews than to Britain, that if America had to choose between
Britain or Zionism she would ally herself with Britain. Ben-Gurion
held that only two forces mattered—Palestine Jewry and American
Jewry—and Weizmann would get nowhere because non-Jewish
politicians would always act in their own national interests. Ben-
Gurion's policy was radically new. It reflected a new spirit that
had been born among the pioneers in Palestine, and Ben-Gurion
was its spokesman. But at first it was not universally accepted. In
1942, Ben-Gurion, except to his disciples, was too raw and too

brash for the more conservative American and British Zionists. The difference between the two men was the difference between the silk glove and the sledgehammer. Although both Weizmann and Ben-Gurion agreed on the Biltmore Program, they differed on how it was to be implemented.

Populist Ben-Gurion made the most of Biltmore. He used it as a rallying cry—to state forthright aims in simple terms, to excite the people into sounding trumpets and waving flags. In the process Ben-Gurion made many enemies; they called him "a wild man" and worse. His protagonists swore by him. But on whichever side one stood, all could acknowledge that a new force, a dynamic leader, ruthless and singleminded, was abroad ready to lead his people to the ramparts. He had the pulse of his people at his fingertips, and he knew they were ready to march.

The Biltmore Program achieved its goal of rallying American Zionists. At the 1942 convention held in New York City, Hadassah gave the program its wholehearted support. For the National Board of Hadassah, however, a serious problem grew from the fact that the founder of Hadassah, Henrietta Szold, and the chairman of the Hadassah Emergency Committee, Judah Magnes, were among the founding members of Ichud (Unity), a new organization proposing the establishment of a bi-national state in which Arabs and Jews would share sovereignty. A bitter debate erupted within the leadership over a proposal to disassociate Hadassah from the stand of Dr. Magnes and Henrietta Szold, both closely identified in the public mind with Hadassah. At this critical stage in Zionist history, Hadassah was in no mood for solutions such as bi-nationalism, and was now mature enough to say so and to put the organization four-square behind the concept of a Jewish commonwealth. This was a significant milestone in Hadassah history. Now Hadassah had taken a firm stand in political affairs. With a membership of around 150,000, Hadassah had grown enormously on the American scene which, until now, was dominated by a male leadership. That growth was irreversible and in time would make the organization the largest single Zionist group in the world.

In the mid-war years Hadassah was so active in so many fields in Palestine that it could justifiably throw a little weight around. Scopus was the center of much of that activity. British army physicians took courses on tropical diseases from Saul Adler, a world authority. That led to a series of regular, formal medical conferences attended by British military doctors who were just out of medical school. "I don't know what we would do without you," the British army medical chief wrote Dr. Yassky. Hundreds of physicians attended lectures. In the labs British army X-ray machines were repaired and its margarine was regularly tested for vitamin content. Hadassah supplied the Royal Air Force in Egypt with drugs that it could not get from its own medical corps. Hadassah sent vaccine and supplies to the Russians, the Turks, the Free French, the Czechs, and the Anglo-Iranian Petroleum Company; trained a lab technician for the Yugoslav partisans; sent eight nurses to care for war wounded at an Alexandria hospital directed by the personal physician of King Farouk.

With the war came the fear of epidemics. By right the health department of the Mandate government should have commanded the battle. But it was Hadassah that inoculated 70,000 school children against typhoid, furnished the department with antityphus vaccines, reduced the incidence of malaria to a point where it no longer posed a risk for troops, even set up small emergency field hospitals.

Then there was the regular regimen of work: combatting tuberculosis brought in by immigrants (the anti-TB hospital in Safad maintained a 110 per cent occupancy rate and Hadassah was planning a new hospital in Jerusalem when new drugs practically eradicated the disease); establishing a home medical service to relieve overcrowding on Scopus; launching two major vocational education centers in Jerusalem and preparing the groundwork for a medical school; opening a pharmacological institute for production of medicines that would one day be turned into a pharmacology school; helping found a soldiers welfare committee; setting up more kindergartens and playgrounds; and supervising nutrition in seventy-seven summer camps.

With it all Hadassah's performance in medical work was impressive: 90 per cent of all war-wounded treated at Hadassah survived. And in Palestine, largely as a result of Hadassah care of the young, the *yishuv* had the world's lowest child mortality rate—27 per 1,000.

To keep the wheels well-oiled Hadassah set up an unusual body called the Hadassah Emergency Committee. With the onset of war it was clear that the National Board, 6,000 miles away, could not keep its hand gripped on the wheel. There was thus need for an independent field command with powers almost equal to that of the board. In 1940, Rose Jacobs, Hadassah trouble-shooter, asked Judah Magnes in Jerusalem to head an emergency committee that would in fact play the role of trustee for the National Board. The eloquent Magnes accepted the task "to imprint upon the community a Hadassah personality."

Hadassah always faced the problem of running affairs with its mind in New York and its heart in Jerusalem. Soon after non-medical projects were begun in the early 1920's, a Palestine council coordinated activities. In 1924, Henrietta Szold urged the Central Committee (predecessor of the National Board) to appoint Nellie Straus Mochenson to be its representative in Palestine. The council had an executive secretary, Yugoslav-born Shari Berger who as a child had witnessed the assassination of Archduke Ferdinand at Sarajevo and after arriving in 1923 helped Henrietta and Jessie Sampter organize the Hebrew Women's Organization which later became WIZO. Rose Halprin came to Jerusalem in 1934 when Shari resigned and remained until 1939. During those years Rose kept a flood of reports moving to New York.

Thus, the Emergency Committee had strong precedents on which to build. It kept firm control over expenditures, and it negotiated for Hadassah with the government and the Jewish Agency. Its long-lasting importance was that it broke down the artificial barriers between the preventive and the curative services. Until 1939, the Hadassah Medical Organization was a power unto itself while the Palestine Council served as a cover for all other services. Now the Emergency Committee was responsible for all.

The committee could only have pulled down the barriers with three persons of stature in command: Magnes, Henrietta, and Julius Simon of the Palestine Economic Corporation. Later on, others were co-opted—Ethel Agron, Rose Viteles, Yassky himself, Yehuda Bromberg—and when the state was finally established the committee's successor, the Hadassah Council in Israel, would become a permanent feature of volunteer service in Jerusalem.

One of the more piquant aspects of Scopus' personality during the war were the salutary relations that existed between Jew and Arab. Feelings between the two communities improved enormously once the fear of invasion diminished. By 1943 Arabic was being taught in Hebrew schools, the League for Jewish-Arab Relations opened joint youth clubs, school children exchanged visits. Part of the reason for this era of good will was that some of the trouble-makers were out of the country. The Mufti of Jerusalem, who fled first to Iraq and Iran, was consorting with the Nazis in Berlin where he worked out a plan with Hitler for the future of Palestine. In 1943 and 1944, there were no serious outbreaks between the two communities. On his discharge from hospital, the Emir Abdullah—soon to become the first King of the Hashimite Kingdom of Jordan—penned on the opening page of the Medical Center's visitors' book words of praise for Hadassah and invited Yassky to visit the palace in Amman. "More than half of our patients in the neurosurgery department were Arab," recalls Professor Aharon Beller.

Although Hadassah was to suffer deeply at the hands of Arab nationalists, no Arab was ever turned away. Abdullah himself—and King Hussein, his grandson—would be responsible for keeping Scopus a lifeless shell for nineteen years after Israel's War of Independence and yet they would not hesitate to allow Jordanians to be treated in Hadassah's wards when specialists were not available at home. Hadassah personnel were killed by Arabs in the 1920's while on mercy missions. Yet one of the prize documents in Hadassah's archives is a letter dated November, 1918, from the British military governor of Beersheba and signed by twenty-seven Bedouin Sheikhs to Joseph Krimsky which thanked him and his nurse for saving the eye sight of Bedouin patients.

During World War II Arab royalty sought out Hadassah's doctors; among them King Feisal of Iraq who had reneged on his agreement with Chaim Weizmann in 1920, and the prince of Saudi Arabia, whose father, King Ibn Saud, would toward the war's end influence President Roosevelt to veer away from a Zionist policy. But it was in the summer of 1944, shortly before the Roosevelt-Ibn Saud meeting that Saudi Prince Mansour in-sisted that his brother-in-law Prince Fahd be hospitalized at Ha-dassah. Ibn Saud objected to a Zionist state but not a Zionist hospital. Said Prince Mansour to Dr. Yassky: "When my brother-in-law fell ill there was a consultation of some twenty physicians in Cairo and it was suggested that he be flown to London. I said,

'Nonsense! Why should he be taken to London if there is Hadassah in Jerusalem?' Now nobody will go anywhere but to Jerusalem."

During the war years—even as the *yishuv* smoldered because of Britain's immigration policy—formal visits were made by the British high commissioner. On those occasions, the hospital would be on its toes as though an admiral were being piped aboard a destroyer. On one such occasion, Esther Passman Epstein, who served as a one-member Hadassah welcoming committee, took the high commissioner, who was a bachelor, into the maternity ward. "He was twirling his walking stick and looking at the infants when a sudden smile crossed his face. He lifted his hand and started waving to the babies. Lord Gort turned to me and said that they were lovely children. Without thinking, I replied, 'Yes, this is our internal immigration department.' He looked at me, his face red and gruff, cleared his throat and said, 'Yes, you have a point there.' Then we looked at each other and broke into laughter. The ice was cracked and after that we were all good friends." It was during Lord Gort's administration that a measure of peace between Arabs and Jews was possible, but he did not remain long.

Immigration was the issue on which the British, the Arabs and the Jews were ready to risk their future. It was the wellspring from which all developments flowed. The Arabs feared inundation. The British feared Arab retribution. The Jews feared neither and by a combination of audacity, terror, skill, and sanguinity decided the issue. In the end the British would take desperate departure of this land; the Arabs who sought to resolve the problem by arms would be soundly defeated.

Even before Hitler came to power, the refugee flood began to accumulate. Some could not wait for British certificates. The first known attempt of a large group to steal into Palestine was carried out successfully by three hundred Polish Zionists who landed in the night in 1934 aboard a small hired Greek boat, the *Vellos*. Quickly they dispersed into the collective settlements where they took on new identities. The second attempt of the *Vellos* failed and no large-scale attempts were made for several years. Finally, in 1937, at a clandestine meeting in Tel Aviv a group of Haganah, labor, and kibbutz leaders set up Mosad l'Aliyah Bet, the Institute for Immigration B, a euphemism for uncertified, or as the British called it "illegal," immigration. In 1938, Mosad agents were operating in Nazi Germany and Austria. They made contact with Adolph Eichmann, then head of the Central Bureau for Jewish Emigration, and won his agreement to help them establish training farms for Jews wishing to live in Palestine. Eichmann, the fiend who transported millions of Jews to death camps, was certainly no lover of Jews. He was merely implementing Hitler's policy to rid the Reich of Jews.

By mid-1939, many hundreds had managed to get by the British. To show they were in earnest the British returned refugees on three small ships to their ports of departure in Nazi Europe— a virtual verdict of death in each case. The resultant worldwide uproar prevented further repatriations. On the day war was declared, the Mosad ship *Tiger Hill*, carrying 1,205 refugees, settled in the sands south of Jaffa. The British had hailed it as it approached the shore and fired on it killing two passengers, one a physician. The senseless shooting was ordered by overanxious officers who suspected that the Gestapo had planted Nazi agents among the immigrants. With the help of the Mosad about 7,000 certificateless Jews arrived by the end of September, 1939. Many others set sail but never reached Palestine's beaches; leaking, rusted, rotten boats that should never have ventured on to a lake tried weathering heavy seas and, like the S.S. *Salvador* carrying three hundred Bulgarian Jews, sank with everyone aboard.

The more the British tried to limit the entry of refugees the more the *yishuv*, directly and indirectly, tried to break through. Because of the unauthorized immigration, the Palestine government on July 12, 1939, proclaimed a stoppage of the entry of all Jews to Palestine for six months from October 1. On January 5, 1940, the British decreed that fleeing refugees with German or Austrian passports would not be allowed to enter Palestine because they were "enemy aliens." In November, 1940, refugees intercepted on their way to Palestine were put in the S.S. *Patria* in Haifa harbor. The *Patria* was to deport these 1,771 Jews to the Indian Ocean island of Mauritius where they were to be held for the duration and presumably repatriated after the war. But the *Patria* never made it out of Haifa harbor. On November 25, an explosion rocked the ship killing 241 persons. In a misguided attempt to prevent the vessel from leaving port, a Haganah agent attempted to immobilize the engines, but the blast was heavier than planned and many lives were lost. The surviving *Patria* refugees were held in detention at Atlit, near Haifa, and finally released. But nearly 1,800 others were sent to Mauritius where they languished for the remainder of the war.

While the Jews were restricted other refugees were permitted entry and colonies of non-Jewish Poles, Serbs, Greeks, Czechs, and others began growing in Tel Aviv and Jerusalem. The British were effective to a greater degree than they might have hoped. On April 1, 1944, when the White Paper's quota restrictions on immigrants ran out, about 20,000 certificates were still unused, and the Jerusalem government extended their validity, offering a visa to anyone who managed to reach Turkey. By the beginning of 1945 they were finally used up and simultaneously the British withdrew its agreement to grant visas automatically on arriving in Turkey. With that the Turks no longer would grant transit rights to stateless Jews en route to Palestine. Knowing that the war would soon end, the Jewish Agency requested permits for 100,000 survivors in Europe. The reply, in February, 1945, was that because of housing difficulties only 1,500 certificates would be available monthly. That was only a slight improvement over the previous 15,000 yearly but not nearly enough to absorb the expected deluge.

One effect of British stubborness on the immigration issue was the rise of Jewish extremism. In 1942, two such groups appeared on the scene. One was the Sternists (or as the British called them the Stern Gang), named for a young poet, Abraham Stern. Their most notorious act was to assassinate Churchill's minister of state in Cairo, Lord Moyne, on November 2, 1944, only two days after Weizmann and Churchill had discussed the partitioning of Palestine. Many believe that Moyne's murder so angered Churchill that he temporarily set aside his pro-Zionist sympathies.

A much larger and older clandestine underground group was the Irgun Tzevai Leumi (National Military Organization) which broke away from the Haganah in 1937. Allied to the Revisionists and to Zev Jabotinsky, it was commanded by Menachem Begin, a Polish soldier who crossed into Palestine from Trans-Jordan in 1942. Although its terrorist character cannot be denied, it respected a truce for most of the war, and allied itself with the Haganah in a number of operations toward the end of the war.

In Europe, Jews tried desperately to break out. Few succeeded. There were examples of incredible endurance such as the ill-fated flight of 1,200 Jews from Vienna, Danzig, and Czechoslovakia who sailed down the Danube in three boats, were delayed on the Yugoslav frontier, and were frozen in for three months. The British agreed to release certificates for 200 children on board and they found their way overland to Palestine. The corpses of the 1,000 adults who remained were discovered by the Serbian government after the war, fully dressed, their passports in their pockets. The Germans had caught up with them.

The most heartening tale of all, because it ended happily, was that of the Teheran children. Their saga began in the Russian-occupied part of Poland shortly after the fall of Warsaw. Hundreds of thousands of Poles, among them thousands of Jews, were deported to Siberia. There they worked in the forests and in labor camps. But when work became scarce, they began to move south toward warmer climes. They spent long days and nights traveling and trudging from village to village. Always their preoccupation was to find food. So scarce were provisions that they took to eating grass, dogs, and fruit pits. Thousands died of malnutrition on the back roads of Russia. They trekked onward into the Asiatic republics and many found shelter in or near the kolkhozes. Nearly one thousand reached Teheran along with the fleeing Polish army. It was now 1942. Henrietta Szold won permits for them, and the Jewish Agency negotiated to have the children sent to Palestine through Iraq, but Baghdad refused. Neutral Turkey likewise refused to give the children passage.

Zionist leaders were incensed, particularly since Iraq was then receiving Allied aid. At that point Hadassah entered the picture in Washington. Denise Tourover had been keeping up on developments through her contacts in the State Department. This is her story:

> We called on the Turkish Ambassador but made no progress. We called on companies that had major oil interests in Iraq. That too failed and I was really incensed that a two-by-four government which was getting lend-lease from us should set its will against a humanitarian effort such as this. I went to the White House. The meeting there was arranged through Mrs. Henry

Morgenthau [wife of the Secretary of the Treasury]. A few days
later the White House said that nothing could move the Iraqis.

Together with Tamar de Sola Pool and Youth Aliyah Chairman
Gisela Warburg, Denise then called on Lord Halifax at the British
embassy. It was now December, 1942. The ambassador told them,
"I am most sad that at this time of the year when the world is
about to celebrate the birth of Jesus that I have not been able to
do something on behalf of Jewish children. But I will make one
last effort."

A few days later Denise heard from British War Ministry chief
John McClay in Washington that the children were to be shipped
out within a short time. So it was done. On January 2, 1943, the
first group of six hundred with sixty guardians left their special
camp in Teheran, where many had been waiting ten months, for
the Iranian port of Ahwaz. They sailed to Karachi, then to Bom-
bay, and after that across the seas to Port Said. On the way, hostile
planes scouted their vessel, but no attacks were made. At Port
Said they entrained for Palestine and arrived at Atlit on February
18—a voyage of nearly seven weeks. For Henrietta, who was
there to meet them, their safe arrival was one of her most ecstatic
moments. The *yishuv* was joyously delirious, for no refugees had
been arriving in large numbers and here at last was a large treasure
of Jewish children snatched from sure death. Wherever the train
stopped on its way to Atlit, it was mobbed by persons seeking
their own children or relatives. They threw flowers, food, and
drink through the windows. The bewildered children looked
down wide-eyed, silent, from the windows, waving little white
and blue flags that they had been given in Port Said. At the
clearance station in Atlit one of the women guardians on the train
fainted. In the crowd she had recognized her husband, an officer
in the Polish army who had been transferred from Russia to the
Middle East. And as fate would have it, one woman among the
greeters found her own child on the train—dazed and sobbing.

"They nearly tore us apart when we landed," recalls one of the
children, Yaacov Or, now a resident of Givatayim, who arrived
at the age of thirteen holding the hands of his eleven-year-old
brother Ron and baby sister Leah. "Everyone fought over us. It
was like a war. The *yishuv* thirsted for immigrants. Wherever we

went we were showered with gifts. If we took in a movie and said we were from Teheran they refused to take money. If we went to a kiosk to buy a drink it was free. We came from Teheran."

Thus, the story ended happily. None was happier than Denise Tourover, whose only gripe was that after the children arrived, she received a bill of $57.46 from the State Department for cables made on Hadassah's behalf. It was paid.

About a year after the first group of Teheran children arrived, rumors began reaching Palestine that Jews were walking out of the desert from remote sections of the Arabian peninsula and showing up in the British Crown Colony of Aden at the confluence of the Red and Arabian seas. The Joint Distribution Committee sent an old hand, Harry Viteles, off to Aden. He reported back that about twelve hundred people were lying in the streets, in courtyards, and in synagogues waiting for the fulfillment of the prophecy that they would be returned to the Promised Land. Medical help was urgently needed. Immediately Hadassah's malaria expert, Jack Kligler, was sent down to do control work. In April, 1944, German-born David Ullmann, the M.D. who worked in a Haifa paint factory before joining Hadassah, with Hadassah nurses Zipporah Friedman, Yehudit Kepara, Rachel Mashat, spent six months caring for the refugees.

Professor Ullmann's account:

> Many of the Yemenite Jews who found their way by donkey and by foot to Aden were puzzled that they needed a permit to enter Eretz Israel which they had not seen for the last 2,500 years. They came in groups of 15 and 20; it took them weeks, even months to reach Aden. They knew Biblical Hebrew from their religious training, and nurses started modern language instruction in the camp that was set up for them. They had many medical problems—relapsing fever, malaria, dysentery, diseases caused by the intense heat. I was their only doctor, and they called me King David. I had brought along a microscope—an unheard of instrument there, and diagnosed relapsing fever. Before that, all fevers were said to be malaria.

Among them were Jews from Haban, perhaps one of the most remote places in the world—somewhere up in the mountains of

Arabia. These Jews lived completely isolated; for them the Yemenites were a highly sophisticated people. They arrived in white flowing gowns, long beards and peculiar headgear. Today, the Habanites live like all other Israelis, most of them in Rishon l'Zion.

Within six months they were put on ships by the Aden administration and taken to Port Said where they went by rail to the Promised Land.

In February, 1945, the war was drawing to its close. In a few weeks the newly organized Jewish Brigade of several thousand men fighting under their own flag would be moved to the front in northern Italy. The brigade would taste only five weeks of battle before V-E Day and would have no serious effect on the course of the war. But by war's end 19,207 Palestinian Jews would have fought with the British forces, including 2,000 women, and 3,000 with other Allied units. In Palestine itself, 7,300 served in police units. By the time the Axis collapsed 30,000 men and women were in uniform, some of them hardened soldiers, and all of them with good basic training. They made a fine cadre for more difficult battles to come.

In that same month of February, the internment of refugees on the island of Mauritius was ended. On August 27 a total of 1,303 had landed; of those, 126 had died, 50 children were born, and 250 were in the Jewish Brigade. They returned with a Hadassah medical unit that arrived a month before.

February was also a sad month for Hadassah despite approaching victory. The organization was bigger, stronger and more energetic than ever and ready to face a new world of challenges. But in a way Hadassah was now orphaned, for on February 13, 1945, her frail heart no longer able to keep pace with her breathless energies, death came in the Mt. Scopus medical center to Henrietta Szold. She was eighty-four.

In her last years Henrietta was grieved that children on arrival were put into detention camps along with adults. As a gift to her, Hadassah had decided to build a $400,000 reception and screening center that would serve Youth Aliyah exclusively. She did not live to see it, although she attended its dedication in 1944. On February 10, 1949 it was opened amid the oak forests in the Hills of Ephraim behind Haifa, not far from Alonim, the first kibbutz to be founded by Youth Aliyah graduates—a site that Henrietta herself had chosen. Ramat Hadassah Szold, two names that would live inseparably in the annals of Youth Aliyah, was perhaps the finest tribute she could have. But inevitably there would be others. Hadassah established the Henrietta Szold Award for Humanitarian Service and conferred the first on Eleanor Roosevelt. The nursing school was named for Henrietta, as was the scenic road that leads to the Ein Karem medical center which would be dedicated on August 3, 1960. So was a social research institute, a forest, a publishing house, a kibbutz, a Tel Aviv taxi company. Henrietta was buried on the Mount of Olives. Later, the Jordanians, who held the Mount of Olives for nineteen years, would build a road over her grave and its precise position would be lost. But nothing could erase her spirit.

14.

Siege!

HITLER was dead. So were 75 per cent of Europe's Jews. Stateless and penniless, 400,000 survivors wandered the face of the continent and finally moved into displaced persons camps while political leaders disputed their fate. Hitler's Holocaust had reaped a dreadful harvest. But it had also begun to generate a terrific creative force among the remnant.

In 1945, Zionists faced a new set of world leaders and a new balance in the power struggle. Britain was shedding its empire; France and Italy, struggling for internal stability, fell to the second echelon in the world order; Germany was prostrate; the United States and the U.S.S.R. now called the turns. In Britain, Clement Attlee succeeded Winston Churchill. Campaigning vigorously, Attlee recklessly promised all things to all peoples. To Jews, his party pledged not only a national home but even an unrealistic exchange of Arab and Jewish populations. In Washington, Harry Truman was now President and Congress was strongly pro-Zionist, even though his administration was not.

At the end of July, an exuberant but untutored Truman flew to Potsdam, outside Berlin, for a summit conference. Genuinely concerned over the fate of European Jews, Truman asked Attlee and his boorish foreign secretary, Ernest Bevin, to permit the Nazis' victims to move to Palestine. By making the request, Truman unknowingly pulled America for the first time into the

Palestine question. When Attlee asked him to help Britain by providing troops for Palestine so that Jewish immigration could be realized without bloodshed, Truman refused.

On August 1, the day the Potsdam Conference closed, Zionists from round the world gathered in London. The scene could best be described as pathetic. Weizmann's fears of August, 1939, had come true. The once great Jewish community of Poland could send only eight delegates, four of them partisan fighters. German Jewry had only the gaunt, noble figure of Rabbi Leo Baeck, a concentration camp survivor. "To be a Jew," he told a stunned conference, "means to be prepared for tragedy. Our people were the objects of a brutally minded gang which developed cruelty into a system, ferocity into a science and bestiality into a philosophy. The question now is, What is to be done?"

Hadassah had four delegates in London. Two—President Judith Epstein and National Political Chairman Rose Halprin—would lead Hadassah on Zionism's political march in the three bitter years to come. From London, Rose reported, "We did not acclaim the victory of the Labor Party as a Zionist victory . . . but still everyone looked forward to an improvement over the Churchill administration which allowed the White Paper to strangle Jewish development."

In the debate, Weizmann and Ben-Gurion disagreed over dealing with the British. Impulsively, Ben-Gurion sped off to the Colonial Office and there, mincing no words, demanded 100,000 immigration permits and a Jewish state forthwith. Aghast, the neophyte colonial secretary spluttered that it was too much to expect the Labor Party to change Palestine policy after being in power only two weeks. In Washington, President Truman received a report that most of the Jews in the displaced persons (DP) camps desired no other home than Palestine, and he pressed openly for the acceptance of 100,000 by the Palestine Mandate government. In Britain, the ruling Labor Party split over the next step. One faction, led by Harold Laski, insisted that the pre-election pledges be honored. But the majority, led by Attlee and Bevin, feared an Arab uprising at a time Britain was trying to sign a treaty with Egypt. The Americans, too, were split. While the White House and Congress were four-square behind the Zionists, the State Department and the military pulled the opposite way.

In Europe, meanwhile, the Mosad was reactivating its agents

to get the stateless out of the camps by hook or by crook and, legally or illegally, on their way to Palestine. So chaotic was the picture at this time that a surreptitious organization like Mosad could work at maximum efficiency. Thus began what became known as Aliyah Bet, or clandestine immigration.

In Palestine, both Jewish and Arab leaders knew that the British could not long hold on. Forces in both camps organized for an underground struggle. As pressures grew for and against mass immigration from Europe, the united Jewish underground struck a first blow. In one coordinated operation the partisans freed two hundred Aliyah Bet immigrants from detention, wrecked railroad lines, damaged the British-run Haifa oil refinery, and hit British naval craft. The struggle for Palestine was now joined.

Anxiously, Foreign Secretary Bevin asked America to help him out of a tight spot by undertaking a joint probe of the immigration problem. Washington agreed to participate in a twelve-member Anglo-American commission. Overjoyed by his success, Ernest Bevin committed himself to accept the body's findings. The members visited the European refugee camps, Palestine, the Arab countries, and Washington. On January 8, 1946, Hadassah President Judith Epstein appeared before it. She represented 200,000 American women now, but she spoke for all Zionists when she said, "The burning need of solving the Jewish problem, of creating a home where those Jews who needed or wanted to rebuild their lives in a Jewish land be given that opportunity, was what moved this large army of Jewish women in America to dedicate their lives to this cause." After four months of travel and toil, the commission reported in April, 1946, that a bi-national state was to be preferred to partition, that 100,000 immigration certificates should be issued to Jews immediately, restrictions on land sales to Jews should be dropped, and the Mandate continued. A happy Truman applauded the immigration recommendation but a flabbergasted Ernest Bevin cried foul, and in Parliament said he would never agree to 100,000 Jews going to Palestine. Now, the magic figure of 100,000 became a cause célèbre in the world press.

A series of events then shook Palestine that turned the country into an armed camp. On a moonless night in mid-June, 1946, the Haganah blew up eleven bridges, all of them connecting Palestine and the neighboring Arab countries. This was the *yishuv*'s reply to Prime Minister Attlee for saying that he, like Bevin, could not go along with the 100,000 immigrants until all the underground forces disbanded. On "Black Saturday," June 24, the British over-reacted. They rounded up the top Jewish Agency and Haganah leaders in Palestine, including "Foreign Minister" Moshe Shertok, and 2,800 young Jews, and sent them all to detention camps. Ben-Gurion was then in Paris and for the rest of the year ran the *yishuv*'s affairs from the French capital.

Two weeks later, the Irgun blew up the southern wing of Jerusalem's King David Hotel, headquarters of the British army. More than ninety Englishmen, Jews, and Arabs died in the blast. The commanding officer in Palestine, General Evelyn Barker, ordered a policy of "non-fraternization" with the Jews (as the Allies had done in Nazi Germany) and made the unhappy state-ment that he would punish the Jews "in a way that race dislikes —by striking at their pockets." Barker was subsequently trans-ferred. The *yishuv* now knew that it was fighting not only anti-Zionism in the British administration but the much deadlier poison of anti-Semitism as well.

Despite British opposition immigrants were pouring on to the shores of Palestine from Mosad ships. Most were caught and sent to the Atlit detention camp south of Haifa but some made it safely inland and lost themselves with fake papers in the kib-butzim. To make it a bit easier for the ships to land, in July, 1946, a Haganah commando platoon led by a young Yugoslav Jew named Haim Bar-Lev (later to be Israeli chief of staff) blew up a British radar station that was tracking the ships. The ships began coming with such frequency that on August 12, the British an-nounced Operation Igloo; henceforth immigrants arriving with-out permits would no longer be sent to Atlit but deported to detention camps on the island of Cyprus from where they would be released at the rate of 1,500 monthly. That same day a ship with 543 on board arrived from a Greek port. She was the *Henrietta Szold* and she was one of 63 ships to be bought clan-destinely for Aliyah Bet with funds quietly collected in the United States. The *Henrietta Szold*'s passengers were the first to be sent to Cyprus. Nearly 40,000 more followed to the end of the Mandate.

Only ten days before the *Henrietta Szold* arrived, the Jewish Agency put Hadassah in charge of the immigrants' health. At that time twenty-five hundred were cooped up in Atlit. Within twenty-four hours, Yassky had a sixty-bed emergency hospital staffed round the clock by a doctor and five nurses. After an inspection trip to immigrant ships in Haifa, Yassky angrily reported, "Beasts are not kept under such conditions."

The Jewish Agency was banned in Cyprus so Jewish teams went in under the aegis of the American Joint Distribution Committee. To organize the welfare work, the JDC sent American-born Rose Viteles, a member of the Hadassah Council in Palestine and, unknown to most, one of the early organizers of the Haganah in Jerusalem. Rose was soon followed by units of Hadassah physicians and nurses. Tamar de Sola Pool arranged for an entire educational foundation for children, including teachers and texts, to be moved from the Abraham Ruttenberg Foundation in Haifa to the camps. The last Hadassah team returned with the last immigrant on February 16, 1949, nine months after the birth of the state.

As more ships challenged the British navy and underground pressure increased to lower the gates, the British committed more troops to Palestine. Eventually they would number 100,000. But Bevin knew force could not settle anything and out of despair he called a conference in London to which he invited both Jews and Arabs. Neither Palestinian Arab nor Jew attended so the British met with delegates of the newly formed Arab League, a loose union of Arab nations formed with British encouragement. The Zionists stayed away because the British refused to put on the agenda a new plan drawn up by Ben-Gurion. The plan was visionary, for it suggested the partition of Palestine along lines that were almost identical with the map drawn in 1949 following the War of Independence. The British recessed the conference after two months of getting nowhere, but Bevin carried on discussions with the two sides nonetheless. Just as he thought he was making some headway, President Truman took the wind out of Bevin's sails by announcing full support of the Ben-Gurion partition plan.

It was now November, 1946. Bevin tried for his second wind by releasing the imprisoned Jewish leaders and the 2,800 youths. In return Haganah severed its ties with the more fanatic Irgun and Sternists. In December, the first postwar Zionist Congress met. It was to be known as the "Confused Congress," for the leadership was divided on how to move forward to independence. At Hadassah's thirty-second national convention in Boston, held prior to the Zionist Congress, Ben-Gurion railed at the British and demanded an autonomous Jewish state. He continued his attacks at the congress. But no one was clear on what to do next or how to do it. Should Zionism encourage a regime of terror to get the British out? The great-maned, voice-of-doom orator from Cleveland, Rabbi Abba Hillel Silver, who was to lead Zionism's battles in the United States as head of the American section of the Zionist Executive, encouraged revolt. The aging Weizmann stuck to the guns of moderation. In the end, the congress voted for a Jewish commonwealth, for unlimited immigration, but against any form of trusteeship and against terror. Without expressly going back on Biltmore, the congress seemed to say partition would be acceptable as the absolute minimum. Hadassah had its own private triumph at the congress. Its "foreign minister," Rose Halprin, was elected to the Jewish Agency Executive's American section and for much of the next quarter of a century she would be its sole female representative.

Zionism may have been perplexed about what route to take but it was not confused about where it was going, nor was it hesitant to look to bolder captains to get it there. At Basel, Chaim Weizmann was not re-elected. As a sign of respect the post of president was left vacant, and by default the leadership of the Zionist Organization fell to the aggressive David Ben-Gurion. Out of office, a man divested of position and a future, Chaim Weizmann would sixteen months hence play a fateful role in the birth of the Jewish state. History would then reward him with the task of appealing at the eleventh hour to the President of the United States for vital American support.

In mid-February, Bevin announced Britain's intention to give up the Palestine Mandate. In consequence, the United Nations Assembly met in special session on May 9 and set up an eleven-nation special committee on Palestine (UNSCOP). The Arabs announced their refusal to cooperate with the committee. The British Foreign Ministry showed no interest, expecting that after UNSCOP's failure the General Assembly would call up Britain to return in order to form order out of chaos. Both the United States and the Jewish Agency held high hopes for the committee, and both backed it fully.

UNSCOP began its work in June, 1947, as terrorism and British counter-terrorism reached heights of insanity. The British made one faux pas after another. While UNSCOP was in Palestine, it committed the worst blunder when Bevin ordered 4,554 refugees in the Aliyah Bet ship *Exodus* to return to Germany. That single act brought widespread sympathy for the Zionist cause, for it dramatized the homelessness of the Nazi victims and the empty-headedness of British policy.

As UNSCOP met in Jerusalem, it heard much the same testimony as the commissions that preceded it. The Hadassah Council in Palestine presented a memo on behalf of 218,000 members in forty-seven of the forty-eight states (only Idaho was not represented among the hundreds of chapters). Hadassah's Zionist effort, said the memo, had transferred $25 million to Palestine since 1921. In that time infant mortality had dropped from 144.3 to 34 per thousand, trachoma was gone, and all-in-all "Palestine is the most healthful area in the Middle East." The memo ended, "The Jewish women represented by Hadassah will continue their un-remitting efforts to help re-create Palestine, the Jewish National Home, as a democratic Jewish Commonwealth." UNSCOP visited Scopus on June 27 and heard Dr. Yassky say, "Everyone is welcome here."

Back in New York on September 1, UNSCOP voted seven to three with one abstention for partition. Its plan was much less than that suggested to the British by Ben-Gurion, but it was by far the best ever offered the Jews. The UNSCOP map cut the country into six interlocking segments—three Arab and three Jewish—and made Jerusalem an international city.

In Zurich, the Zionist General Council, meeting in place of the congress, accepted the plan. The Arabs announced they would go to war to kill it. The British said they would leave Palestine so the two sides could fight over the map. And as it turned out, UNSCOP had not created two states so much as it had unintentionally drawn up the battle lines for the coming war.

For the next two months the U.N. was a labyrinth of confusion. The battle to win sufficient votes in the General Assembly of the United Nations was fought by Jews on all continents. Jewish Agency representatives used every stratagem, every contact, every argument to get the necessary two-thirds majority. In the

United States, the head of the Jewish Agency delegation, Moshe Shertok, had the help of a vast array of volunteers. Booming out over all else was the stentorian voice of Abba Hillel Silver. Working in every single state to turn public opinion were nearly a quarter of a million Hadassah members. "We had something no one else had—grass roots," President Judith Epstein said. "We were everywhere. I remember one period when I had a midnight call from the Hadassah president of Philadelphia. 'We are still in the office,' she said. 'What can we do? We don't want to go home if there is something we can do.' They had written personal letters to every member of Congress, phoned, sent telegrams, and they still wanted to know what they could do!"

As if to anticipate the historic events that were now about to occur, Hadassah, meeting in its thirty-third convention in Atlantic City in late October, adopted a record budget—$4,070,000. Speaking to the convention, Guatemala's UNSCOP delegate Dr. Jorge Garcia-Granados, compared the opposing positions: "There is a fundamental reason why the Jewish case is stronger than the Arab case. It is not a question of nationalism fighting for a land or a territory. It is a question of giving thousands of human beings hope and a reason for living. . . . The human case in unanswerable."

Retiring President Epstein turned her office over to veteran political fighter Rose Halprin with a simple equation of Hadassah philosophy: "From the very beginning of Hadassah—whether it was the establishment of a playground or the introduction of new hospital methods—we have always had before us the compulsion of a great idea—The Jewish State."

One month later, on Saturday, November 29, 1947, the U.N. General Assembly firmly implanted the seeds of a Jewish state in Palestine by passing the partition resolution, thirty-three to thirteen, five more votes than the required two-thirds. Ten states abstained. The news hit Palestine late at night. Unrestrained joy splashed over the *yishuv* and over Jews everywhere. The Arabs called a day of mourning and the Mufti, appearing on the scene like an evil genie, called a three-day general strike.

After the rejoicing over the U.N. decision, individual survival became a matter of fortitude, luck, and ingenuity. One Hadassah board member who saw the radical change on partition night was Palestine Committee Chairman Bertha Schoolman, who had ar-

rived only a week earlier to help plan for educating and settling
six thousand Youth Aliyah children about to be freed from the
Cyprus camps.

> I went down the street from my hotel to the Jewish Agency
> building. There were thousands in the streets—the old, the young,
> even British Tommies. They were in a joyous mood. Laughing
> British soldiers drove Jewish boys and girls on their vehicles; they
> thought everything was over now and they would be going home.
> At 2:00 A.M. Golda Meir, the highest ranking Agency member
> in Jerusalem—Ben-Gurion was resting at the Dead Sea—came out
> of the building and spoke to the crowds about the possibility
> of peace with the Arabs.

On Mt. Scopus life had been a pleasant routine until November
29. Rumanian-born pathologist Alexander Laufer, who had joined
Hadassah as a volunteer in 1941, recalled how it was in the
bachelor quarters.

> We had a cozy, warm atmosphere. We became a closely-knit
> group. Our social life was limited; our contacts being primarily
> with the nurses or nursing students. Our lifeline to the city was
> Hamekasher's Number 9 bus which made its last trip up to
> Scopus at midnight. We had walks to the university buildings or
> strolled to the nearby Arab village where we drank coffee at
> the El Tur cafe. The Arab bus drivers knew us and would often
> stop to give us a lift. Then the tension began . . .

On November 30 there erupted a reign of terror. An ambulance on the way to Scopus was fired on at Nashashibi Bend in
the Sheikh Jarrah Quarter. Located between the Jewish part of
the city and Scopus, a half-mile of narrow roadway that wound
through this Arab Quarter was to be the scene of high tragedy
and to bring to an early end Scopus' use as a world center of
healing and education. The Nashashibi house, a colonnaded manor
of a wealthy Arab family, was to serve as a focal point from
which continual attacks were launched on traffic. Several hundred yards farther on at an L-curve that led down into a valley
at the bottom of Scopus was another manor set back from the
road in a lovely garden that belonged to the Mufti. Rented by
the well-known Arab nationalists, George and Kate Antonius, the
dwelling was known as the Antonius House and would be another
key point for the tragedy to come.

Arab rioting, under the Mufti's orders, broke out elsewhere on that last day in November. Two buses were gunned down near Lydda Airport; one of the six killed was Hadassah pathologist Nehama Zelutovsky. That night Arabs began shooting at buses on Route 9 to Scopus. On the first day of the Arab general strike frenzied young Arabs stormed out of Jerusalem's Jaffa Gate, targeted in on workshops in the New Commercial Center where they looted, burned, stabbed, and stoned, and then headed for the center of the city. British troops did not interfere until the mobs approached city center. There, Haganah men stood ready to make their first open stand, but the British arrested sixteen, and only then moved to stop the mob. A torch having struck the tinder, the Jewish leadership ordered "a census" of all seventeen to twenty-five year olds for "public service." Eventually, men up to age fifty-five would be mobilized. Major attacks were launched against Jewish neighborhoods and against isolated settlements in all sections of the country.

For the first seven months of the war Scopus would be Jerusalem's principal medical facility. Dr. Laufer recalled:

> It was distressing for us to see the wounded Haganah men being brought into hospital from the surrounding Jewish settlements of Atarot and Neve Ya'acov where they had been caught by the Arabs. I remember one day we had to watch from Scopus behind the hills as smoke came from one of the Haganah cars that had accompanied the bus on its routine trip to Scopus. A British officer came later with the bodies which had been mutilated.

Hadassah's local governing bodies—the Council in Palestine and the Medical Organization Board—met almost daily for the remainder of the crisis. Director Yassky was abroad from November until February to attend the national convention and to help plan Palestine's first medical school. That left the direction of Hadassah's hospital activities to British-born Deputy Medical Director Eli Davis and Deputy Administrator Mendel Krupnik. Acting for the National Board, the Council in Palestine was chaired by Hebrew University Chancellor Magnes, and in mid-1948 by Ethel Agronsky (Agron). Bertha Schoolman's presence in Jerusalem gave the board an extra representative.

As fighting became certain, the legislature of the *yishuv*—the Va'ad Leumi—immediately urged Hadassah to prepare for the

worst and appointed a national medical board on which Eli Davis
was a representative.

Uppermost in the minds of the Hadassah people was the
security of the road to Scopus. Within the week following the
partition vote, Davis reported that all departments in the medical
center had augmented emergency services and that while the
Hadassah station wagon had a military escort through Sheikh
Jarrah, only essential journeys were being made. On matters concerning Scopus, the University, represented by Administrator
David Werner Senator, and Hadassah acted in unison. On December 8, Senator and Davis asked the police for more guards at
the hospital and for permission to provide Hadassah staff with
arms. The request for more security was made the day after a
bus jammed with Scopus-bound workers narrowly missed death
when a grenade crashed through one window and went out another to explode on the ground. But twenty bullets hit the bus,
wounding two doctors. Bus Number 9 windows were henceforth
screened with steel netting. One hundred staff members bedded
down on Scopus rather than risk the ride while patients went
elsewhere for treatment. Despite the increase in war casualties, the
number of admissions on Scopus declined in December. Davis
judiciously set up an independent operating theater at Hadassah's
downtown clinic.

Constant attacks indicated that the Arabs were intent on
neutralizing Scopus to make an assault on Jewish Jerusalem that
much easier. Before the year was out five doctors miraculously
escaped injury when their car was set afire on the Scopus road.
But fifteen staff members were wounded in an attack on a bus,
and for the first time, on December 30, the magnificent foyer of
the medical center was turned into a clearing station and shock
room. In another shocking attack, Szold Nursing School Professor
Hugo Lehrs was murdered by three Arab gunmen at Jerusalem's
Hospital for Contagious Diseases while walking in the compound
with an Arab doctor and nurse. The Arabs asked them, "Which
of you is a Jew?" and when the Arab doctor and nurse stepped
aside, Lehrs was slain. The year ended with a personal tragedy
for Hadassah. On Friday, December 26, Bertha Schoolman and
Youth Aliyah director Hans Beyth were returning to Jerusalem
from the coast where they observed the arrival of children from
Cyprus camps. The long battle for control of the forty-mile road

to Jerusalem was now in progress. As their convoy headed up the steep Judean Hills, past hostile Arab villages, the buses absorbed heavy Arab fire from the crests of the mountains on either side of the serpentine, two-lane highway.

Bertha was riding in a car with Golda Meir and two Jewish Agency members. She recalled: "Yitzhak Gruenbaum, one of the Agency men, had a small pistol and he kept shooting back through the window as we drove. Fifteen minutes from Jerusalem the bus ahead of us was hit. Hans was in the bus. He, too, had a gun and shot back. He was a good target when he stood, and he was killed." From then on, Bertha shared the management of Youth Aliyah with Moshe Kol, who later joined the Israeli cabinet.

January of 1948 began badly. Prospects for a military victory were dim. Arabs in Palestine outnumbered Jews 1,250,000 to 650,000. Arab armies had a two to one advantage (115,000 to 50,000). Although the Jews did have a well-trained core of 20,000 who had fought in World War II, they had only one gun for every four men, no air force, and no navy to speak of. The Arabs on the other hand, had planes, ships, tanks, and heavy artillery. They also had defense treaties with Britain and, in Abdullah's Arab Legion, British officers. The United States put an arms embargo on the Middle East in December; Britain announced in January it would supply arms to Egypt, Iraq, and Jordan. Secretly, Ben-Gurion sent agents to Prague to buy weapons, but Arab agents were there doing the same, and before the arms arrived the fighting could well be finished. The Zionists could not have been in a grimmer position. Their scattered forces were surrounded on three sides by hostile Arab nations and in the west by an unconcerned sea. Triumph would emerge out of tragedy nevertheless, but at a tremendous price in casualties: 10 per cent of the entire Jewish population.

Aware of the looming struggle, Hadassah called an extraordinary meeting of the full National Board on January 4 in New York. Yassky informed the members that all 105 Hadassah doctors in Palestine were at the service of the *yishuv* and in fact 30 were put into uniform. In response to the *yishuv*'s request that Hadassah coordinate all medical services for the emergency, the board voted extra allocations including an immediate grant of $100,000 to help develop the central military hospital at Tel Litwinsky, near Tel Aviv. In so doing, Hadassah became a founder of the Israel Army Medical Corps. By the end of 1948 the extra disbursements would reach nearly $1 million.

The first heavy attack against a Jewish settlement outside the Jerusalem area was launched against Kfar Szold, a new kibbutz only two hundred yards from the Syrian frontier. Nine hundred Arabs rushed the tiny outpost, but British armor drove off the attackers. Isolated settlements everywhere were pounded.

Battle-hardened by war, riot, and plague, Hadassah was on the out-lying front lines in two urban areas where the *yishuv* was most vulnerable—in Safad and in Jerusalem. In Safad, on the mountains of eastern Galilee, Hadassah's tuberculosis hospital lay between the Jewish and Arab quarters. Most of the TB patients were sent home as fighting began and the hospital—the only one in town—was used for casualties. Safad was a key to upper Galilee and the vital waters of the Jordan River. Arabs outnumbered Jews ten to one. As in Jerusalem, the Arabs began a war of attrition, blowing up houses, firing on traffic, encircling the Jewish area. The British left in April and turned over the main forts of the city to the Arabs. Before they left, an officer warned Hadassah's chief nurse, Russian-born, Pittsburgh-trained Nellie Helfand, a Safad veteran of eleven years, to run away. Nellie replied, "What would you think of a matron in London if she were advised to evacuate under similar circumstances and did so?"

The officer reddened and whispered, "My apologies."

Bitter fighting by the Palmach finally captured Safad on May 11. The hospital cared for 250 casualties.

In the Jerusalem area, in January, the war was rapidly moving in favor of the Arabs. Near Hebron, south of the capital, the four kibbutzim of the Kfar Etzion Bloc were under pressure from one thousand Arabs. A rescue platoon of thirty-five men set out afoot to help the defenders but was massacred on the way. One of the thirty-five was an American volunteer, Moshe Pearlstein, son of Ella, a prominent Hadassah member in the Borough Park section of Brooklyn. The Kfar Etzion fighters held out until mid-May and by so doing relieved the pressure on Jerusalem.

In Jerusalem itself, the Arabs doggedly tried to stop the flow of traffic to Scopus. Davis reported to Yassky early in January that the staff no longer had confidence in British assurances of security. While Davis wrote one report to Yassky, he had to stop to read an urgent communication. Then he went back to writing:

"We have just been informed . . . that a car with bullet-proof sides, with 25 of our personnel, an ambulance and a police escort going to Hadassah were attacked near St. George's Road. A bomb was thrown. Shots were fired and a bullet pierced the roof. A student nurse, class of '48, Hannah Gardi was killed."

Hannah's death was followed by a three-hour battle between Arabs and the Haganah during which all eight phone lines to the hospital went dead. Morale on Scopus plummeted. After prolonged pleading by Davis and Magnes, the British finally replaced the police with army units on the road. Spirits rose, but not for long.

Rationing went into effect at the medical center. Nurses pitched in to carry out menial tasks because of the larger number of persons remaining on the hill. As the starkness of the situation became evident, Magnes brought up the possibility for the first time of moving off Scopus to downtown Jerusalem. The faint-hearted had begun whispering that it might be best to abandon Scopus. But the hospital's management committee at the time firmly decided to stand fast "even though absolute security is no longer possible." They anticipated Jewish Agency Chairman David Ben-Gurion who, one month later, appointed David Shaltiel as commander of Jerusalem, and gave him orders not to surrender one inch of ground anywhere in Jerusalem. The possibility that the Arabs would launch a frontal attack to capture Scopus was real. With more than seven hundred persons, mostly civilians, on the hill, the decision to stay put was not a light one to take. But there is no doubt that it was the right one since it was instrumental in helping save most of Jerusalem for Israel. Wrote Davis to Hadassah Medical Organization Chairman Etta Rosensohn on January 20: "The most important fact of all is that the hospital remains open, is carrying on much as usual. . . . Were Mt. Scopus cut off, the Arabs would have a very much smaller Jewish area to besiege and against which to deploy their forces."

The role of the British in the quickly deteriorating situation in Jerusalem was ambiguous. Some were strongly pro-Arab, others —probably a minority—were pro-Jewish. The bureaucracy continued to function for the most part as though the crisis facing it was of no matter. Nothing was done to prepare an orderly transfer of government. The Mandate administration was interested only in safeguarding British interests until evacuation.

The British stoutly turned down university pleas to remove an Arab Legion camp stationed a few hundred yards from the medical center, or even install a "hot line" to the camp from the university. Even less comprehensible was the British refusal to permit the Jews to build a short $88,000 ring road—at Hadassah's expense—that would bypass the Sheikh Jarrah Quarter and Nashashibi Bend.

By the end of January the war in Jerusalem accounted for three hundred Jewish casualties. Nearly all were treated at Hadassah. On the night of February 1, Hadassah itself became a casualty. Early in the day Eli Davis escorted a Red Cross delegation through the clinic in Hasolel Street and through the Scopus hospital. They parted in high spirits; the delegation complimented Davis for the high level of excellence he had achieved under battle conditions. At 10:58 that night, a stolen British police truck that was parked outside the offices of *The Palestine Post*, the country's English-language daily, blew sky high and laid waste the building. The Hadassah clinic across the street was badly damaged as was the entire street. Two British deserters hired by the Mufti and an Arab accomplice had done the job. The explosion, which rattled windows two miles away, was so forceful that closed drawers in editorial room desks opened, filled with broken glass falling from the window panes, and closed tight again. Three persons were killed and about fifty were injured.

By February 3, Yassky was again at his post. Angered that his beautiful medical center had to be turned into what amounted to an army base hospital, he recalled in a letter to Etta Rosensohn how British medical personnel had benefited from the hospital during the World War and how British personnel "were now forced by a treacherous policy of their Government to take the road of treason." However, he added, "Mt. Scopus should not be abandoned." He gave orders to brick up operating theaters and halls, fortify windows, build blast walls, dig wells for water reservoirs, build storage huts for food stocks. Yassky was preparing for a siege—and none too soon. The Arabs intensified their attacks. No one was spared. They even exploded a mine under a truck escorting a funeral.

The Trojan Horse trick used against the *The Palestine Post* was to be used twice more inside Jewish Jerusalem with devastating effect. Shortly after dawn on Washington's Birthday, the two

British deserters were back with more Mufti agents. This time they planted three trucks loaded with three tons of TNT in the middle of Ben Yehuda Street, the city's main shopping district. The resulting detonation smashed the thoroughfare along its entire length, caved in buildings, killed 50 and injured more than 150. Hadassah took the 70 most serious cases, and while they were being treated, the hospital came under attack. A guard on the hospital roof was killed, and a bullet narrowly missed Yassky's head in his office.

Mines on the roads and bullets in the air moved Magnes and Davis to ask the board in New York to ask the State Department to intervene. The university's David Senator addressed a confidential memo to Magnes saying that since the British were unwilling to provide adequate security, the presence of the attackers "makes active Jewish defense unfeasible." Again, the voice of alarm. Magnes turned to the British commander of Jerusalem, Brigadier C. P. Jones, with a new plea for help. Jones replied through a subordinate that nothing could be done about the Sheikh Jarrah Quarter and fatuously suggested that the Arab and Jewish medical associations should work out a deal. By the end of February, Magnes cabled the National Board, "Road impassable." Hadassah replied reassuringly, "Preparing memorandum to present to State Department."

Thus ended the worst month so far in Jerusalem.

Zionist fortunes elsewhere had reached their nadir. At Lake Success, the United Nations grappled unsuccessfully with the Palestine problem. Now that partition was decided upon the United Nations was at a loss to find a way to ensure its implementation. The State Department, never happy over the resolution, tried to convince the United Nations to retreat on partition. U.S. delegate Warren Austin declared that the U.N. Charter did not empower the Security Council to enforce the resolution, and one month later suggested that statehood for Jews and Arabs should be held up and be replaced by a temporary U.N. trusteeship. In Palestine, the fighting *yishuv* looked with disbelief over its shoulder at America's acrobatics. Twice the United States would reverse its field on the question of trusteeship.

Fearing a political disaster at the very moment of triumph, Chaim Weizmann rushed to New York on February 4 hoping to see President Truman. But Truman, weary from constant pressure by Zionists, held Weizmann at bay. Then, in what is now a well-told tale, he finally got to the White House through the intervention of Truman's gutsy former haberdashery partner, Eddie Jacobson. On March 18, Weizmann, in the greatest performance of his career, convinced Truman of the urgent need for a Jewish state. The crunching argument was humanitarian—multitudes in Europe were heading for Zion's gate and would go nowhere else, he said. The following day Austin put forth his trusteeship proposal. A double-cross? No, the State Department simply had not informed Truman of the change. The sky fell in on the Zionists. But in retrospect the State Department's action was fortunate, for it apparently sealed once and for all Truman's mind on his own independent course. Spitting fire at the "striped-pants boys," Truman asked an aide how this could have happened after his assurance to Weizmann that he was for partition. The following month during Passover Weizmann was told secretly by the White House that Truman would stand by his promise. The old statesman kept it to himself but advised the *yishuv's* leaders to go on with the planned declaration of the state come what may. Within eleven minutes after the State of Israel was established on May 14, the White House startled Washington and the world by announcing de facto recognition. America thus became the first nation to grant status to the Jewish nation.

15.

Tragedy and Triumph

At 2:05 p.m. on March 2 the operator at the Hadassah exchange in Jerusalem heard an Arab voice warn that the hospital would be blown up within ninety minutes. The warning was not carried out but it was a clear giveaway of Arab intentions. Two days later, Hadassah President Halprin and Denise Tourover called on the State Department and the British embassy in Washington to secure Scopus, then followed up with strong protests to U.N. Secretary-General Trygve Lie and the International Red Cross. Shortly afterward, the commander of Palestine Arab forces, Abdul Kader Husseini, spoke on-the-record to correspondents: "Since Jews have been attacking us and blowing up our houses containing women and children from bases in Hadassah Hospital and Hebrew University, I have given orders to occupy or even demolish them." Showing he meant business he placed a cannon on top of the Rockefeller Museum of Archaeology opposite Mt. Scopus, and he began using armor-piercing ammunition and electrically-detonated mines against Scopus traffic. Surgeon Edward Joseph penned a note to Yassky that he could no longer take the responsibility of transferring cases to Scopus. Yassky replied sharply: "The time has not yet come to evacuate Mt. Scopus. . . . There is no security anywhere."

But reality won out. Yassky carried on negotiations quietly for the use of the Anglican Mission Hospice a few blocks away from the Hasolel Street clinic that Hadassah ran in downtown Jerusalem. On March 15, ten beds were set up for maternity cases and the site became known as Hadassah "A." History had played another of its pranks. One hundred years earlier Jews in Jerusalem were running away from mission hospitals; now they were running back into them.

By mid-March the Hadassah Emergency Committee resolved that supplies would no longer be concentrated on Scopus but would be dispersed in the center of town. A meeting held at the home of Myriam Granott considered the possibility, never implemented, of returning to the old Rothschild building where Hadassah's vocational school was located. Magnes noted that the Red Cross had offered to put Scopus under its flag on condition that Hadassah and the university agreed to demilitarize the area. To Hadassah, the Red Cross banner was the white flag of surrender, and persistently refused.

On March 22, a crucial meeting of the Hadassah council was held in the living room of Ethel Agron's split level home in Jerusalem. (Most of the members present were unaware that in another room of the house English-speaking Haganah agents, some of them former Junior Hadassah members now living in Jerusalem, were monitoring British police and army radio traffic.) Topic A was the extent of Hadassah's evacuation of Scopus.

Ethel Agron warned: "There will be complaints against the transfer of casualties to Scopus if Hadassah opens departments in town."

Rose Viteles: "No other road has so far been given up by the *yishuv*. Hadassah cannot be first."

Krupnik: "After the British leave even a partial transfer will be most difficult."

Magnes weakly held out hope that the new trusteeship proposal at Lake Success "might ease the situation."

Yassky asked Bertha Schoolman to take a confidential note to Jewish Agency Treasurer Eliezer Kaplan in Tel Aviv. Unless the agency did something at once to secure the road to Scopus, the memo said, the hospital would have to cease operations.

Fatigue and stiffer rationing added weight to the arguments to move down off the hill despite a determination to remain as long as possible. In Jewish Jerusalem, the supply situation was so bad that Jews were reduced to scrounging in the fields for a weed called *khubeizeh* to supplement their diets which now consisted of a few slices of bread, an occasional egg, a handful of noodles, some jam, and an orange. On Scopus and in the Hasolel clinic, reported Davis, "Our surgeons have been on the job night and day since the end of November and not one of them has had a weekend off since then." Dr. Laufer recalled life on Scopus, "In our little time off we listened to the news and the firing of bullets. One of our colleagues would read to us from Sholom Aleichem. All personnel put in their spell of guard duty." Dr. Magnes informed British Chief Secretary Sir Henry Gurney, "I am afraid our devoted doctors, nurses and patients are being subjected to a strain too great to bear."

Yassky now had an evacuation plan ready. At a joint Hadassah-Hebrew University meeting with Golda Meir, she was told that unless a minimum of three convoys could safely pass daily, the hospital would close. The only alternative was to accept the Red Cross offer. Golda agreed to raise Scopus at a Zionist Executive meeting in Tel Aviv. Meantime, the Zionist General Council, popularly called the Actions Committee, was in session to debate the proclamation of the Jewish state and to authorize the formation of a cabinet and legislature for the new state's functioning. For that historic session Hadassah had flown a delegation in from New York; President Rose Halprin, Judith Epstein, Tamar de Sola Pool, and Rebecca Shulman. Rose asked Yassky to join them in Tel Aviv, but he was too anxious about Scopus' fate to leave. On April 10, Yassky replied:

> Much as I wanted to do it I thought I cannot leave my post for a few days. The situation in Jerusalem is very serious and that of Scopus much more so. I do not exaggerate when I say that 100,000 Jews of Jerusalem depend on Hadassah's functioning somehow, somewhere. I am very pessimistic about Scopus. . . . It is our duty to prepare emergency arrangements in the city. We will do our best to hang on.

To Mrs. Schoolman who was to leave for the United States on April 12, he reported,

> Transport to Scopus did not improve in spite of all the promises of B.G. [Ben-Gurion] and G.M. [Golda Meir]. At best we have one convoy a day. With the number of casualties in town one convoy is an absurd situation. I am afraid we will not be able

to continue to operate the Hospital very much longer. . . . I hope that we will meet again in not a too distant future.

That hope was not to be. Three days later Dr. Haim Yassky was dead, shot through the liver in an Arab ambush on the road that he and Hadassah leaders had tried valiantly to make safe.

Five days earlier, on April 8, in the northern outskirts of Jerusalem, the Irgun attacked the Arab village of Deir Yassin, a base for Arab irregulars. As many as 250 Arabs, mostly civilians, were slain. The effect was not, as so many commentators have claimed, to encourage the Arabs to retaliate by hitting a civilian convoy to Scopus, because the Arabs had planned the ambush before Deir Yassin; but the massacre was cited to justify the Arab attack on the convoy. The Arab leadership had three goals in mind in planning the attack on the Mt. Scopus convoy: to strike a decisive blow that would force the Jews to abandon Scopus and make Jerusalem more vulnerable, to destroy the Jews' will to resist an Arab invasion of the city proper, and to deprive the Jews of their largest medical facility. And there was another factor. On April 8, in hand-to-hand fighting for control of Qastel Hill, which dominated the Tel Aviv–Jerusalem highway, the Arab hero and ace military commander, Abdul Kader Husseini, was killed by Meir Carmiel, a mobilized Hadassah worker. Shortly thereafter, Carmiel himself died in action.

Conditions for an ambush were ideal in the Sheikh Jarrah Quarter. Over a stretch of a few hundred yards between Nashashibi Bend and Antonius House, there were stone walls on either side of the narrow road. The convoy would be traveling slowly uphill at this point and ahead at Antonius House there was a 90-degree bend. Caught in that stretch of road the machines would be tin ducks in a shooting gallery. The plan was as old as Thermopylae. Possible intervention could come only from the Haganah escort and from a small unit of Scots' Highland Light Infantry stationed in the Antonius House. But the British there would not shoot unless they received orders to do so, a possibility that was remote.

On April 11, the British military commander in Jerusalem assured Magnes and a Jewish Agency man that the road was safe, though, because of Deir Yassin, the general area was tense. Even as Jones spoke, the Arabs were consulting expert British officer friends on the logistics of the operation. Subsequent events indicate that the Arabs had an understanding whereby they would not be disturbed in their mission so long as they did not shoot at British soldiers. The Arabs could not—and would not—lose this one.

On April 12, Deputy Medical Director Eli Davis returned to town from Scopus. Wryly he commented, "It was not comfortable on the way down." Customarily Yassky and he took turns up on the hill, but on the evening of the twelfth Yassky had a social engagement and did not go up that morning. Gynecologist Yehuda Bromberg was with him that evening. "I was struck by the great depression which had overcome Dr. Yassky," Bromberg wrote three days later. "It was clear that his depression arose from his deep concern over the fate of our hospital. The dangers confronting the hospital because of the difficulties of transport were clear to him and the fear of the destruction of the hospital to which he dedicated his life."

On Tuesday, April 13, the largest Scopus convoy yet assembled was to take personnel, patients, visitors, workers, and supplies up to the hospital and university. At 8:00 A.M., people began converging on the clinic in Hasolel Street where a university bus and a Hadassah bus, both lightly armored, waited. Three blocks away, outside Hadassah "A" two armored ambulances were parked. Haim and Fanny Yassky entered one of the ambulances, a converted Dodge truck which only the day before had been painted a glaring white with a big red Star of David on the body.

Back at the clinic the buses quickly filled. Hadassah Social Director Esther Passman, her arms brimming over with magazines and sweets for the patients, was so determined to get to her wards that she left behind her beloved ginger-topped son David, who was recuperating from an accident when explosives with which he experimented went off in his hands. At the clinic Esther met the noted cancer specialist Leonid Doljansky, who urged Esther to sit beside him. She was his "mascot" ever since, three weeks previously, she moved next to him on a bus and during the ride got a bullet through her hat. Had he, the much taller of the two, been sitting in her place he would have died. But this day Esther was not permitted to board the bus and the ill-fated doctor would have to ride without his lucky mascot. Swearing under her breath,

Esther ran three blocks to find a seat on one of the ambulances; she would live to tell about it.

Dr. Moshe Ben-David, administrator of the planned medical school, got a late start from home, hailed a cab, finally caught one of the buses, and so sealed his own fate. Shelev Truck Company manager Moshe Lazar had a safe seat in the six-ton Brockway truck of veteran driver Benjamin Adin, but in a move that cost him his life, Lazar changed at the last moment to one of the buses.

By 9:00 o'clock the vehicles were on their way. Three trucks, filled with supplies for the hospital and for fortification work, joined the two Haganah escort cars, two ambulances, and two buses. The exact number of people in the vehicles is not known because precise lists were not kept, but there were well over one hundred.

At the final checkpost outside Hadassah's Tipat Halav station, which served as a Haganah outpost, the convoy halted to await the customary order to proceed from the Haganah. At Tipat Halav, Haganah officer Moshe Hillman phoned British inspector Robert J. Webb, chief of the Mea Shearim police station, who said the road was safe. Webb was known as a friend to both Arabs and Jews and was said to be well-rewarded by both. One job Webb did outside his official duties for the Jews was to drive over the road to Scopus before a convoy left. Webb would stop at Nashashibi Bend, have a look around, and sometimes wait there till the convoy passed. On this day, Hillman said, he called Webb as usual and Webb answered that the way was clear. But Webb did not station himself at Nashashibi Bend on April 13, and all efforts made by the Haganah to contact him throughout the day were fruitless.

Commander of the convoy was Jerusalem-born Lieutenant Asher "Zizi" Rahav, a British army sergeant during World War II. Now he was in Company Noam of the Jerusalem Haganah, the only Jewish unit in the city to wear uniforms and black berets. His assignment was to escort convoys in the Jerusalem area in an armored Ford truck.

It was 9:30. Rahav was in the lead in his escort vehicle with ten men and two young Haganah women hitchhikers. "When we proceeded a short way through Arab territory on Nablus Road, near a mosque, I had an odd feeling that something was wrong, because there was no traffic. I thought of turning back but instead I told my men to load their weapons and keep their eyes open."

The car had peepholes through which the gunners shot and a winged roof of meshed steel covered by canvas.

"Step on it," Rahav told his civilian driver. At the first turn in the road the Arab grocery shop was shuttered—another bad omen. The cars began to climb. Ahead, Zizi saw Nashashibi Bend curving on itself like a snake. Rahav held his breath. Through his peephole he spied the hurried movements of Arabs wearing green Iraqi uniforms with bandoliers. To his left, Rahav noticed that the road was broken. The driver had to swing slightly right to miss it. It was 9:45 on Rahav's watch. Suddenly the Ford truck shook violently, throwing the men forward. A mine was electrically detonated five feet in front of them, creating a narrow four-foot deep ditch. The car's front wheels nosed into the hole and the car settled at a steep angle. The mesh roof and canvas slid back, partly off the vehicle, obscuring the view of the rest of the convoy. Bullets pounded on the armored car. "Bullets came through the armor like bees swarming around us," Rahav recalled later. Zizi shot holes in the canvas to see what was happening to the convoy behind. He saw the last cars trying to turn around. At Nashashibi Bend, two British armored cars blocked the retreat. Rahav gave orders to his armorer, Baruch Nussbaum, to fire a few bursts at the British cars to get them to move out of the way. He did not know then that in one of those cars, sitting as a spectator, was Lieutenant-General G. H. A. MacMillan, commander of all British forces in Palestine. MacMillan ordered his driver to move away from the convoy. Two days later MacMillan would reply to a protest by University Chancellor Magnes in words that unintentionally admitted British neglect in the convoy tragedy:

> I myself motored through the area, passing under the fire of an automatic weapon in a Jewish armored car at 09:45 on my way to Kalandia [Jerusalem's airport] . . . I assumed that the situation was clearing up and my inference at the time was that it would have cleared up much quicker, had the Jewish armored car stopped firing.

Five vehicles managed to extricate themselves and get back to Jewish quarters. The Haganah escort car in the rear, its tires punctured, inexplicably turned tail and returned. Driving blindly with only a crack to see through, Benjamin Adin reversed, advanced, reversed, backed into the wall of the Nashashibi House and finally turned his six-ton Brockway toward the city. His foot brakes were gone, his tires were flat, the steering wheel worked only partially. On the floor of the cabin was a weeping male passenger who hopped on at the last moment in an effort to see his wife and newly born son on Scopus. "I never shall see them again," he cried over and over. Adin pushed his pedal to the floor and arrived safely at Mandelbaum Gate where his passenger fell out of the cab in a deep faint.

The driver of the larger of the two ambulances, Yosef Levy, was wounded in the head. Surgeon Edward Joseph took a quick look, found it was only superficial and urged him to get moving toward Scopus. Reported Joseph, "We thought the driver was going on but instead he wisely turned the car around and returned to Jerusalem. It was the first to get back." Dr. Joseph then crawled to join the Haganah men who were trying to edge close to the besieged convoy.

> We were being attacked by a tremendous amount of shooting. It was impossible to lift one's head. The bullets were whizzing everywhere. I asked the soldier nearest me, "Are these Arabs shooting at us?" He replied, "No. They are English soldiers." I knew it had to be true because it was the kind of shooting that only a proper army could do. They were shooting at the Haganah boys. If they had not, we could have reached the convoy.

The surgeon then joined a few men who had been in the Haganah vehicle that retreated and ran to the roof of the Tipat Halav station. Esther Epstein, who had been in Joseph's ambulance, joined the men. With his old pistol Joseph ran from roof to roof trying to get close enough to get in a shot. It was a hopeless act. As the ambush appeared to be succeeding, Arab volunteers from the region ran to the scene to get in on the kill. Esther could only sob at the end of the day, "It was horrible—all that shooting and shelling. Later we saw the burning—it was horrible to see."

On the spot, blood was beginning to flow in Zizi Rahav's thinly armored escort car. Private Shlomo Mizrahi got two bullets in the stomach and fell on his commander. Rahav himself caught a steel splinter in the temple, his eye swelled, and blood gushed.

He kept shooting, aiming with his one good eye. Around noon-time one of the hitchhiking Haganah girls, Shoshana Ben-Ari, of Kibbutz Yagur, rose from the floor to help a wounded man, was hit in the mouth by a bullet and died shortly thereafter. At 12:15 Zizi dispatched his armorer, Baruch Nussbaum, to Antonius House about two hundred yards farther on to get help from the Highland Light Infantry officers who were observing the battle, their heavy weapons silent. Baruch, who had a slight limp from a case of childhood polio, jumped into the deep ditch made by the mine and crawled along the wall. Baruch's body was later found in a wadi in Arab territory.

Back in Jerusalem proper at Haganah headquarters, Commander David Shaltiel called twenty-one-year old Baruch Gilboa, who had arrived in Jerusalem early that morning from Tel Aviv. Gilboa was a commander of an armored unit that had escorted over 150 trucks of supplies to the city, following the capture of Qastel Hill on the city's outskirts. Shaltiel ordered him to take some men in his armored car to the Sheikh Jarrah Quarter and try to tow out the four vehicles that were under Arab fire.

"I don't know where Sheikh Jarrah is," said Gilboa.

"Take my operations officer with you," Shaltiel ordered.

It was obvious that Shaltiel's intelligence from the scene of battle was faulty; otherwise he would not have ordered a lone escort car into that trap. Gilboa and his men were fatigued from fourteen hours on the road. His civilian driver, apparently shocked by the battle, saw the ditch made by the mine across the road, decided to try to drive the car over it, put on speed as he came up to the left of Zizi Rahav's embattled vehicle and landed with a thud in the ditch, injuring some of the men. Had he gone to the right of Rahav, he would have missed the ditch, gone on to Antonius House, and the men could then have engaged Arabs who were firing at the convoy from a house across the street. Now, two Haganah cars were stuck at the head of the convoy.

Close behind was Yassky's ambulance, its tires were shot out, standing breadthwise across the road where it got good protection from the two Haganah cars just ahead. About fifty yards behind were the two buses. They were most open to attack from both sides of the road.

One attempt was made by a British friend of the Haganah to extricate the buses. Major Jack Churchill, of the Highland Light

Infantry, on his own initiative drove an open-fronted armored car to the scene, and was about to put a tow-line on one of the buses when his driver was killed by a bullet in the neck. Churchill pulled in the tow and drove out of the area but before doing so banged on one bus and shouted to the occupants to risk getting out and returning with him. He later reported they refused to do so.

By early afternoon the two buses were sieves. Only one man from each vehicle survived. Shalom Nissan, a university student, jumped when the Arabs began lobbing grenades at his stricken bus. Miraculously, he dodged the rain of fire and ran all the way to Mt. Scopus where he was to provide the first on-scene account of events.

In the other bus was a guard, Nathan Sandowsky, who told a ghastly story that has since been verified. Nathan said that from the initial fire the driver was wounded and lost control. The second driver was lightly wounded but froze from fear and could not function. Nathan reported:

> The fire grew ever stronger. I heard the Arabs approaching with wild singing. In our car Yitzhak Berger had a Mauser pistol with eight bullets which at first did not work. We transferred all the suitcases to the rear of the car and tried to keep the shutter [of the peephole] in place. Dr. Ben-David held the shutter with all his strength but finally was overcome by the heat and asked to be relieved.

The bus had three lookouts inside. One was Nathan. Another was Dr. Avraham Freiman, lecturer in Jewish Law, and a third was University employee Zev Mariasin.

> From the rear opening I saw that all the time the British army passed in large convoys. They continued on their way. We shouted "Help! We have wounded women and men!" But they did not stop. Armored cars of the police arrived and stood for a time without extending any help whatever and without even communicating with us. We were sure that at least they would not let the Arabs approach so close as to burn the vehicles.

From inside the buses could be heard clearly over and over again Arabs shouting, *Minshan Deir Yassin* ("For Deir Yassin"). Nathan reported that the arrival of Gilboa's armored car caused rejoicing in the bus. "We saw that our people were at last coming. But the Arabs derived courage from the fact that the police and army cars which passed did not raise a finger."

From the early hours on, bullets found their marks. Gas fumes began to seep in as the Arabs made ready to burn the bus. Molotov cocktails were being thrown. Some of the unhurt passengers tried to make a dash to safety. But the Arabs, only a few yards away, picked them off as they jumped out. As four men ran, a girl in the bus cried, "They are being killed." Nathan deliberated:

> I sat at the side of the opening of the bus with a scalpel—my only weapon. Fire started from the rear of the bus. There were cries, "We are burning alive." I dived. The blade of the scalpel broke. I ran the length of the road zig-zag. I passed the ambulance and approached an escort car waving the broken knife in my hand. I pounded on the door shouting, "I am one of you." The door opened. Inside all the men were dead or wounded.

It was now about 2:30 P.M. Inside Gilboa's armored car Sandowsky saw Safad-born David Bar-Ner with a grenade in his hand. The pin was out and primed to explode. Recalls Bar-Ner:

> When Sandowsky climbed in we were waiting for the final assault. It was now a tradition in the Haganah not to be caught alive. We had five dead. Gilboa was paralyzed by a head wound. I had three bullets in my arm. I piled up the six grenades left in the car and pulled the pin on one to blow us up if the Arabs tried to take us prisoner. We had plenty of ammunition left but there was no one left to fire it. Then Sandowsky appeared. His face was blackened from the fire in his bus. He grabbed the grenade from my hand and threw it outside where it went off. Then he took one of our two machine-guns and kept shooting short bursts. That kept the Arabs at bay since they knew we could still shoot back. He saved our lives, for soon after, the British picked us up.

One further feeble and futile attempt was made in the afternoon by the Haganah to try to save the convoy. Haganah Squad Sergeant Haim Kimron took an armored car to Sheikh Jarrah to tow out the vehicles. As Kimron entered the ambush he saw the buses burning. His vehicle stalled in a ditch. Almost immediately from the fire overhead he had two killed and three wounded.

> Hysterically, I ordered my driver to get the hell out of the ditch. He reversed and we went around to the right of the road, past the two armored cars, and beat it up to Mt. Scopus. My

tires were shot full of holes. When I reached Scopus I was so enraged, I ran to the top of one of the buildings and shot off my machine-gun in frustration and revenge at a nearby Arab village.

No one at this time knew what was happening in the white ambulance with the big red Magen David Adom. Its armor being the thickest of all the vehicles, this wagon was the safest place to be in that corridor of hell. Next to driver Zecharya Levitan sat Yassky. Behind him on the benches were Mrs. Yassky, six doctors, a nurse, and a wounded soldier. The position of the ambulance behind the two armored cars was such that it was a poor target for the Arabs and so absorbed the least punishment. Yassky, who sat by the driver because he had a revolver and could more easily use it, concerned himself with appraising the situation by looking through the tiny window in the vehicle.

"Everytime he opened the window," Yehuda Bromberg reported later, "a rain of shots was fired at him. At 2:00 P.M., Yassky informed us that everyone had been killed in the burning buses."

After the buses turned into pyres Yassky announced, "Now our time has come. No escape from our fate is left. We must bid one another farewell."

Yassky took leave of his wife and, Bromberg reported, thanked her for the happy life which they had lived. At 2:30 Yassky was wounded in the liver by a bullet that must have ricocheted through the ambulance's engine.

"I'm hit," he said, and then after a few minutes of continuous chatter, he whispered to Fanny, "Shalom, my beloved." He lost consciousness and was dead five minute later. There was nothing the six physicians and one nurse in the ambulance could do. Ironically, there was not even a first-aid kit in the vehicle.

Pediatrician Yehuda Mattot, who sat on a bench behind Yassky, recalls: "Fanny Yassky took off her blouse and with it I bandaged Yassky. Only an immediate blood transfusion and an operation could have saved him."

Fanny remained strong. Someone began to weep. Fanny asked, "Why do you cry? Soon we shall follow him."

Zecharya, the driver, suddenly got up, opened the door and jumped out. He was shot dead a few yards away.

Dermatologist Haim Cohen asked gynecologist Bruno Berkovitz to join him in an attempt to run for it. But Dr. Ullmann said firmly, "Cohen, we have survived this together from nine o'clock. You can wait another few hours."

Mattot, who missed sure death by changing at the last minute from a bus to the ambulance, tried his luck a second time.

> I thought that if I stayed it would be the end. My wife later thought I did it because I could not stand to be without a cigarette. I jumped into the ditch and began to crawl. The Arabs spotted me and began shooting. I got one bullet next to my spine. I kept going and got to Antonius House where the British troops welcomed me. Just opposite on the other side of the road were Arabs, apparently the leaders of the whole thing. The British took me in and bandaged me. They were apologetic. They said they were a small unit and they could not do anything. They had been asking for reinforcements but could not get any. I was not able to convince the British to do anything for the convoy.

Throughout the day pleas to intercede were directed to the British by the Jewish Agency, Haganah, Magnes, Davis, and others. The British authorities suggested a truce to both sides and waited. The few troops at Antonius House were consistently refused permission to use their heavy machine-gun and bazookas; a few bursts from these weapons could have smothered the Arab initiative. Monitoring by Hadassah volunteers followed the British radio conversations throughout the day. This exchange was noted at a critical point:

Forward British observer: "The buses are burning. Someone has put out a white flag. Request permission to intercede."

British headquarters: "Reinforcements are on the way. Keep everything steady."

But reinforcements, which were only a few minutes away, took seven hours to get to the site.

Lieutenant-General MacMillan returned to the site at 4:30 P.M. Incredibly, he admitted to Magnes by letter that he had been uninformed all day about events in Sheikh Jarrah. Wrote MacMillan:

> I was surprised . . . to find heavy firing in progress on the spot and my own car, which had been back to barracks and returned again to meet me, had been pierced by a bullet. On arrival

once more on the spot, I found that Brigadier Jones had got the matter in hand and had persuaded the Arabs to stop firing but had not been able to achieve this until after he had been forced to fire heavily upon them and kill fifteen.

At about 4:00 P.M. General Jones had given permission to open up with bazookas. Another army post fired off a few mortars. Then under a smokescreen, half-tracks were sent in to pick up the survivors. A British Intelligence captain, who had befriended the Jews, arrived under his own steam from military headquarters at the King David Hotel. Wounded Zizi Rahav was already in Antonius House. Asking Zizi what he could do to help, the captain acceded to a request to return to the scene to bring back the weapons and secret operational papers on the body of one of the men. The captain did just that.

The captain, now living in Israel, would never forget the scene.

> It was grotesque. People were standing over the body of Dr. Yassky, screaming and yelling, while a little farther back beside the two burned-out buses the dead were piled in heaps. The corpses were burning and it was at least twenty minutes after the shooting finally stopped that someone thought to douse them with water.

How many were killed and wounded in the convoy? No one will ever know. A marble memorial stands today near Nashashibi Bend with seventy-six names. A seventy-seventh inscription merely says "Unknown." So badly burned were the bodies from the buses that the remains were buried in a common grave in nearby Sanhedria. On April 16, Hadassah handed the Red Cross a list of thirty persons whose bodies were identified and a list of forty-seven "still unaccounted for." Sixteen were listed as hospitalized on Mt. Scopus, nine at Hadassah "A." That made 102 dead and wounded. Eight from Yassky's ambulance came through practically unscathed.

Only the night before the massacre, Rose Halprin and Bertha Schoolman flew home and heard the news on their arrival in New York. Judith Epstein and Rebecca Shulman, who remained in Tel Aviv, were having dinner at their hotel when a newspaperman came up to their table: "I have terrible news for you. Yassky was killed today."

Rebecca on her return told the board in New York, "I doubt whether we will be able to use Scopus again soon. I recommend that we start building somewhere else."

To Ethel Agron and Eli Davis the board cabled in May: "We dedicate ourselves to the task of maintaining services and rebuilding Hadassah."

The British reinforced Antonius House and warned both Jews and Arabs they could countenance no further military activity in Sheikh Jarrah. On April 25, the Haganah under a young Palmach officer named Yitzhak Rabin occupied Nashashibi House nevertheless. But next day he was shelled out by the British. The Israelis would not return for good until nineteen years later when, under Chief of Staff Yitzhak Rabin, they occupied all of the Arab sector of Jerusalem.

Shelling and sniping made life on Scopus impossible and the road impassable despite the British presence. Fresh food and water were near to vanishing point on the hill. Davis had to find a way to get the more than seven hundred people down. He contacted Major Jack Churchill. This is Davis' account:

> Major Churchill told me there was a slight chance of getting through to Mt. Scopus, because the Arabs saw the British meant business. He agreed to make the trip up to Scopus and invited me along. The Major took a Jeep and his driver. I sat while he stood in the Jeep twirling his stick. He looked as though he were on parade in London. Nothing happened as we went through Sheikh Jarrah. On Scopus we were embraced. We had shown it was possible to get through.

Davis decided on the spot to risk a major evacuation because of the low morale. Ben-Gurion had told Hadassah and university representatives several days before the disaster that the hill was to be held at all costs. But Ahron Brezinsky, who was acting as medical director of the hospital, reported to Davis, "You cannot hold a frontline with sick people who do not want to stay. The atmosphere here is of a refugee camp. With all the strategic importance of this place, we must get out with what we can."

Davis returned to town to organize the evacuation and to consult. A decision was taken to retain a fifty-bed hospital on Scopus and thus demonstrate that the hospital was not being abandoned.

Davis scrounged the impoverished city for fuel for the partial evacuation. So empty was the city that he was reduced to collecting gasoline from private homes, institutions, friends—bottle by bottle. Four convoys made it. The last on May 5 was the biggest because Churchill pleaded with Davis, "I've exceeded my orders. I am in trouble with my superiors." Brought into town were 200 patients, 100 student nurses, and 300 staff members, as well as 600 tons of equipment and supplies. Not a shot was fired. Left behind were 150 persons, including 8 student nurses who ran the kitchen, and 40 patients. In the university buildings were another 150 men.

Now in charge of Hadassah's destiny were Davis and Ethel Agron, as chairwoman of the council. Magnes, broken and sick, shattered by British nonchalance over the convoy ("This happened not out in the desert but in plain sight of Jerusalem," he wrote indignantly to General MacMillan), left Jerusalem for the United States where he died in October, 1948.

On May 6, Haim Halevy, who administered the hospital, reported, "The hospital no longer exists for all practical purposes." Water and flour were sufficient for two weeks, power was rationed to only four hours daily and "soon there won't be refrigeration." Compounding the problem were intelligence reports that King Abdullah was about to shell Scopus preparatory to assaulting it.

By the beginning of May, Davis and the Hadassah Council in Jerusalem had managed to set up reasonably good facilities in Hadassah "A" and, two blocks down the street in St. Joseph's Convent, now known as Hadassah "B," but the accommodations were hardly luxurious. St. Joseph's, leased on April 29, had been a school for six hundred Arab girls, run by French nuns. After shells hit the converted hospital, the top floor was evacuated and patients were removed to the dank basements where there was neither water nor electricity. Shelves that stored potatoes were cleaned and became emergency beds. Nurses knelt on the stone floor to change bandages, and physicians sat on the floor to examine patients. Together with "A" and "B," the Straus Health Center and the Hasolel Street Clinic, Hadassah improvised three hundred beds, or nearly as many as it had on Scopus. Heroic volunteer work temporarily made up the difference. Nurse Madeline Lewin-Epstein, who had come with AZMU in 1918, turned her large apartment into a twenty-bed hospital, often braved snipers' bullets and mortars to pick up the wounded in the streets and pull them into her home. Hers was the first military hospital in Jerusalem, and many of her patients were wounded underground soldiers who could go nowhere else. British police officials would be sitting in a chair in the dental clinic of her popular husband, Sam Lewin-Epstein, while in the living room only a few yards away from them were the men they were hunting.

At the height of all Hadassah's problems, the Old City of Jerusalem fell to the Arabs on May 28. Hadassah had staffed the hospital in the Old City's Jewish Quarter since early in the fighting. But the Jews' position had been hopeless against overwhelming numbers of Arabs. They fought until they were too few, too starved, too fatigued to go on. Avraham Laufer, one of the surgeons who was sent into the Jewish Quarter, reported a week before the surrender that the top floors of the hospital had been shelled and seventy patients had to share mattresses and wooden benches in a synagogue and in basements.

Laufer told of one young soldier who had shrapnel in an eye but refused to wait fifteen minutes for an operation to remove it because the situation at his post was desperate. "An hour later they carried him back. His handsome face was blown away by a shell."

Thirteen hundred aged women and children were evacuated to the Jewish side of the city, while the men were taken to a prison camp in the Jordanian desert. Three among the POW's were Hadassah physicians: Egon Rys, Eli Peiser, and Laufer. Two weeks later, while Rys was in a Trans-Jordanian prison camp, his wife, Hava, a Hadassah nurse, was killed in the last pre-truce shelling of the city.

The refugees from the Old City were housed in the abandoned houses of the Katamon Quarter, a large neighborhood of Arab villas that was conquered in bloody fighting by the Haganah. There, Jerusalem's meager food supplies were tightly rationed by Hadassah volunteers, who themselves were now on starvation diets. Under the supervision of Sara Bavli, head of Hadassah Nutrition, these 1,300 and 20,000 others were having frugal daily meals in what was known as a "battle of the calories."

In the turbulence of siege, Friday, May 14, 1948, was no more than just another day of hunger and death in Jerusalem. No street celebrations marked David Ben-Gurion's proclamation in the Tel

Aviv Museum of the State of Israel. Few knew about it until the following day, for few in the city had electricity, and news had to be passed by word of mouth. *The Palestine Post* appeared with its headline "STATE OF ISRAEL BORN" only on Sunday, May 16.

The highway to Tel Aviv had been cut again by the Arab armies. Daily rations were down to slow starvation level. The Holy City's only link with the outside world was a small one-engined plane that landed under fire in the Valley of the Cross. While great advances were being made in the rest of the country, Jerusalem at the end of May appeared to be doomed. The last British had left Jerusalem on May 14—except for those officers who remained behind to command Abdullah's Arab Legion. Residents of the city knew they were in command because the merciless shelling would stop precisely at 4:00 P.M. daily so that the British officers could enjoy their tea. It was during that hour that most Israelis dared go outside for their rations. Scopus was no exception to the bombardment. The buildings suffered badly, but casualties were few because the underground tunnel between the nursing school and the hospital served as a perfect shelter.

Born under fire was a new Hadassah service for Israel—orthopedic surgery. One of its pioneers was British-born Myer Makin, who had been a medical officer with the troops when they landed on the Normandy shore in 1944 during the Allied invasion of Nazi Europe. Soon after demobilization in 1946, he joined Hadassah as a surgeon. Battle casualties were nothing new to him:

> We worked twenty-four hours on and twenty-four hours off. The main trouble was getting to work through the shelling. I would borrow my neighbor's bicycle and dash like hell through the streets. The shelling of Jerusalem was much worse than any I had gone through in France. In France we were at the front for three or four days and then were taken by for a week's rest. Here it went on constantly. No let up.

In mid-April, the U.N. Security Council had authorized the consuls general of the United States, France, and Belgium to try to arrange a truce in Jerusalem after a British effort was rejected by the Mufti. At the same time American Consul-General Thomas Wasson, the most congenial and effective diplomat in the city, worked to secure Mt. Scopus from attack, but at the end of the month he was killed by Arab fire near his consulate. Hadassah doctors fought twelve hours in vain to save his life.

Immediately after May 15, the British established a consulate in Jerusalem and appointed two consuls to handle Arab and Israeli affairs. Consul John Guy Tempest Sheringham applied himself to the Scopus problem and on May 31 in a phone conversation with Hebrew University Administrator Senator he advised Israel to surrender Scopus. Senator left a record of the talk:

> Sheringham: "The best way to safeguard the University and Hadassah buildings would be to accept King Abdullah's offer to put them under the protection of the Arab Legion."
>
> Senator: "The best way it seems to me would be to advise King Abdullah not to shell the University and Hadassah."
>
> Sheringham: "Your military situation is not very bright. You have not succeeded in driving the Arabs out of Jerusalem."
>
> Senator: "The responsibility for the Legion's acts against the University and Hadassah lay with the British Government."

In Washington, innumerable pleas were made to every imaginable source to help relieve Scopus. The State Department was helpful in one respect: Secretary of State George Marshall agreed that cables from the National Board be relayed through the consulate in Jerusalem to Davis and Ethel Agron.

In the end an agreement was worked out by all parties whereby the United Nations would assume control of Scopus over which it would fly its flag and provide observers to maintain the area as a demilitarized zone. Eighty-four Jewish police would guard installations at Hadassah and the Hebrew University, while forty Arabs would guard Arab property on Scopus. The United Nations agreed to supply and exchange the Jewish police in regular fortnightly convoys through the Arab Sheikh Jarrah Quarter. Hadassah and the university were evacuated on July 6 and demilitarization was completed on July 7, when the first police, who in fact were Israeli soldiers in police uniform, went up.

Out of tragedy and fortitude had come triumph. While the price—an entire medical center and university—had been high, Mt. Scopus had not fallen into Arab hands, and it would serve as a base for Israeli forces to win the entire city in 1967. On balance, Scopus was the pawn Hadassah sacrificed to save the queen.

Jewish Jerusalem was rescued at the eleventh hour by a month-long truce that went into effect on June 11. In another twenty-four hours not another scrap of food would have been available. Battered and bloody, the city stood—most of it in Israeli hands. Looking back, Davis hardly knew how he had made it. Tetanus antitoxin was near the vanishing point and could no longer be given routinely; two wounded died for lack of the drug. X-ray film was short; morphium low; hypodermic needles, alcohol, adhesive plaster, and catgut silk practically gone. "We were forced to keep one eye on stocks and one eye on the patient," Davis reported. He pleaded for help from the Red Cross but aid first came dramatically from New York where the National Board was trying frantically to help.

Hadassah's Margaret Doniger set up blood plasma collecting centers on America's east and west coasts. But a more immediate act of first aid was to organize an airlift of 15,675 pounds of medicines and supplies under the direction of Purchasing Committee Chairman Miriam Handler. The supplies were only a drop compared to the more than two million pounds of supplies sent by Hadassah that year, but these arrived at a critical time.

On the plane was Lola Kramarsky, the first European-born member who was later to be elected Hadassah president (1960). Lola and Siegfried Kramarsky, both committed Zionists and close friends of the Weizmanns', arrived in the United States in 1940 as refugees from Hitler's Europe. Lola had been active in the Youth Aliyah movement, and in 1935 was present with Henrietta Szold as she greeted the first group of Youth Aliyah children to reach Palestine. With Lola on the plane was Jeanette Leibel Lourie, Hadassah's meticulous executive director. It was now the beginning of July, 1948, and the one-month truce was about to end. The chartered craft landed in Amsterdam where the supplies had to be reloaded on to a C-54 cargo plane. Israel had no airfield that at that time could take a larger craft. After long and harrowing hours in flight during which the pilot of the plane had to radio several times for landing instructions, Lola and Jeanette and the supplies bumped down at Ein Shemer, south of Haifa. The date appropriately was July 4. Forty Israeli soldiers rushed the craft and began unloading. The scene was one of great relief and hilarity. Arthur Lourie, a South African-born diplomat, ran out in underwear to greet his wife; he had been bathing when he heard the plane land. Next day, the convoy of trucks arrived in Jerusalem, only four days before the resumption of war.

The next phase of the fighting lasted only ten days but it was sufficient for the Army of Israel, resupplied during the thirty-day truce, to take the initiative. Jerusalem was no longer in danger although it was again being continuously shelled. Twenty-four hours before the war was renewed on July 9, Davis had completed a fully equipped underground operating theater in St. Joseph's Convent—the first of its kind in the country. Forty-six direct hits were suffered by St. Joseph's. On the third day Dr. Shlomo Gorfunkel, a Hadassah X-ray specialist who had organized the Vilna Ghetto uprising and served with the partisans in the Vilna forests, was killed in the streets of Jerusalem.

The fighting finally ended in Jerusalem on July 19, although sniping and occasional shelling would continue for several years. From the beginning of the shooting in December to July 19, Hadassah had treated most of the Jewish casualties in the city—a total of 3,550.

In Jerusalem at the time was United Nations peace mediator Count Folke Bernadotte. As he offered compromise solutions—among them a considerable withdrawal by Israeli forces—he was cut down in Jerusalem on September 17 by the assassins' bullets of an extreme faction of the old Stern Group. On arrival at Hadassah there was no hope for his life. The provisional government of Israel under David Ben-Gurion abhorred the act. Three days after Bernadotte's assassination, the Mufti proclaimed a Palestine Arab state—one he could have had less than a year earlier without bloodshed—but now it was too late. King Abdullah outfoxed him and in October got five thousand notables to agree to his being sovereign over all Arab Palestine. In another year he would annex the West Bank and East Jerusalem to his newly named Kingdom of Jordan.

But the war was still not over. In mid-October, Israeli forces, now an organized army, moved south to take a Bedouin village called Beersheba. Hadassah would soon follow the troops to open a hospital there—the first in the Negev—as a memorial to Haim Yassky. And at October's end, the Israelis consolidated gains in Galilee.

The final campaign of Israel's War of Independence occurred as the year ended. Forces moved deep into the Negev and Sinai, and on January 19, 1949, the shooting war came to an ironic end. Hours before a ceasefire went into effect five British-piloted Spitfires flew from Egypt to determine whether the Israelis had, as agreed, withdrawn from Sinai. Mistaking the planes for Egyptians, the Israelis brought four of them down in air-to-air combat and one by ground fire. The word was flashed around the world, and for a few days it seemed as though the triumphant Israelis might have to fight the British. President Truman and others including friendly British leaders scolded the Royal Air Force for having stuck its nose where it did not belong and the crisis subsided. In Rehovot, home of Chaim Weizmann, the soon-to-be president informed a British friend and member of Parliament, Richard Crossman, of the incident. Crossman is said to have replied, "Don't worry. This means that you are now a state. Britain will recognize you within the month." On January 30, a chastised and humiliated British Foreign Secretary Bevin accorded de facto recognition to the State of Israel.

Succeeding Count Bernadotte, American mediator Ralph Bunche negotiated armistice agreements with Egypt, Lebanon, Jordan, and Syria in the months of February, March, April, and July. Iraq refused and removed its troops from the West Bank. While the armistice lines would be the frontiers of Israel for the next nineteen years, the agreements were flimsy and did not, as hoped, lead to peace pacts. But they were a measure of the state's permanence, and no one who had gone through the War of Independence in Israel now doubted that the incubating state would live.

Hadassah had been a midwife to the state all through its difficult birth, and in recognition of that service, Prime Minister David Ben-Gurion, after having been brought to office by the first elections on January 25, 1949, said:

> The achievements of Hadassah in Zionism generally; its invaluable contribution to our war of liberation and independence; the work of its people here under fire on Mt. Scopus and on the fronts, will live in the history of our nation forever.

16.

The Web and the Woof

ISRAEL, the state of the Jews, appeared so abruptly that it took the breath out of the world. Zionists and most other Jews could not immediately rationalize the event and for years thereafter would speak of the state in metaphysical terms—as the miraculous rebirth of the Jewish commonwealth or as the advent of the Messianic Age. Even some Christians greeted Israel as prophecy fulfilled and prepared for the coming of the Messiah.

Zionists could therefore be forgiven for not having realized that their political mission had now terminated and that their further participation on that level had diminished. Worse, they were confounded by abuse emanating from Israel. Angry that Zionist leaders did not rush to settle in Israel, Prime Minister Ben-Gurion would belittle those who remained abroad, referring to them merely as "friends of Israel." Great names in the movement gave up their roles like actors on closing night. The noble Chaim Weizmann was elected first president, a post that had no political power, and in 1952, almost thirty-five years to the day after the issuance of the Balfour Declaration, he died. Others like Abba Hillel Silver, who waited in Cleveland for a summons from Jerusalem to join the cabinet; Stephen Wise, who died within a year of statehood, and Louis Lipsky, the once powerful head of the Zionist Organization of America, would play no part in the political affairs of the state for which they had so valiantly fought.

To all this, Hadassah was an exception—and for good reason.

Hadassah had been on the scene from the beginning. Like a sapling wintering in the snow, it had weathered well in the Middle East's wars and plagues. Henrietta Szold said in 1929, "Hadassah entered into the fabric of Palestinian life, into its web and woof." While other Zionist groups decreased in size or importance after 1948, Hadassah, because of its deep roots in the Land of Israel, would flourish. By the end of Israel's first quarter of a century, the membership of Hadassah would number 325,000, organized in 692 chapters in all fifty states and Puerto Rico.

None of this was yet evident on a searing August morning in 1948 when three board members—President Rose Halprin, Rebecca Shulman, and Anna Tulin—met in Jerusalem with the Hadassah council and the hospital administration to map a new course for the organization's work in Israel. The task was not easy since Israel itself, still taking form in the crucible of war, was embarked on an uncharted and unpredictable future.

For five days under the chairmanship of Ethel Agron, who headed Hadassah's council in Israel, they tried to plan for an unpredictable future. Ethel posed some of the alternatives:

> Will we return to Scopus? Should Hadassah take over the health department of Jerusalem if the city is to be internationalized or should it now limit its services to preventive services? Should Hadassah expand outside Jerusalem? Does the Medical School have an absolute priority?

With the political destiny of the state unsure, with masses of poor, ill, uneducated immigrants crowding into the country, Hadassah once again faced an old problem that repeatedly nagged Henrietta Szold—everything had to be done at once.

Some of the leaders meeting in Jerusalem insisted that Hadassah should concentrate on immigrant care. But Eli Davis spoke up against Hadassah's providing across-the-board care for newcomers. That was now the Israeli government's task. Hadassah should do only what it knew best—provide service in specialized fields.

"Hadassah's duty is to administer the medical services for immigrants," retorted Rose Halprin.

"Whatever we do we must not desert Jerusalem," said Rebecca Shulman.

A compromise solution came from Davis. "The best way of becoming a factor in Jerusalem and in the state is through the·

medical school. The medical school must get priority." And so it did.

The concept of a school of medicine in Palestine is almost as old as political Zionism itself. In 1913, the Zionist Congress accepted "as a matter of urgency" the establishment of a medical faculty at the projected Hebrew University. After World War I, the American Jewish Physicians Committee was organized to raise funds for the school. In the 1920's, a parasitology department under British-born Saul Adler and other medical research facilities opened at the university, but no serious thought could be entertained until Hadassah built the hospital center on Mt. Scopus. Preparing for that moment, a post-graduate teaching and research center for doctors developed and served physicians attached to the Allied armies during World War II. Clinical departments formed and the university granted status to heads of Hadassah departments. In December, 1945, a $4 million building fund took shape, and as the exhausted world laid down its arms, the university and Hadassah finally looked forward to accepting the first students in 1947 or 1948. But these were crisis years. The new generation of physicians would wear uniforms of khaki rather than white.

Soon after World War II Director Haim Yassky, knowing that a successful school depended on a corps of bright young physicians, initiated a fellowship program. He chose his best and sent them to the finest medical institutions in the United States. The first was Polish-born neurosurgeon Aharon Beller: he left on a troopship in April, 1946, and returned to Jerusalem two years later because the country was without a neurosurgeon.

One of America's most prominent physicians, Johns Hopkins' Jonas Friedenwald, visited Jerusalem to size up the needs. In March, 1946, he reported to Hadassah:

> Virtually the whole of European medicine has been wiped out. Work in Switzerland and the recovery of medical schools in Holland and Denmark are tiny oases in the desert. In short, there is no first class medical center east of London. Jerusalem is the obvious place. On Mt. Scopus there are enthusiasm, devotion and scientific maturity.

Friedenwald was only one of a few score physicians and Hadassah women who labored to create the school. In the United States, Hadassah took counsel from its Medical Reference Board headed by Dr. E. M. Bluestone, who had gathered together some of the best names in American medicine: Duke University's William Perlzweig, the U.S. Public Health Service's Harry Eagle and Henry Makover, educator and author Abraham Flexner, Columbia's Israel Wechsler, Harvard's Charles Wilinsky, and Johns Hopkins' Abel Wolman. In Israel, there were Bernhard Zondek, Arieh Dostrovsky, Leonid Doljansky, Moshe Ben-David, Saul Adler, Arieh Feigenbaum. But above all there was Haim Yassky, of whom Eli Davis would say, "He had the vision of a great modern healing-teaching center. For that he worked always. Before his death he had been working on the blueprints of the school. It was the most natural thing in the world, when we had come down from Scopus, to carry on with the healing-teaching hospital idea."

But there was also one other who was only a distant relative of the Hadassah family. He was the first surgeon-general of the Israel Defense Forces; his name was Haim Sheba and he served as a catalyst.

As the head of the Haganah medical services in January, 1948, Sheba wrote to all Palestinian Jewish students studying medicine abroad to return home. About fifty answered the call and immediately went into uniform. They were joined by medical students from Russia, Lithuania, and Rumania who left their schools and emigrated to Israel. Recalled Sheba:

> I suggested that we ask Hadassah not to wait with the medical school until they could begin with the first year but take the boys and girls who had already completed three years, give them a refresher course and proceed with the fourth year. Those who did not respond to the call to return would have to serve an extra year in uniform before they could receive their licenses so as not to give them an unfair advantage.

On September 10, 1948, Sheba formalized his suggestion in writing to Medical Director Davis.

"I felt when I wrote that letter," Sheba recalled later, "we would not only be creating a medical school but we would also be saving Hadassah from losing some of its most valuable senior members who might not have had the stamina to remain in Jerusalem while the city was under fire. A few of them had made it clear that they could no longer continue after five months of continual siege."

Davis replied with a qualified approval saying that the students could begin in April, 1949. But the students did not want to wait that long. Taking matters into their own hands, they went to Jerusalem to protest. They started a rumor that the army was about to begin a medical school since Hadassah and the university were dragging their feet. Sheba himself gave some credence to the rumor by forming a medical school preparatory unit in the army hospital in Jerusalem. He had ordered four senior officers to begin screening prospective students, but he had no intention of opening a school. The result was that Hadassah and university representatives quickly cooperated. One hundred and twenty candidates passed before the committee, a third were accepted, and by November, 1948, a three-month preparatory course began. Sheba, in the meantime had come a-cropper with the army. The Ministry of Defense only learned much later that Sheba, at his own initiative, had excused soldiers from regular duties to start studies. Not surprisingly, Sheba was soon in civilian clothes. He organized Israel's Ministry of Health, set the foundations of the state's health services, and co-opted three Hadassah senior administrators to assist him.

In February, 1949, studies started informally. The scene for the official opening of the school, on May 17, 1949—the holiday of Lag b'Omer in the Hebrew calendar—was foreboding. Claps of thunder and occasional streaks of lightning in an overcast sky interrupted the proceedings. Only a few hundred yards away, across the coils of barbed wire that delineated the divided city, King Abdullah's Arab Legion shot off a few rounds at the thick-walled, shell-pocked building which a year earlier served as the base for attacks against Arab positions. In one respect this was a homecoming. Three decades previously the building had been the Hotel de France—Hadassah's first official home in Jerusalem. In the municipal garden before the school sat two thousand guests. The forty-four members of the first class were all in army uniform. David Ben-Gurion was the principal speaker, and he spoke of a far-off day when the nation would be at peace. No medical school ever had an inauguration quite like it. At the end of 1949 a second class of sixty-three was formed with many Zionist medical students from Bulgaria, who needed only one year to receive their degrees. Thus, in premises on a hostile border, with students in military dress using texts in English, Polish, Russian, and Bulgarian and hearing lectures in Hebrew, did the medical school begin.

While most of the professors were European-trained, the influence of American medicine was strong because of the Hadassah Medical Reference Board. Polish-born Moshe Prywes, who spent five years as a prisoner-of-war in a Russian concentration camp in Siberia before emigrating to Israel, and served as associate dean of the school until 1965, considered the American-European synthesis beneficial:

> The Americans brought a new informal approach that gave the students more freedom and produced better teamwork. Our curriculum was European—a six-year course which includes premedical sciences—but we applied the American system of preselection. We did not, as did the Europeans, allow everyone to enter and then permit only the best to continue.

One innovation was wholly Israeli. The first graduating class on May 13, 1952, took the Oath of the Hebrew Physician. It was written for the occasion by neurologist Lipmann Halpern, the school's fifth dean. Addressed as "New Men of Medicine in Israel," the graduates were blessed "to enhance the heritage of medicine in Israel." While the best of the traditional Hippocratic oath was retained, the Greek gods played no part in the Israeli doctor's obligation to his patients and to his profession.

With the graduation of the first class in 1952, undergraduate studies began, and since then the medical school has provided the State of Israel with 1,400 physicians.

Says dermatologist Arieh Dostrovsky, first dean of the medical school, "At the beginning we felt that the medical school could only have been established by Hadassah in Israel, for it was the only hospital that had a standard of any significance."

The logical consequence of a functioning medical school was the appearance soon thereafter of a school of dentistry. Veteran dental surgeon Samuel Lewin-Epstein, who arrived with the American Medical Zionist Unit, urged the creation of a school in the early 1930's. Finding little interest, he contacted professional fraternities in the United States for support. His determination won not only the backing of Alpha Omega but Hadassah's as well. The first class of fifteen students was opened in 1953. Two years later the faculty opened a clinic in the crowded Straus Health Center where Hadassah ran a dental service for Jerusalem's school children. It was then that Hadassah gave the school its own home and equipment and joined hands with the Hebrew University to provide budget for staffs and teaching facilities. Later on, Alpha Omega would top its original contributions with a fund of $1 million for a permanent site in the new medical center complex at Ein Karem.

In that same year of 1953, an old dream of Akiva Kosviner came true. Akiva was born in Galilee in 1892, studied pharmacology in Beirut and after practicing briefly in Egypt, settled down in the Rothschild Hospital in Safad as pharmacist. When his Egyptian employer asked him why he was returning to "that desert" in Palestine, Kosviner replied, "Even though I will be making only half the salary, I feel I must contribute something of myself to that desert now."

During World War I, Kosviner spent much of his service at a small Turkish army hospital in a death hole called Tabuk in northern Saudi Arabia. Thankful to be back in Palestine after the war, Kosviner moved his family to Jerusalem and opened a pharmacy, the first in the city outside the ancient walls. Soon, Kosviner became Hadassah's chief pharmacist and began teaching at the nursing school. But always he dreamed of a school of pharmacology. The school finally began in 1953 with Kosviner as executive secretary. Strictly speaking it was not the first. Kosviner himself had rented a room in a hotel in the early 1920's and there gave a one-year course to Jews, Arabs, and Christians.

Hadassah served as teacher and healer not only in Israel but also in underdeveloped lands far beyond, providing experts in many fields for the nation's foreign-aid program. Two of the most successful were in the fields of eye care and mental health. In 1959, much of black Africa had specialists in neither, and many natives had only witch doctors to resort to. Hadassah's chief opthalmologist, Scottish-born Isaac Chesar Michaelson, toured Africa's oldest republic, Liberia, and some of the newer ones. In the early 1960's, Michaelson sent twenty-five eye doctors to Africa to set up hospitals in urban areas and to organize clinics in the bush.

On October, 1961, Hadassah psychiatrist Dan Hertz arrived in Monrovia to direct the black continent's first modern psychiatric hospital and lived three years in Africa introducing therapeutic methods in four countries. For his work in mental health the Liberian president awarded Hertz the Star of Africa.

The medical school's associate dean, Moshe Prywes, traveled

widely advising on teaching programs—to Guatemala in 1959, to Singapore, Ceylon, and India in 1960, to Argentina in 1961, to Ghana in 1964. Between 1960 and 1964 the medical school brought French and English-speaking Africans to study; seventy-three of them were graduated as physicians in Israel's capital. They returned to their home countries to teach other physicians and with them these Jerusalem alumni took a fluency in the Hebrew language which they used to communicate with each other. Few medical schools have had such an exotic alumni as those of the Jerusalem medical school.

Dentistry's first dean, Ino Sciaky, was called to the island republic of Malagasay in 1964, and later to Senegal and Congo (Brazzaville), to teach his profession. His successor, Jacob Lewin-Epstein, would make numerous visits to Iran.

One unplanned visit of a Hadassah physician to Africa had an immediate political reward. In October, 1961, heart specialist Moshe Rachmilewitz was on his way home from South Africa when his plane made an unscheduled stop at Addis Ababa. Israel's consul was there waiting for him and rushed the doctor to the palace of Emperor Haile Selassie, Lion of Judah, where the empress lay ill. She was being treated by Jordanian and Yugoslavian doctors but the medical complications were difficult. After Rachmilewitz put the empress on the road to recovery, he was given a formal dinner at the palace. Rachmilewitz noted:

> The Emperor emphasized that the Jews and his people were related. On the floor I noticed a huge carpet with a large Magen David. We talked about many things, including politics, and after an hour's conversation he said to me, "I want to tell you something that will please you. Your country was not recognized *de jure* by us. You are leaving tomorrow. On your way to Israel, recognition by Ethiopia of Israel will be announced—this will be in appreciation of the service you gave my wife."

At home there were tens of thousands of disadvantaged and culturally deprived to care for. The immigrants brought with them their poverty and their sicknesses, their superstitions and their illiteracy. First they came from the Cyprus camps and from the displaced persons camps in Europe. Then from Poland and Rumania. After that they came from Yemen on the wings of chartered eagles and from Iraq in an airlift named "Operation Ezra and Nehemia"—800,000 in all by the end of 1952.

Strict rationing went into effect throughout the country. So poor was the nation that ships loaded with food and goods went straight from the docks to empty market stalls and shop counters. *Tzena* was the byword—"austerity." Hadassah worried about getting large amounts of emergency staples into the larders of the poorest of the poor; it provided healing to the sickest of the sick immigrant children; it offered teen-agers an opportunity to take up a dignified vocation. It even arranged large loans for the government. In the first years after independence, Israelis were unashamedly and painfully hungry. In Washington, Hadassah representative Denise Tourover was put to work to get food from government warehouses to the Israeli housewife. By virtue of its membership on the President's Advisory Committee on Voluntary Foreign Aid, Hadassah had the right to receive government surplus foods for free distribution. Immediately available at the time, Denise learned, were tons of potatoes stored at Presque Isle, Maine. The Israeli embassy in Washington said that it would gladly take them provided they were fumigated against the red potato bug. Hadassah fumigated them and sent shipload after shipload to Haifa harbor. Meat followed. In 1953, Hadassah undertook Operation Reindeer —a one-time project that provided $12 million of kosher meat, dried fruits, and staples. They were placed into bags inscribed with American and Hadassah insignia and distributed free. The U.S. government sent the rations as a Christmas gift. Among the recipients were both Israeli Arabs and Jews. The project was something to ponder: an American Christmas gift handed out by a Zionist organization to Palestinian Arabs.

Butter followed meat, but here there was a major slip. The Israeli government understood that it could sell the butter on the free market, but in fact the sales were a technical violation of the American law. One diplomat at the American embassy in Tel Aviv acknowledged later, "There had been some sort of agreement [with the Israel government to sell the butter]." Whatever the case, visiting Congresswoman Frances Bolton noted that butter was fetching high prices in grocery stores and protested loudly when she returned home. Denise Tourover was called before the Foreign Aid Committee to explain. Fortunately, Denise was able to report that she had already mentioned the sales to the American embassy in Tel Aviv. The statement was accepted and Hadassah was off the hook. But long negotiations between the two governments followed and finally, after demanding $6 million, the United States accepted $800,000 as compensation. The butter crisis was over and surplus foods continued to arrive. In the first twenty-five years of the program—now under the direction in Jerusalem of Rhoda Cohen—about $30 million in foodstuffs have passed through Hadassah's hands to hospitals and welfare institutions.

No less a problem for Israel was the lack of shelter. The government was determined that no one would sleep on beaches under the open skies as immigrants did in the mid-1930's. The answer, provided by Jewish Agency official Levi Eshkol, was to set up transit camps. By the end of 1952, one-quarter of a million persons were living in tent and shanty towns up and down the country. One of the largest and in winter muddiest was set up east of Tel Aviv at Rosh Ha-ayin for the Yemenite immigrants. It was there in 1950 that Hadassah pediatricians Yehuda Mattot and Zvi Shamir headed a children's hospital, set up in an abandoned army camp. Shamir reported:

> We were dealing with terribly ill children. Almost everyone who came to the hospital suffered badly from malnutrition and acute intestinal infection. These people had no natural immunity. On the way from Yemen to Aden they contracted a severe type of malaria. The youngsters needed care twenty-four hours a day. At the beginning the staff was enthusiastic; they were accustomed to dealing with sick children. But these were more dead than alive and after making the round each evening we found many dead in their beds. They died like flies. They had reached the point of no return. We soon became depressed.

Routine treatment of children in such conditions was to give large quantities of intravenous fluids. But the doctors quickly came to realize from post-mortem examinations that these children were so exhausted and malnourished, their bodies could not absorb large amounts of nourishing fluids. Their enervated, overtaxed hearts simply gave out. The amounts of fluids were accordingly reduced and with the aid of antibiotics, the death rate plummeted from 50 to 5 per cent. Other problems arose. Reported Mattot:

We could not keep them long in hospital because of the large numbers and we grudgingly sent them back to their huts where there was insufficient food and horrible living conditions. We tried distributing food to the families for the children but we soon learned that the fathers were taking it all. We set up a feeding center so the kids could have at least one cooked meal a day. Then we found that the children had strict orders to throw the food over the fence for their fathers. We called in the police to stop it, but this started riots.

Accommodations for the medical staffs were very bad. Shamir recalled:

The rats from a nearby stream crawled over us at night. We started a new sport—trying to kill them with shoes and brooms. The summers were unbearable. The heat and the lack of proper water facilities made work impossible. Diapers had to be washed by hand. Nurses covered the huts with sheets and poured water over them in an attempt to cool the huts which were steaming ovens.

Hadassah staffed the hospital for two years. Then, the state's health service was sufficiently organized to move in.

Talpiot camp, on the other side of the railroad tracks in southern Jerusalem, was even larger than Rosh Ha-ayin. Ten thousand would crowd into the wooded area. There, Hadassah was to do a job it knew well from start to finish—mother and child care. It was in Talpiot that an energetic young Jerusalem-born physician, Kalman Mann, medical deputy to Eli Davis, spoke up for a different approach to medicine. He said,

We usually emphasize disease in our hospital but as a medical organization we should emphasize health. Because we cater to disease, the emphasis is on diagnosis and treatment. It should be on prevention and promotion of health. Most of the illnesses we meet are really emotional and social—particularly among immigrant communities.

Mann urged the creation of a community health center to monitor all the families in the neighborhood. The family, not the individual, was to be considered the unit of care and all problems —not only medical—would come under the trained staffs in the center. Thus began, in 1953, in Jerusalem's immigrant suburb of

Kiryat Yovel, a unique experiment in social medicine. A five-year study carried out by Mann and the center's South African-born director, Jack Medalie, would show that the immigrant community —representing newcomers from thirty countries—had achieved one of the lowest mortality rates in the country.

Other community health centers developed under Hadassah's planning. The community idea worked to such an extent that it spread to Arab communities and even to South America.

The newcomers only needed training and direction to become productive. Because Hadassah faced the problem of vocational education nearly two decades earlier it was ready for that task, too. In the early 1930's Henrietta Szold worried much over the problem of wayward Jewish children who were sent by the British courts to dubious institutions housing delinquents of all communities. Her attitude was that delinquent Jewish children should be cared for in Jewish homes. She was especially vexed about young Jewish prostitutes and the fact that many Eastern girls became child brides or servants. In 1940, she received $25,000 as an eightieth birthday gift from Hadassah. With it she established the highly-successful home for disturbed, delinquent girls at Ein Vered, east of Tel Aviv. In her search for the right kind of institution, she also came upon the idea of training girls for vocations as preventive therapy.

On one of her Youth Aliyah trips to Haifa she had met a robust, energetic home economics school principal named Helen Kittner. At the time Henrietta felt that Youth Aliyah children need not be sent only to farms but could also be integrated into urban life providing they had a vocation. After consulting the Hadassah council's first vocational education chairman, Rose Viteles, Henrietta dispatched a fifteen-page memo to the National Board suggesting the establishment of a vocational girls' school in Jerusalem. By coincidence the board was then considering a memorial project for Henrietta's closest friend, Alice Seligsberg. The board accepted the idea, and Henrietta asked Helen Kittner to head the school. The official opening took place in two converted wards of the old Rothschild Hospital on October 14, 1942, the day that Hadassah met in national convention in New York City.

In 1944, the hospital compound also housed not only the Seligsberg School but workshops for one hundred and sixty boys and girls under the direction of an unsung pioneer of progressive education in Jerusalem, Deborah Kallen, and a new vocational center named for Justice Brandeis. But within eight years, Helen Kittner had taken over the entire building. The workshops were moved and Miss Kallen was retired.

Helen Kittner, who was skilled at knitting stockings for her family at the age of four, was often ahead of her time in later life, too. In 1949, when Jerusalem had no tourist trade, she opened a school to train hotel personnel. But hotels in the capital in the early 1950's were closing, and the school had to be transferred in 1956 to the government. Likewise, in 1949, when the country could not feed its burgeoning population properly, much less dress them in haute couture, Helen started a fashion school. It was discontinued after the graduation of the first class. Nevertheless, Seligsberg School was responsible for highly successful fashion shows that Hadassah sent to the United States to raise funds.

The Alice Seligsberg School outgrew its converted wards and sixteen years later had a $1 million, five-story edifice. In its first twenty-five years the school graduated 2,200 girls. Henrietta Szold had said, "I see the school as a big school with every girl in a blue dress and every girl in a white apron . . . bringing honor to an apron." Helen Kittner fulfilled Henrietta's wish.

In 1944, three teen-age boys were taken into a hut in the Rothschild Hospital compound under Hadassah's sponsorship and taught precision mechanics by German-born, Czech-trained Tunia Gladstein. Within three years the Brandeis Training Center's fifteen students and their teachers were turning out weapons and ammunition for the Haganah. They produced heads for the Haganah's secret weapon—a heavy, noisy mortar called the Davidka. They made hand grenades and mechanisms to set off mines. During the fighting early in 1948, Arab agents learned that Brandeis was the center of an arms workshop and directed shells against it from positions in the Old City. The Rothschild building's thick stone walls gave good protection and no one inside was hurt, but one student was killed in the street on the way to his bench. Conditions became impossible and the workshops moved first to a nearby cellar cafe, then farther away to the Bezalel Art School where the boys had their own electric generator and could work in two twelve-hour shifts.

Brandeis' technical designer Yitzhak Schneider invented a flame-thrower for which the boys made most of the parts. They also turned out muzzles for smoke bombs used to screen Jerusalem's lone landing strip from Arab gunners. With the battle raging around them, the school went on to produce more and more complicated products as the Haganah, cut off from supplies outside Jerusalem, made more and more demands. Schneider together with handwork technician Yitzhak Moshieff even put together binocular telescopes. When materials were difficult to obtain, one of the Brandeis men endangered his life by going to the Jerusalem railroad station under fire and ripping up tracks for metal. The school, only a few years old, thus played a key part in the battle for Jerusalem.

Brandeis taught more than precision instruments. In 1949, the country's first printing school was begun. The school's director was French-born Henry Friedlander who distinguished himself by designing a new Hebrew script—the result of thirty years' research. He named the script Hadassah. It was the first original Hebrew type of modern times. Beautiful in its classical design, yet uncomplicated, Hadassah fonts were adopted for the Swiss-made Hermes typewriter and were widely used by the Israeli government printers and by public institutions.

With money bequeathed by the Brandeis family, new quarters were built in northern Jerusalem in 1951. Then it became possible to introduce such sophisticated courses as industrial electronics under director Edgar Freund. On the eve of the Six-Day War, Brandeis could convert immediately to the production of complicated components for the Israeli Defense Forces, among them vital parts used in the bombing of Egypt on June 5, 1967.

But by no means was the school a war factory. Characteristically Israeli, it was civilian but was subject to call-up at short notice. In civilian life Brandeis would not only teach but it would build instruments to measure avocado peels and sections of the heart-lung machine used by Hadassah for its first open heart operations.

In 1969, Seligsberg and Brandeis amalgamated into a comprehensive high school. At the same time, the idea of a junior college was born and developed under the chairman of the Hadassah Israel Education Services, Esther Gottesman. And in November, 1972—precisely three decades after the Seligsberg School was founded—Hadassah graduated the nation's first junior college students.

While it was well and good that Hadassah provided vocational education to students who had no talent or desire to become scholars, it was another matter when young people could not decide what they wanted to do or what they could do. Research carried out among Jerusalem's high school seniors would show that only 25 per cent knew their own minds as regards education and occupation. The others were in a state of indecision.

To test, to counsel, to direct students became the function of Hadassah's Vocational Guidance Bureau, founded in 1944. Its first director was Haim Ormian, one of the country's pioneer educators. Although founded to do testing, the bureau branched out in recent years under Director Zev Sardi into counseling, teaching, and research. Says Hadassah's former Education Services Chairman Esther Gottesman,

> Our Vocational Guidance Bureau is one of a kind. We do the job that at least four agencies in America would do. The Department of Labor would put out statistical information and resource material that we put out. Psychological counseling would be done by another agency, group counseling by a third and still another would be giving the tests.

Testing and therapy for emotionally disturbed school children required an institution of its own. That need was filled in 1949 with the opening of the Lasker Mental Hygiene Clinic.

Important as Hadassah's educational function was in the 1950's the main preoccupation was the medical organization. With the end of the War of Independence, hospital facilities expanded in a makeshift way down the alphabet. Hadassah "A" and "B" were war-born, as we have seen. They were soon followed by "C" for tuberculosis patients; "D" in a derelict building that once housed the harem of the Turkish governor served internal medicine patients; "E" in an old German Lutheran Hospital took in surgical cases. One unlettered institution that Hadassah inherited as a result of the war was an Arab leprosarium. When the Arabs abandoned it, the dermatology department assumed responsibility and did notable work there in alleviating the pains of leprosy. By 1951, Hadassah was spread out in at least a dozen buildings over the face of the city.

All together Hadassah had put together places for 452 beds in Jerusalem in the 1950's, but if one included the hospitals in Beersheba, Safad, and Rosh Ha-ayin, they numbered 700. Occupancy at one point, reported the statisticians, was an unbelievable 298.4 per cent.

Without Scopus, however, Hadassah was bereft of its crown. Rebecca Shulman had said at the August, 1948, meeting in Jerusalem, "We will have to build anew." The loss of Scopus was too fresh to begin immediately, but by 1951, the shock had eased and Hadassah leaders began to plan for a new medical center.

One had only to visit the scattered premises to appreciate the need. Working conditions were almost laughable. So cramped were the facilities at the mission now called Hadassah "A" that they expanded into the private quarters of Canon Jones, the mission's director. The delivery room was put into his bathroom and an expensive cobalt unit for cancer therapy was set up in a room the reverend used for prayer meetings. In a small kitchen next door, Hadassah opened Israel's first medical isotope center. Down in the damp basements, the walls covered with fungi, were the X-ray labs.

The time had now come not only for a new center but for new management. Eli Davis, the British-born physician who had gone to Jerusalem on a promise from Yassky that he would be able to keep in touch with medicine while serving as deputy administrator, found that administration at Hadassah was a twenty-hour-a-day job. Eli Davis had worn Yassky's mantle with great fortitude at Hadassah's most trying hour. Davis was a man who spoke directly, plainly, and rarely wavered. If these characteristics sometimes brought him into head-on collisions with the Hadassah leadership, they also brought him the board's deep respect; so much so that when in 1950 he decided that, the war being over, he could now return to his first love of medicine, Hadassah dispatched President Rose Halprin and President-to-be Etta Rosensohn to Jerusalem to change his mind. Throughout a snowy night in the winter of 1950 even their considerable powers of persuasion failed. Davis, fortified by his wife's resolution and support, had made up his mind, and that was that.

Hadassah was now left without Scopus and without a director. Fortunately for the deputy director the task at that moment looked like an impossible one—few qualified men in American medicine would entertain moving to poverty-stricken Israel to take over a hospital dispersed in dilapidated buildings. And so the directorship fell to Davis' deputy Kalman Jacob Mann, son of the city's first

Jewish building contractor, seventh generation Jerusalemite, born in the year Hadassah was founded. The house he lived in as a child also served Ray Landy and Rose Kaplan as an eye care station in 1914. Mann himself went through the treatment for trachoma ("I used to run away because of the painful treatment and they would run after me, catch me and drag me back. This did not endear the nurse or the physician to me. But it did cure me"). He was graduated from a teachers' college at nineteen, went off to England to study medicine with the aim of entering psychiatry. Instead he took four degrees in medicine, a diploma in tropical medicine, and specialized in chest diseases. During the war he served as a resuscitation officer at Hendon airfield in charge of chest cases. It was an experience that would prove useful in the Six-Day War.

Mann returned to Jerusalem in 1948 on the promise of a position at Hadassah. But by the time he arrived, Scopus was lost and Eli Davis told him, "It's a shame you came. We have no job for you now." Mann was about to leave to establish a group practice when one day, as he crossed the Street of the Prophets, he met Rebecca Shulman who spent much of Israel's first year in Jerusalem and Haifa.

"How are you getting along at Hadassah?" she asked.

"I'm not."

Under St. Joseph's galvanized roof they sat and they talked. A week later Kalman Mann began as Davis' deputy. He explains, "My mother thought it was an honor and Rebecca Shulman kept after me. Dr. Davis was a good teacher, and I felt a partnership growing in the building of Hadassah."

Hadassah sent Mann to the United States under its fellowship program, to study hospital administration under Dr. E. M. Bluestone. While he was in Rochester, New York, in 1950, Mann received word from Davis that he was about to resign. So it was that at thirty-eight years of age Kalman Mann became Hadassah's eighth director. He was the first to come from native soil and he would serve much longer than any of his predecessors. Under Kalman Mann's steady hand the Hadassah Medical Organization would build a new home and keep faith with an old one.

Above: Henrietta Szold with members of Junior Hadassah in 1930. In 1967 Hadassah assumed sole sponsorship for the expanded American Zionist youth movement, Hashachar, which comprises Young, Intermediate, and Senior Judaea for 8-19 year olds, and Hamagshimim up to 25.

Below: At eight Young Judaea camps, sports, Jewish culture, and training for Zionist leadership are combined.

Young Judaeans have year-round activities including participation in parades, actions for Soviet Jewry, exchange programs with Israeli Boy and Girl Scouts. In addition to the American camp program, the Hadassah Zionist Youth Commission sponsors summer and year-courses in Israel. Hamagshimim group *(below)* are at Hadassah Riklis Youth Center on Mt. Scopus.

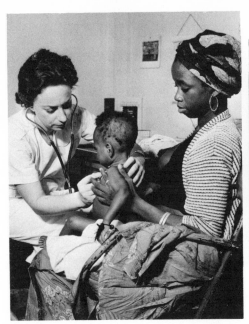

Above, left: When Hadassah moved into its new medical center, it initiated programs of healing, teaching, and research with developing Afro-Asian countries. A Hadassah pediatrician examines baby in Monrovia, Liberia, maternity clinic. The merged Seligsberg-Brandeis Comprehensive High School (*right*) became coeducational, breaking down one more barrier in the thrust toward modern education.

Below: The Hadassah Israel Education Services complex is centrally located in Jerusalem and includes Israel's first community college.

Above: Hadassah national annual conventions are full-house events averaging 2,500 delegates from 1,400 chapters and groups from every state and Puerto Rico (where there are both Spanish and English groups). The agenda ranges from American to foreign affairs, medicine, education, and fund-raising and membership workshops. The late Whitney Young *(inset)* addresses a session.

Hadassah headquarters at 65 East 52 Street, New York City, where *Hadassah Magazine* is published and its national officers work as professional volunteers.

MEMBERS OF THE EXECUTIVE COMMITTEE, 1973: *Front row, left to right:* Tamar Pool, Zip Szold, past presidents; Rose E. Matzkin, president; Judith Epstein, Rose L. Halprin, Rebecca Shulman, past presidents. *Second row:* Lola Kramarsky, Miriam Freund, Charlotte Jacobson, Faye L. Schenck, past presidents; Roslyn Brecher, Bess Katz, Aileen Schacht, vice presidents. *Third row:* Florence Perlman, treasurer; Rose Goldman, recording secretary; Isabel Marks, secretary; Rose Dorfman, Bea Feldman, Esther Gottesman, Frieda Lewis, Helen Lusterman. *Standing:* Aline Kaplan, executive director; Pauline Mack; Betty Bienstock, vice president; Bernice Salpeter, Bea Usdan, Gladys Zales, Fannie Cohen; Hannah L. Goldberg, assistant to the president; Elsie Kairys, Madlyn Barnett, vice presidents.

17.

Ein Karem

"You are crazy, Mann!"

With that the distinguished rector of the Hebrew University turned on his heels and tramped down the slope to the parked Jeep. He had been invited to the top of the mountain by Hadassah's enthusiastic medical director. Spread out before the two men in a majestic panorama was the Valley of Sorek, the lair where Delilah snared Samson. It was here that the Philistines planned to break through to subdue Judea and not far away the youthful David foiled them by slaying Goliath. Peaceful, even primeval, the blue-tinted Judean Hills were ideal for quiet study and research. In time, Kalman Mann had explained to the rector, Jerusalem lying five miles to the north had nowhere to grow but southward. A broad highway from Tel Aviv would one day be cut through the valley, and this spot would be the city's grand new entrance. What could be more fitting, he suggested, than to build fortresses of healing and teaching on opposite hills to guard the gateway to the City of Peace.

The realistic rector was unimpressed. This place was good for goats or for Philistines or even for prophets but definitely not for serious students who had to rush to jobs in the city after classes or for sick people in urgent need of a specialist.

Disconsolate, Mann began feeling a little silly that he had supported this site as the successor to Mt. Scopus. But before he would surrender to goats and Philistines, he was determined to get one last opinion, and that from a latter-day prophet.

The year was 1951 and by then the loss of Scopus lay as heavy as a dirge on the soul of Jerusalem's physicians and professors. No one doubted any longer that the Hebrew University and Hadassah must build anew. The problem was where. Jerusalem offered no easy locations. Fashioned by nature in the shape of an outstretched hand—of ridges and valleys—the city was further limited for reasons of security. Jewish Jerusalem was the end of a salient that began in the Judean foothills to the west and stuck like a thumb in the gut of the heavily populated sections of Arab Palestine that had been annexed by Jordan. Arab artillery positions dominated the city from high points to the south and north. On the eastern border, which cut through the middle of Jerusalem's commercial section, Jordanian sentries sat perched on roof tops. Few sites anywhere were at that time beyond the effective range of Arab guns. Ein Karem was one.

Hadassah and the university considered four sites. For Hadassah each had its disadvantage: one was too small for expansion, another was out of the mainstream of the developing city, and a third was needed for an airport. That left Ein Karem—distant but enticing. Ein Karem—the Well of the Vineyard—is a quaint village snugly held in the Valley of Sorek, an artist's dream of statuesque cypresses, crooked lanes, and stone-walled churches. Tradition tells that St. John the Baptist was born there.

Long, hard-fought sessions between Hadassah and Hebrew University representatives over sharing the new site came to naught. Always before the university was the specter of the ill-fated Scopus convoy trapped on hostile ground between the city and the campus. Hadassah was torn between the desire to remain with the university inside urban Jerusalem and to strike out independently on the edge of a wilderness where it could expand without limit. The final decision was put in the hands of David Ben-Gurion, Israel's political seer. At the site, the security-minded prime minister turned to his Hadassah escort and said, "Magnificent! Build here."

From that moment Hadassah and the university went their separate ways. Not even a compromise worked out later by Defense Minister Pinhas Lavon, who suggested that the university's science faculties remain at Ein Karem, could bridge the gap. In the end the medical school and the schools of dentistry and pharmacy as well as the microbiology and biochemistry departments voted to stay with Hadassah. The university built its campus on the Givat Ram ridge which soon became the geographical center of Jerusalem.

The issue having been decided, Hadassah received through the Jewish National Fund 315 acres above Ein Karem. The first problem was to carve a road to the site. Working with primitive equipment, the state's Public Works Department set out bravely. But on the way the workers ran into a political barrier that could not be budged with TNT. Part of the land belonged to the Russian Orthodox Church which took its orders from the vicars in the Kremlin. Israel could not then afford diplomatic crises with major powers, so it agreed to stop the work while lawyers fought the issue.

In the autumn of 1956, everyone expected Israel to launch an attack against Jordan. Repeated Arab raids against Israeli towns and farms on the frontiers had made life unbearable. The crisis peaked on October 25 when Jordan joined Syria and Egypt in a military alliance against Israel. On October 29, the Israeli army struck deep into Sinai in an attack that was coordinated with Britain and France. In one hundred hours Israel occupied the entire peninsula, broke Nasser's blockade of Eilat, and smashed Nasser's army. Militarily, Israel's operation was a resounding success. Politically, it was a failure. President Eisenhower condemned the action and forced Israel's withdrawal.

Hadassah had prepared for heavy military casualties, but when the front opened in Sinai rather than in Jordan, the hospitals in Jerusalem were not needed. Most of the wounded were taken to Beersheba where Hadassah organized and staffed a field hospital.

Golda Meir was then foreign minister. After the Russians broke relations with Israel because of the war, Mrs. Meir told Hadassah, "Finish the road quickly. Our relations with the Russians could hardly be worse." Before Moscow could return to Tel Aviv, the Henrietta Szold Road was completed to the plateau. And there, four years later, at the southernmost limit of Jerusalem, the medical center complex stood.

Not all Hadassah's expectations were fulfilled. The projected highway through the Valley of Sorek that was to open a new gateway to Jerusalem turned out to be a seldom-used secondary

two-lane road. Down in the valley an agricultural school was
built, a far cry from a university. And near the site that the university rejected, the city fathers dumped and burned Jerusalem's
garbage. These shortcomings, however, had no effect on the development of the center. And, as Ben-Gurion had promised, the
city did indeed grow toward Ein Karem and even beyond.

The Ein Karem site inspired grandiose dreams among department chiefs that would have required an 800-bed hospital, a 450-
student medical school, a 120-student dental school, 4 acres of
space to teach basic sciences, and an out-patient clinic to handle
1,000 patients a day.

In New York, the National Board was stunned by these proposals. To build a medical center of such proportions went far
beyond anything Hadassah had ever attempted. The shock was not
so much over the expanse as over the expense. The original building budget amounted to nearly $8 million with an additional $2.5
million to be provided by the university for the professional
schools. What Jerusalem was asking for would, at prices current
then, have amounted to three times the sum. As it turned out,
soaring costs and needs did force Hadassah to spend an astronom-
ical $30 million by 1971, a decade after the center was opened, in
addition to $6 million provided by the university.

Hadassah turned to its Medical-Advisory Board to study Jerusalem's program for the center. Dr. Harry Eagle, an advocate of
modest medical centers, was sent to Jerusalem. His presence there
stirred a hornet's nest among Hadassah's equally distinguished
physicians. Men such as gynecologist Bernhard Zondek, pathologist Henry Ungar, and others protested indignantly that their
concepts were questioned.

Sandwiched in the middle was Kalman Mann. On the one
hand, New York complained that Jerusalem's doctors were "building personal empires." On the other, his staff insisted that Jerusalem's medical center must be large enough to stand on its own
with the best in modern medicine. Permission for the program was
finally granted by the National Board, and Architect Joseph Neufeld was given the green light to prepare blueprints for actual
construction.

Both sides had grudgingly compromised. Mann had scaled his
staff's demands down to a 540-bed hospital. But that clashed with
the board's insistence on 350 beds. The center finally opened with
420. Yet a decade later the number would reach 680 with plans

to take it up to 740 by 1975. What broke the ice was a basic compromise whereby construction would begin modestly but allow for constant expansion. Fortunately this was possible at Ein Karem. The choice of site was justified.

In New York, a vigorous building-fund campaign was begun. To raise the money for the single largest project in Hadassah's history, the medical center was "sold" in bits and pieces. Donors could buy a brick or a square foot in the center or could be listed as a Founder for $10,000. Out of the Founder's program emerged Hadassah's Big Gift project ($5,000 and up) which has since been an important source of funds. The largest single gift, $1 million, came from Siegfried and Irma Ullmann, of New York, for the establishment of Hadassah's sixty-bed oncology institute. Named for Moshe Sharett, Israel's second prime minister, who died of cancer, the institute, under Director Avraham Hochman, is designed to be one of the most modern in the world, complete with a department of nuclear medicine.

From the corner stone laying of the Ein Karem center on June 5, 1952, to the projected completion of the Sharett Institute in 1975, Hadassah jumped into a new age of medical care.

To design the center, Hadassah chose Vienna-educated Joseph Neufeld. It had long been realized that the accepted shoe-box form of most hospitals was inefficient, dismal, and hard on nurses' feet. Neufeld substituted a semicircular shape which he called "radial." Thus, the distinguishing feature of the medical center came to be the eleven-floor radial unit. Inside, on each floor, the nurses' station was located in the center of the half circle and from there nurses and attendants were within easy reach of all the eight-bed wards. To eliminate the gloom of the ordinary hospital, Neufeld put the corridors in the adjoining recovery wings on the outside— one facing north and one facing south. In summer, the north corridor, opposite the picturesque Sorek Valley and the village of Ein Karem, became a lounge. In winter when the north side was buffeted by wind and rain, the sunlit south corridor became the lounge. Neufeld prescribed red and white bricks and pink Jerusalem stone for the building's exterior to blend in with the constantly changing colors of Jerusalem's landscape. The over-all cheerful effect and the awesome view impressed Rebecca Shulman to remark, "This center has been designed so that people will be able to enjoy their bad health."

Neufeld was beset with unusual problems. One was to secure

the building against war damage. Surgery, for example, had to be located two floors above ground—high enough to minimize the effect of near-misses of shells and bombs and low enough to be insulated from a direct hit. Three floors, built underground with connecting tunnels, could be converted into emergency wards.

Inevitably, mistakes would be made in the planning. Large windows facing east and south were sun collectors. In the Mediterranean where the light is blinding during hot dry summers, planners have learned to plan small windows. Neufeld assumed that the hospital would be air-conditioned, but in 1957 a decision was taken to save $1 million by eliminating artificial cooling. The result was that until air conditioners were finally installed staffs and patients suffered during hot spells.

Jerusalem's water, heavy with sedimentation, wreaked havoc with the American-engineered boilers and pipes. The current Medical Center Building Chairman, Pauline Mack, says, "I spent long sleepless nights because of Jerusalem's water. We had to spend enormous amounts of money on retubing, reconditioning, and cleaning the boilers. Finally, we put in a whole new water system."

But no problem was as ticklish as that which involved the pathologists and the rabbis. Religious law forbids kohanim (men belonging to the priestly class) from entering a building in which a corpse is lying. Since pathology was an integral part of the center, and it was the only hospital in Jerusalem to dare have a pathology department, Director Mann took the problem to Chief Rabbi of Israel Isaac Nissim, and received a facile reply, "Erect a separate building for pathology." Mann blanched; he did not have the extra $5 million. Like a patient seeking a more effective cure, he went off to consult another sage (without telling Nissim). The consultant was the chief rabbi of Jerusalem, who suggested that if the post-mortem room had electronic doors that opened when one approached and closed before others opened, then the pathology department would be sealed off as though it were not part of the rest of the building.

Happily Mann went back and ordered electronic doors for the hospital. But the cure failed. Staff and visitors did not have the patience to wait until one door closed and the other opened, and even broke the equipment. Mann was left with the problem of how to make the hospital on-bounds for observant kohanim. The solution was deceptively simple—revolving doors were installed.

Problems notwithstanding, the medical center slowly took shape as the 1950's ended. When it was completed, even the critics could agree that no similar institution existed in the Middle East.

One day in the spring of 1959, as construction moved forward, Hadassah President Miriam Freund sat with Neufeld in her New York office discussing the shape of a small synagogue to be built at the center. She commented that just that week she had read a newspaper item that Marc Chagall had done some windows for a French cathedral. "Both Neufeld and I had the thought at once that it would be a wonderful thing if Chagall would do windows for our synagogue. I took the idea to the board."

On the plane to Paris to negotiate with Chagall, Miriam met violinist Isaac Stern, and she asked him to come along with Neufeld and her. In Chagall's apartment near Notre Dame the trio tried to convince Chagall in Yiddish, Russian, and French. Miriam recalls:

> While the men were studying the plans for the synagogue, I spoke with Marc's wife. She said, "Chagall is unhappy that the whole world has come to him but not the Jewish people." In my broken Yiddish I went over to Chagall and said, "I have come on behalf of the Jewish people." I took a deep breath and plunged on, "We could never repay you enough for doing these windows. I cannot even ask you what your price is since all I can spend is $100,000. That has to cover everything. I know this is no fee for you . . . but you will be shaping the art history of a new country. All young Israelis are interested in art. You will be their lodestar." He listened intently, but his only reply was, "I shall see."

That was in June, 1959. The following December, Miriam and Neufeld flew to Chagall's home in Vence. There they saw already completed drawings for twelve windows: each bore the name of an ancient tribe of Israel and its symbol. Subsequently, the windows were painted in striking blues, greens, yellows, and reds. The glass was made at the Simone atelier of Charles and Brigitte Marq in Rheims. Says Miriam: "When the windows were finished, it was much more than we had ever bargained for. They were so beautiful that Culture Minister André Malraux insisted on showing them in the garden of the Louvre. After that we put them on show at the Museum of Modern Art [New York City]." That was in November, 1961.

Hundreds of thousands packed into the museum to see what

was the hit show of the season. Then the windows were packed and flown for security on three planes to Jerusalem. Replacement glass was sent along in case of breakage. The windows arrived in Jerusalem in perfect shape; the replacement pieces were shattered. They became one of Israel's most valuable art treasures and one of its greatest tourist attractions, drawing several million tourists to the medical center.

The tiny synagogue which houses them was a modest structure, and critics carped that it was much too poor to wear so priceless a diadem. Chagall himself was patently disturbed when in 1962 he attended the dedication ceremony. The artist from Vitebsk should have remembered that some of Italy's greatest art works repose in far shabbier churches, but he suggested that they be transferred to the Israel Museum. Chagall promised to replace them with other windows. He had a few supporters, Miriam Freund among them, but the National Board rejected the idea and they remained at the center.

The dedication of the Ein Karem Center took place on August 3, 1960. The day began routinely for Hadassah's 254 physicians, 514 nurses, and 1,352 staff. In ophthalmology, red-haired Professor Walter Kornbleuth operated on three cross-eyed children. A housewife from Athens began to receive massive doses of steroids in dermatology to fight an advanced case of pemphigus, a fatal disease until only ten years previous. "Cancer patients who are incurable are never hopeless," Oncology Department Chief Hochman told his students that day. "We can always add time to their lives." Then carrying his pipe, which he stopped filling with tobacco for the last month, he went on to check patients whose tumors were being bombarded by cobalt. Orthopedic surgeon Myer Makin removed a torn cartilage from the knee of a football player. Then he turned the leg of a club-footed boy. Green-uniformed Nurse Haya Dorit, a thirty-five-year veteran who directed one of Hadassah's fourteen Tipat Halav mother-and-infant welfare stations, reassured Hassida Frumkin. Hassida was eight month's pregnant with her first child and suffered from swollen legs. In the Kiryat Yovel Community Health Center, Dr. Charlotte Hopp spent part of the morning reviewing the case of fifteen-year-old Rahamim, a hemophiliac who had lately developed asthma.

Thus was Hadassah occupied on August 3. In the late afternoon nearly all workers left their stations to troop out to the plateau above Ein Karem. There, they joined Israeli notables and four hundred overseas guests on the red flagstone plaza. President Freund began with a prayer in which she noted that Hadassah had entered into "a partnership with Him in the healing of the sick, in the rescuing of the homeless and in the mothering of the motherless." A Freedom Bell, shaped like the Liberty Bell, on which was inscribed "Proclaim Ye Healing Throughout the Land," was ceremoniously rung by Fanny Cohen, former Medical Center Chairman. American Ambassador Ogden Reid addressed the gathering in perfect, if halting, Hebrew, but switched to English to note that $100,000 was provided by the U.S. government to build the premature baby wards.

Prime Minister Ben-Gurion, the featured guest, complained that he was asked to speak English whereas the Gentile ambassador could get away with Hebrew. "I have two wishes," said Ben-Gurion. "One is that I hope we go back to Scopus. And the other is that I hope Hadassah women learn the Hebrew language." He went on to chide American Jews for not sending their children to settle in Israel, but more to the point, he paid tribute to Hadassah's founder:

> Henrietta Szold who was not only the greatest woman America has yet produced, but undoubtedly one of the noblest personalities of our generation, had two great qualities: her profound knowledge of the Hebrew language and culture, and her great desire to work in Israel. . . . May the memory and life's work of Henrietta Szold be a light to guide your path. She gave herself to our country.

Ben-Gurion sat down to polite applause. The dedication was over.

Moving Day followed on June 6, 1961. In May advance parties had transferred the administration and 250,000 individual records, the huge cobalt therapy unit and medical stores. The army provided twenty ambulances to shuttle three hundred patients. Director Mann remembers the day with something less than glee:

> I knew we were not completely ready, I was asked to postpone the operation but Hadassah chapters were celebrating the day. We simply had to go. Top administrative people actually shook me and if others had not interfered I might have been mauled, I was accused of "killing them," of "sucking blood" from

them. This was a great psychological crisis in the life of our people because so many changes were involved.

Mann frankly admitted that he had not properly prepared his staffs. In the United States, hospital directors trained for such moves for up to two years. But, he explained, "We could not afford the time." A few were indeed sent abroad to learn how to use new equipment. But even the head of the kitchen, who was thoroughly trained, had a revolt on her hands over a new belt system. But finally when the day was over, Mann cabled New York:

> PROUDLY REPORT SUPERBLY SUCCESSFUL COMPLE-
> TION OPERATION MD DAY. 6 A.M. NURSES PREPARED
> PATIENTS TRANSFER. 7:30 HADASSAH FLAGS UN-
> FURLED AT MEDICAL CENTER; MRS. PERLMAN CUT
> RIBBON TO ADMIT FIRST CONVOY OF ARMY AMBU-
> LANCES BEDECKED WITH CHAPTER FLAGS. FIRST
> CAME WORST CASES TO AVOID THE MIDDAY HEAT.
> MEDICAL CORPSMEN CLOSING IN TENDERLY TO
> TRANSFER STRETCHER AND TRANSFUSION CASES TO
> PREVIOUSLY DESIGNATED BEDS UNDER SUPERVISION
> OF DOCTORS AND NURSES. NEXT CAME CHILDREN,
> SOME JUMPING WITH EXCITEMENT; BABIES IN ARMS,
> OF GIRL SOLDIERS, YAAL VOLUNTEERS. 45 MINUTES
> AFTER LEAVING TOWN PATIENTS COMFORTABLY
> SETTLED FLOWER-DECKED WARDS, ADMIRING
> BREATH-TAKING VIEW, RECITING BENEDICTIONS. AS
> CONVOY FOLLOWED CONVOY, DEPARTMENT AFTER
> DEPARTMENT RESUMED NORMAL WORKING, TREAT-
> MENTS, XRAYS, EXAMINATIONS: AS KITCHEN PRO-
> SAICALLY PREPARED MEATBALLS. 1 P.M. ARMY HAD
> TRANSFERRED 300 PATIENTS, HALF STRETCHER
> CASES, COMPLETING THIS STAGE OF MOVE. IMPOS-
> SIBLE EXPRESS BOUNDLESS JOY, GRATITUDE OF
> STAFF PATIENTS TO EVERY MEMBER OF HADASSAH
> WHO MADE THIS GREAT DAY POSSIBLE.

For Hadassah in America this great event in its history left a deep impact. Three hundred thousand Hadassah members had been preparing for M-Day by raising an additional $300,000 to meet the extra cost. Each chapter undertook to contribute a share of the total and this effort was symbolized by a blue satin pennant on which the name of the chapter was stamped in gold. A duplicate of each banner had been sent to Jerusalem to be affixed to the army trucks transporting the patients. At the 1961 national convention in Denver, the hall was darkened and the pennants distributed to the achieving chapters. As the lights went on, the hall was a sea of pennants.

For the chapters there was an additional reward, for the film *Fifty Miracle Minutes* picturing the move was shown at the evening meeting and there projected on the screen, they saw the flags flying atop the army trucks as they moved from the town of Jerusalem to the hills. Arthur Goldberg, then secretary of labor, was a guest of the Hadassah convention. He watched in the darkened room and caught something electric, unique, from the assemblage in that hall. When the lights went up and the women cheered and wept, he too was visibly moved.

In Jerusalem once the jitters of moving passed and everyone had accustomed himself to the elephantine elevators, the intercom systems, and the push buttons at the new hospital, Hadassah settled down to its primary tasks of healing, teaching, and research. The years to mid-1967 were relatively calm and richly productive. Hadassah physicians were doing 90 per cent of all medical research carried out in Israel. Much of it was too technically complex for laymen to grasp, but some of the projects did manage to fascinate them.

Gynecologist Bernhard Zondek worked toward the development of a new contraceptive. He had already produced a series of pregnancy tests, a urine analysis to determine whether a fetus was alive, and a test to find the dominant sex in hermaphrodites. Now he and his associates had found that when an alarm clock was rung regularly within the hearing of mice during their mating sessions, they became temporarily sterile. Zondek achieved the same results with a supersonic device. The obvious continuation was to develop an audio-contraceptive for humans, but Zondek died before that result was reached.

Zondek's student and successor, Wolfe Polishuk, concentrated on the most serious problem facing gynecology in the Middle East—sterility. In one aspect of the work he and his colleagues found a way to replace a nonfunctioning fallopian tube with the appendix.

Heart Surgeon Joseph Borman's cardiac surgery unit developed an electronic defibrillator that controlled irregular heart beats during open chest operations.

Neurologist Lipman Halpern did major experimentation into color medicine. In a rare sickness which he called unilateral disequilibrium—a condition in which patients see abnormally on the affected side of the brain—Halpern found that red-colored glasses aggravated the symptoms while green or blue glasses corrected them. The result of a blow on the head or sclerosis, the disease made patients stumble while walking or see pictures tilted on walls.

Orthopedic surgeon Myer Makin, who won a British medical medal for introducing bone formation through bladder transplants, developed a procedure to lengthen shortened legs by as much as two and one-half inches.

Dental School Dean Jacob Lewin-Epstein together with pharmacologist Edward Superstine pioneered in the use of a preanesthetic suppository for children undergoing dental surgery. Children fall asleep and wake up without any recollection of undergoing an unhappy experience.

Dermatologist Jacob Sheskin prescribed the drug Thalidomide, which had been responsible for causing deformed babies, to help lepers. He found that while Thalidomide did not cure leprosy it did alleviate pain, skin eruptions, and fevers to such an extent that at least half of the patients could be released from the hospital.

Former Medical Director Eli Davis and ophthalmologist Jacob Landau reported on a method to diagnose such ills as arteriosclerosis, hypertension, diabetes, and rheumatic fever by placing a patient's fingertip under a microscope. Called clinical capillary microscopy, the test became routine at Hadassah for the first time anywhere.

Ringworm, which was usually treated by first shaving heads, affected about 20,000 persons in the late 1950's. Then, dermatology chief Felix Sagher turned up with a new remedy that eliminated the shaving and the disease.

In the chest disease department, Professor Joseph Rakower reported that if one had to smoke, the safest of all was an old-fashioned narghileh, the water pipe of the Arabs.

And so, these accomplishments among others were proof that Hadassah was back to normal in its new quarters.

18.

Six Days in June

In June, 1967, Israel was again at war and, as usual, the unexpected happened. The bitterest fighting and the heaviest casualties occurred in the City of Peace. Hadassah did not foresee a war in Jerusalem any more than anyone else until the latter part of May, but like the entire nation it was prepared for what it did not expect. As early as December, 1964, in conjunction with the army, Hadassah administrators drew up a secret manual that detailed Hadassah's role in time of national emergency down to the last safety pin. Periodic drills tested the manual's instructions. Unexpectedly hospital chiefs would receive a call from an army officer who would say, "In a few minutes you will be receiving fifty wounded soldiers." A short while later, fifty serious-faced school children would be brought up in ambulances, each wearing a tag describing his imaginary wounds. Says Deputy Medical Director Jack Karpas, "We learned to spot our weaknesses from those drills. When the Six-Day War came we were ready."

On May 15, Israel celebrated its twenty-first anniversary with a military show in Jerusalem. In Egypt soldiers began to march too, but not in parade. They were headed for Sinai. By May 26, war appeared to be inevitable. On that day the Hadassah Hospital pharmacy, under the direction of Detroit-born Edward Superstine, began preparing massive amounts of sterile solutions, analgesics, and antibiotics. Says Superstine, "Our 20-member staff worked 20 hours a day. In our storerooms we kept 5,000 different types of pharmaceuticals. Drug trucks were fitted out to be sent to other areas in case the war went on for a long time and we could not accommodate all the wounded."

Military intelligence passed the word that the Egyptians might use gas as they had done in the Yemen war. (Gas installations later captured in Sinai justified the report.) Superstine had quantities of one antidote, atropin, on hand, but it was useless against nerve gas. Cables were sent to Supplies Purchasing Chairman Gladys Zales to buy up supplies of the effective antidote. Recalls Gladys, "We were told everywhere it simply was not available. The Red Cross told us to try the military. We called the Pentagon but they said that we must first get permission from the inventor in Paris. We got a call from the FBI wanting to know who we were and why we wanted this antigas medicine. In the end we failed." But on June 4, one day before war began, a supply sufficient for about five thousand casualties arrived at Ein Karem. The supposedly secret formula was produced by scientists of the Weizmann Institute of Science. Fortunately it was never needed.

The weekend before the storm broke was unusually quiet. Israeli synagogues were more than normally crowded. Coincidentally, perhaps, the portion of the Law to be read that Sabbath was the beginning of the Book of Numbers wherein Moses is commanded by God to take a census of all military-aged men fit to fight for the Promised Land. But not everyone was in synagogue. Large numbers of soldiers, who had been given leave to confuse the enemy, spent their time on the Mediterranean beaches. In Tel Aviv, Prime Minister Levi Eshkol's cabinet, having determined that the big power intervention against Nasser's blockade of Israeli shipping through the Tiran Straits was not in the cards and that the 100,000 battle-ready Egyptians poised in the Sinai desert were a death threat to the State of Israel, authorized Eshkol and the new defense minister, Moshe Dayan, to resolve the problem at their own discretion.

In Jerusalem on Sunday, June 4, some householders busied themselves filling sandbags, preparing air-raid shelters, and taping up windows. At Ein Karem, Director Mann and Deputy Karpas had two thousand windowpanes to worry about. Workers and student volunteers labored throughout the day and night filling sacks and hanging blackout material. Says Mann,

The day before the war I asked all personnel to volunteer to work an additional two hours. The Workers Committee complained that I was creating panic. This is one of the times I thought I would have a heart attack. I blew up. "Don't you see a war is coming?" I shouted. The head of the committee replied there was no war and I was only getting panicky. But they finally agreed to work the extra hours. . . . At the end of the week the committee came to drink *l'hayyim* and to apologize.

Of particular concern were the Chagall windows. To extricate them without damaging the glass was difficult. Mann cabled Charles Marq in Rheims to fly to Israel to remove them. He arrived on Saturday night, June 3. On Sunday, Marq and Jerusalem architect Dan Ben-Dor studied the problem. Each of the twelve windows was divided into twelve sections. Each section was made up of between forty and fifty individual pieces of glass. The glass in the center was held fast by putty but around the frames where the glass was set into concrete they were reinforced with cement. Ben-Dor carefully tried a dentist's drill with no success. He tried other types of saws equally with little result. That night, Mann visited Marq at the King David Hotel. The only other tourist in the city's largest hotel was former Hadassah president Rebecca Shulman who had been on the way to the airport to fly home when her son Paul informed her that war was imminent. She turned back on the spot.

Mann recalls, "Marq felt we were all doomed. I tried to assure him that we would survive but he did not believe me. I left the hotel with a heavy heart and he departed next morning on the last plane. Rebecca remained throughout the war."

This same sense of doom pervaded the Western world. Marc Chagall cabled Hadassah, "I am not worried about the windows, only about the safety of Israel. Let Israel be safe and I will make you better windows."

To some extent the threat to Israel's survival was illusory for the nation was sufficiently strong militarily to withstand the onslaught of all its hostile neighbors. The unanswerable question for Israelis on June 4, 1967, was not whether they would fall but how badly they would bleed.

In New York, Hadassah reacted to the crisis on two levels— the political and the material. President Charlotte Jacobson set up

an operations room at National Hadassah headquarters on 52nd
Street. Says Charlotte:

> We went to Washington at the end of May and we came away
> with a sense of frustration. We saw every senator and congress-
> man. Everyone said that he would never let Israel down. They
> all made beautiful speeches. When we pressed them, they ad-
> mitted that the United States would not act alone but in concert
> with the United Nations. We came away with a terrible feeling.
> Although no one doubted American friendship, nothing moved.
> This gave us the sense of urgency. We had to see to it that every-
> thing was well-prepared in Israel.

If the leadership in Washington could do nothing to prevent
the war, the alerted American citizen did everything to ensure its
outcome. Medical institutions and personnel throughout the country called Hadassah to offer supplies and volunteers. An additional
switchboard operating night and day in Hadassah headquarters was
swamped with calls. During the crisis Treasurer Faye Schenk did
not have to spend an extra cent from the normal budget. "Everything," she said, "was contributed." After hostilities ended, Dr.
Mann reported that not one of the thousands of items required by
physicians to treat the casualties was missing except for the single
exception of a Number 7 cannula needed for insertion into a
soldier's windpipe. "The surgeon managed with a larger size,"
Mann reassured Gladys Zales, Hadassah's purchasing director. For
one operation ophthalmologist Michaelson needed a pair of human
eyes and got them. One morning during the war Gladys was
startled by a call from the executive director of the International
Eye Foundation in Washington.

"Mrs. Zales," he said, "I have two fresh eyes to send to Jerusalem. They must be there within twenty-four hours."

A National Board member was assigned to meet an Eastern
Airlines flight from Washington, pick up the seven-pound vacuum
jug containing the eyes, and put it on an El Al flight. The transfer was accomplished, and the eyes were in Michaelson's hands
with little time to spare.

The staff of volunteers at New York headquarters worked
twenty-hour days for two weeks.

Johnson and Johnson, the pharmaceutical firm, like many
others, donated supplies. Upon receiving Hadassah's thanks for the

1,200 cases of surgical dressings, they said they planned to make their gift for Israel a yearly event. An El Al spokesman assured Hadassah that next to ammunition Hadassah had top priority to move its supplies. TWA and KLM topped that by taking freight free of charge.

The stories of giving and helping during the war are now part of American-Jewish folklore. Some Jews signed their social security checks over to Hadassah. One man said: "If Israel loses, I won't need it. If Israel wins, I am sure to get it back."

Treasurer, and later president, Schenk received $1.2 million in cash. One envelope arrived with a $100 bill and a newspaper clipping from *The New York Times* advertising the opening of Peter Ustinov's new play, *An Unknown Soldier and His Wife*. A check for $250 was sent by the Fifth Avenue Presbyterian Church with a simple message: "We want to help." From Chicago, an eight-year-old girl sent in several dollars with an apologetic note, "This is all the cash I have on hand."

A young man appeared at Hadassah headquarters on June 5 saying he had just finished medical school and would organize thirty young doctors to help. They spent the week of the war determining priorities for shipping medicines. There were humorous sidelights, like the man who sent in a huge consignment of pyjamas with pop art flowers blazoned on them, thinking they would help cheer up soldier patients. One late afternoon toward the end of the war, Gladys got a call from S. Klein, a New York department store.

"I understand you need linens," said the Klein official.

Wearily, Gladys replied, "Yes, yes. Send them right over."

"They will be there in one hour," he replied blandly.

An hour later a truck driver interrupted Gladys. "Ma'am, I have some linens for you."

"Fine," she smiled mechanically. "Just put them there on the right of the receiving area."

The driver looked perturbed. "Lady, I don't want to bother you but I think maybe you better come outside and have a look."

Gladys, somewhat annoyed at the interruption, stepped outside and almost fainted. There before her was parked a 50-foot trailer filled to the roof with 7,500 sheets, 4,500 pillow cases, and 1,200 blankets. She asked the driver to take them to a garage, and the following week they were on a ship to Israel.

In Israel, three weeks of escalating tensions broke in a crescendo of violence at the breakfast hour on June 5. At 0810, the Voice of Israel gave a terse report that fighting had broken out on the southern front. At that very moment the first wave of Israeli jets screeching percariously low over the Mediterranean had surprised the Egyptian air force and by the end of the morning would smash it out of existence. At about 0900 hours, the Israeli Army Chief Medical Officer called Deputy Director Karpas: "Fighting has broken out in the Negev. Prepare to receive wounded." This time it was no exercise. Hadassah was put immediately into a Phase IV emergency, the highest state of preparedness provided for in its manual.

Outside at the synagogue Dan Ben-Dor and an assistant had been busy with buzz saws carefully grinding away at the cement. Slowly they lifted the small pieces of glass from the Chagall windows and placed them in the original packing cases which had been brought up from the storerooms. Dan began work on the north side because he feared that the first shelling would come from Jordanian positions on Nebi Samwil in the north.

Director Mann arrived early at the hospital that morning.

> I gazed from my window and could see the sandbags being filled. I heard the bells pealing from the churches of Ein Karem. The picture seemed serene. When I saw tanks crossing the road in the distance, I gave the order to bring the patients down. Then, I saw shells begin to fall in the valley, first near the Agricultural School and then inching toward the hospital. I could not believe my eyes. It was as though I was watching a movie. I could not believe they were aiming at us. But they were.

As Ben-Dor buzzed away with his saw out in the open, a tremendous blast shook the synagogue on the east side. The shells —probably mortars—had come not from Nebi Samwil but from Beit Jala to the southeast of Jerusalem, near Bethlehem. "If I had started on the windows on the east side I would not have been here today," Ben-Dor said later. Fragments of shells bounced up from the paving stones and punctured five of Chagall's windows. But the damage was not serious. Altogether six shells hit the center. Ben-Dor took cover till the shelling stopped, then returned to his work. By Wednesday, working night and day, he removed nine whole windows. At that point, he realized there was no longer need to continue. All Jerusalem was in Israeli hands.

In pediatrics, department chief Alex Russell was sitting in his chair by the window when a mortar shell burst outside. Shrapnel sprayed through the aluminum window blind. "Over my desk," he recalls, "a beam of light shone. That was the window crashing through." Russell rushed off to the maternity pavillion.

> Windows were shattered on both sides. The last of the babies had been evacuated within minutes before we were hit. Their empty cots were full of splintered glass. In pediatrics, all the children were taken to shelters just in time, except for three children having blood transfusions. None was hurt.

In that long day at Hadassah, five normal births would be registered and three circumcisions would be performed.

After the sixth shell had fallen, all was quiet. The Jordanians now concentrated on the center of the city. Mann and his emergency staff had to determine whether to evacuate the hospital of its civilian patients. War casualties would soon be arriving. According to plan, they had to leave, but with the shelling going on in the city could he risk sending them away? He did. The time chosen, in mid-afternoon, could not have been better. A lull in the firing had occurred as the buses and private cars moved out of the Ein Karem compound. Not one of the three hundred evacuees was hurt. About one hundred and fifty who could not be moved were left behind.

Nine teams of surgeons were ready when the first war casualties from fighting in southern Jerusalem were hurried in. A total of 1,200 beds were available at Hadassah and 17 operating theaters stood by, 8 of them underground. During peacetime the hospital had room for less than 700 patients and ran 9 operating theaters. Pediatricians, psychiatrists, dentists, biochemists, not normally needed for casualty work, were pressed into service as assistants to surgeons and as anesthetists. All had taken special courses for emergency work.

The casualties were rushed to the out-patient department, which had been turned into a receiving station. There, while being registered, two of Hadassah's most senior surgeons—Nathan Saltz and Nathan Rabinowitz—personally examined them and made the basic decisions for their care. Says Karpas, "The fact that we had these senior men in charge saved many lives because a patient who is properly prepared for an operation stands a much greater chance of survival."

What concerned the surgeons most was shock. Physical shock is the result of severe tissue injury or heavy loss of blood and can be a major cause of death. During shock, blood pressure falls and because of the insufficiency of blood to carry oxygen to the tissue, it dies. Physicians do not know clinically when shock is no longer reversible or what causes the condition to be halted. But they do know that in many cases of shock, infusions of blood plasma can make the difference. In the Six-Day War at Hadassah, the surgeons made much greater use of another fluid called Hartman's Solution. Says chief surgeon Saltz, "Before the war we learned that tissue destruction resulted from the contraction of a certain amount of the actual tissue fluids in the spaces of the body, not in the bloodstream. In addition to the bloodstream there was a contraction of fluid that surrounds the cells."

Twelve thousand bottles of Hartman's Solution, a modified salt formula containing lactate, had been prepared in the hospital's pharmacy. Ten thousand bottles were used on the 927 cases that were admitted within three days. On the other hand only 1,000 bottles of blood were used. The result was phenomenal. Says Saltz, "No patient who came to our hospital without an absolute mortal wound was lost in shock."

In the first day of fighting Hadassah received eighty-six casualties. They were well-spaced and Saltz thought that the hospital would have no trouble coping from then on. But he did not know that during the first day in the Jerusalem area the troops were only organizing for the big confrontation.

Jordan had four full brigades ready to do battle. Facing them in Jerusalem, Israel had a brigade of reservists, many of them middle-aged, with orders not to shoot unless they were shot at and not to escalate the firing. The big action was expected in the south; Sinai was the objective. Jordan was not thought likely to become involved and so Jerusalem, lightly held, became a calculated risk. Prime Minister Eshkol made repeated attempts to assure King Hussein that he need not worry about an Israeli attack on his front. But Hussein, who had signed a defense pact with Nasser and had put his forces under an Egyptian commander, was receiving enthusiastic messages from Nasser that the Egyptians were bombing Israel into submission. Thus, Hussein agreed that the front be opened in the east, and the Jordanian shelling of Jerusalem began at about 10:15 on the morning of June 5. A brigade of Israeli paratroops under Colonel Mota Gur was brought hastily up from the Southern Command and thrown into the battle which did not begin in earnest until early on the morning of June 6. That day was a grievously memorable one. Savage hand-to-hand fighting at such places as Ammunition Hill, Mivtar Hill, and the Police School were among the most bitter acts of combat in Israeli history. Companies of men were decimated on both sides. At the end of the day, however, Sheikh Jarrah was taken and the road up to Mt. Scopus was opened. Fate gave the victory to Jerusalem-born Chief of Staff Yitzhak Rabin, who nineteen years earlier had been forced by the British to abandon Sheikh Jarrah and Mt. Scopus.

Recalls Saltz,

> On that Tuesday morning the wounded suddenly started pouring in and by afternoon we had every single hall of the first and second floors filled with casualties—Jordanians among them. I remember looking over some that I had not managed to get to and I was in despair. I wondered how we were ever going to manage. But we did and everything was ready. No one was lost.

Operations went on around the clock—310 in three days. And some lasted four hours. Says Saltz, "I never believed it was possible to go three days without sleep but I proved it to myself."

Neurosurgeon Aharon Beller was abroad when the wars broke out in 1948 and 1956. He was in Madrid for a meeting of neurosurgeons when the Tiran Straits were closed. "I packed up and returned fast this time and arrived less than two weeks before it broke out. We did not have as much work as in 1948 but it was so concentrated we had to work day and night. I operated nonstop for fifty hours. We had forty head and ten spinal cord cases."

Ear-nose-throat chief Moshe Feinmesser's team worked on fifty soldiers with ruptured ear drums and inner ear damage. Only 5 per cent were left with severe handicaps. Ophthalmologist Michaelson and his colleagues had fifty major eye operations in four days, about twenty-five of them to remove foreign bodies.

Good as the results were, bottlenecks developed. One of the most difficult to handle was the appearance at Ein Karem of about 1,200 volunteers. Says Karpas, "All our well-prepared plans were nearly spoiled because there were so many. We had to put a special person on duty to direct them." Yaal (Hebrew acronym for "A Helping Hand to the Ill"), an organization of white-smocked Israeli ladies, during the Six-Day War cleaned floors and cupboards, made bandages, assisted mothers in the maternity hospital to move into shelter, worked in the emergency wards, and ran the cafeterias. Over five hundred members are registered at Hadassah. Other hospitals adopted the idea and now there are altogether more than three thousand Yaalites throughout Israel.

A strange story of one volunteer is told by orthopedic surgeon Makin. He rushed back to Jerusalem from New York, where he had been on sabbatical leave, as soon as the war broke out, arriving on Thursday, June 7. He found that most of the casualties needed orthopedic attention and that his colleague Gordon Robin had worked continuously for more than two days. Two members of an orthopedic team were so fatigued they were sleeping on the floor.

> First thing I did was to take Robin off and start work. After about 12 hours, a Canadian Gentile appeared and said, "My name is John Hall. Can I lend a hand?" He had been a professor of orthopedic surgery in Saigon during the war and was just the person we needed. He had been back in Toronto only a week and when he heard the war was on he boarded the first plane. . . . When he was no longer needed, he left and we never heard from him again.

On Wednesday, June 7, the war in Jerusalem ended. That day, after the walls of the divided city were breached, the Western Wall of the Temple Mount was won. The inflow of casualties slowed. And by the end of the sixth day Hadassah had treated one-third of all the nation's casualties.

On the seventh day, Israelis rejoiced and much of the world rejoiced with them. In Washington, recalls Hadassah's fifteenth president, Rose Matzkin, "Jews from every walk of life—from the *hasidim* to the most assimilated—felt very much involved. It was a kind of spontaneous uproar of joy, of dancing and praying, all outbursts of great emotion and relief."

At Ein Karem, Prime Minister Eshkol addressed the doctors, nurses and staff:

> I wish to thank you from the bottom of my heart for all that you have done and are doing to treat the wounded and to return

them to a productive life, and I am speaking for the families of
the wounded Arab soldiers, too.

God knows that in our hearts we have no hatred for the
Arabs and I hope that we can work out some system of peaceful
co-existence for the benefit of both peoples. The proof of this
lack of hatred is the extreme care that is being given to these
Arab prisoners of war here at Hadassah. I am sure that the same
spirit can prevail and be extended to all our relations in peacetime.

To Hadassah, the Six-Day War offered a special prize—Mt.
Scopus. After nineteen years of separation, Scopus was once again
part of Jewish Jerusalem. On June 8, Hadassah's flag rose once
again on the roof of the hospital. Eli Davis and Rebecca Shulman
were there as Kalman Mann spoke over a closed circuit to the staff
at Ein Karem.

This flag symbolizes an unusual type of war—the war against
disease and ignorance; it is a flag of peace. We here vow that
we will revive this hospital—a vital stream of life will imbue these
buildings that have been dead for so many years.

On June 21 in a formal ceremony, the army handed the keys
over to Hadassah President Charlotte Jacobson who, with former
president Lola Kramarsky, had received special permission from
the State Department to fly into the forbidden war zone. Veterans
wept when they saw the hospital building, broken and defaced,
littered with rusted beds, windows smashed, Henrietta Szold's
garden overgrown with weeds. Then they saw a message scribbled
on a wall by an Israeli guard, one of those who had stood lonely
watch under the U.N. flag those nineteen years: "If the day comes
and this building is filled again with patients, let them remember
those who watched over this place in difficult years."

Charlotte Jacobson returned to her quarters and overcome
with emotion addressed a letter to Hadassah leaders throughout
the nation. She wrote of visiting hundreds of soldiers recuperating
at Ein Karem and of one who told her with a smile, despite his
wounds, "When we entered Hadassah we knew we were in good
hands." She wrote of her visit to Scopus and of her first pilgrimage
to the Western Wall where, like thousands of others, she could
hardly believe she was not dreaming. "Verily," she wrote, "the age
of miracles is not over." And in her call to the membership to

match "with unflagging devotion the spirit of the people of Israel," she expressed a verity, "This is indeed an age of renaissance for the Jewish people."

Many believed that Israel's third decisive military victory in two decades would finally lead to peace. But within six weeks the Egyptians resumed hostilities despite their strategic disadvantage. They now held only one bank of the Suez Canal; Israel proper was beyond the range of their guns. Still, Nasser retained faith in an ultimate victory over Israel by a combination of massive retaliation and big power politics. Negotiation with Israel, in his eyes, was tantamount to surrender. For its part, Israel felt more secure than ever, dug in behind logical lines of defense on the Golan Heights and along the Jordan River and Suez Canal. Nasser declared at an Arab summit meeting in Khartoum there would be no negotiation, no peace, and no recognition. Israel replied: no negotiation, no peace. The result was deadlock and more fighting. Concurrent with vain attempts by Arab irregulars to sabotage Israel to its knees, Nasser declared a war of attrition along the Suez Canal with the aim of wearing Israel down and finally taking Sinai back by invasion. Against these threats, Israel hermetically sealed the eastern front to saboteurs and built the Bar Lev Line (named for Chief of Staff Haim Bar Lev) to withstand eighteen months of murderous bombing and shelling. This fourth Arab war against Israel was the most enervating of all.

The Israel army did not try to conceal the truth during the war of attrition. Hourly, the state radio broadcast names of the soldier dead. Citizens worked with transistors held to their ears. In shops, restaurants, and in parlors conversation stopped every hour on the hour. In Jerusalem, all eyes lifted skyward when a military helicopter appeared heading southward toward Hadassah. The city then knew a battle was in progress. On Yom Kippur, 1969, the service in one synagogue was halted when a helicopter was heard overhead so that prayers for the wounded it bore could be recited. The military established a liaison office in the hospital at Ein Karem to give the alert of incoming casualties. A helicopter pad was built on the western flank to receive them. During the war of attrition, when the casualty list was as great as during the all-out war of June, 1967, half of all the casualties were taken to Hadassah. Fifteen teams of physicians and nurses remained constantly prepared as the hospital built up its capacity to treat as many as 1,800 in case of total emergency. Partly because of the wars, Hadassah built up its orthopedic and rehabilitation departments, and instituted units for intensive care.

After long deliberation, Hadassah decided to reopen Mt. Scopus as a general hospital which, because of its proximity to eastern Jerusalem, would cater primarily to the city's 75,000 Arab residents. The hospital, which is to be opened by 1975, was to make available 300 beds and was to absorb the 110 Arab staff members of an old-fashioned hospital located in the Via Dolorosa. For Jerusalem, Scopus would thus become a community where Jew and Arab would work in close harmony, perhaps signaling an end to fifty years of fratricide and serving as a pacesetter in bringing unity to reunified Jerusalem.

As Hadassah entered its seventh decade of service in Jerusalem, a new era in the affairs of the city had begun. While Israel had not yet achieved a formal peace with its neighbors, a measure of co-existence was apparent. Zion was physically united. Its Jewish and Arab residents were not only on speaking terms, they were often working together. Hadassah had taken its inspiration and challenge from Jeremiah who poetically lamented how badly Zion had deteriorated. Was there no help for the city and the nation, he asked.

> Is there no balm in Gilead?
> Is there no physician there?
> Why then is not the health
> Of the daughter of my people restored?
> Oh that my head were waters,
> And my eyes a fountain of tears,
> That I might weep day and night
> For the slain of the daughter of my people!

> Is there no physician there?
> There is. Indeed there is.

Purim, 1973
Jerusalem

HADASSAH ORGANIZATION CHART

Appendixes

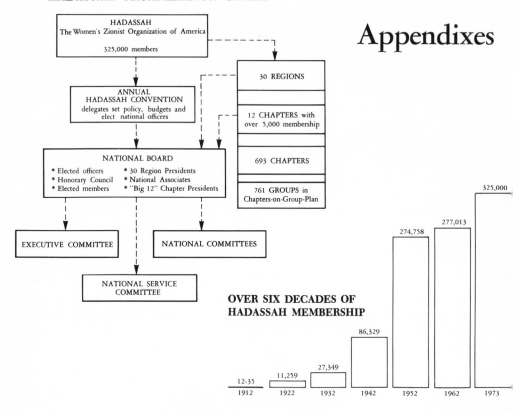

OVER SIX DECADES OF HADASSAH MEMBERSHIP

Membership figures by year:
- 1912: 12-35
- 1922: 11,259
- 1932: 27,349
- 1942: 86,329
- 1952: 274,758
- 1962: 277,013
- 1973: 325,000

NATIONAL PRESIDENTS OF HADASSAH

HENRIETTA SZOLD
Founder
1912–1921, 1923–1926

ALICE SELIGSBERG
1921–1923

MRS. IRMA LINDHEIM
1926–1928

MRS. ROBERT SZOLD
1928–1930

MRS. EDWARD JACOBS
1930–1932, 1934–1937

MRS. SAMUEL W. HALPRIN
1932–1934, 1947–1952

MRS. MOSES P. EPSTEIN
1937–1939, 1943–1947

MRS. DAVID DE SOLA POOL
1939–1943

MRS. SAMUEL J. ROSENSOHN
1952–1953

MRS. HERMAN SHULMAN
1953–1956

DR. MIRIAM FREUND
1956–1960

MRS. SIEGFRIED KRAMARSKY
1960–1964

MRS. CHARLOTTE JACOBSON
1964–1968

MRS. MAX SCHENK
1968–1972

MRS. MAX N. MATZKIN
1972–

Executive Directors
(Post of top staff officer, established in 1935)

1935–1953	Jeanette Leibel (Mrs. Arthur Lourie)
1953–1971	Hannah Goldberg
1971–	Aline Kaplan

HADASSAH COUNCIL IN ISRAEL

Mr. Shlomo Arazi
Mrs. Zmira Baker
Mrs. Dora Camrass
Mrs. Rhoda Cohen
Mrs. Julia Dushkin
Mrs. Anna Eiges
Mrs. Myriam Granott
Mrs. Esther Grunwald
Mrs. Rosa Krongold

Mrs. Marian Lewin-Epstein
Mrs. Jeannette Lourie
Mrs. Leah Landau
Professor Kalman J. Mann
Mrs. Sylvia Mann
Mrs. Simi Olshan
Mrs. Esther Reifenberg
Mrs. Mary Sanders
Mrs. Sylvia Shapiro

Mrs. Rachel Shwarz
Mrs. Vera Tsur
Mrs. Rose Weinberg
Mrs. Tybie Yermish
Mr. S. B. Yeshaya
Mrs. Annabelle Yuval
Mrs. Lillian Gold-Shpiro,
Executive Secretary

Index